D0936638

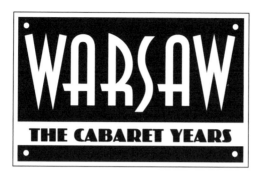

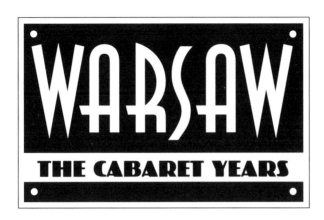

THE CABARET YEARS

by RON NOWICKI

MERCURY HOUSE
San Francisco

Published in the United States by
Mercury House
San Francisco, California

United States Constitution, First Amendment: Congress shall make no law respecting an establishment of religion, or prohibiting the free exercise thereof; or abridging the freedom of speech, or of the press; or the right of the people peaceably to assemble, and to petition the Government for a redress of grievances.

Mercury House and colophon are registered trademarks
of Mercury House, Incorporated

Printed on acid-free paper
Manufactured in the United States of America

Library of Congress Cataloging-in-Publication Data

Nowicki, Ron.
　Warsaw: the cabaret years / Ron Nowicki.
　　p.　cm.
　Includes bibliographical references and index.
　ISBN 1-56279-030-7
　1. Warsaw (Poland) — Civilization.　I. Title.
DK4633.N69　　1992
943.8'4 — dc20　　　　　　　　　　　　　　　　　　92-16660
　　　　　　　　　　　　　　　　　　　　　　　　　　　　CIP

5　　4　　3　　2　　1

To Diana

for her love and support

You may forget but
Let me tell you
this: someone in
some future time
will think of us.

Sappho

Contents

Author's Note

For purposes of historical accuracy the names Danzig, Teschen, and Wilno are used instead of Gdańsk, Cieszyn, and Vilnius. I have also used the Polish spelling of Kraków rather than the common English spelling Cracow.

For events in the life of Hanka Ordonówna I have relied for background on the biography of her by Tadeusz Wittlin, *Pieśnarka Warszawy: Hanka Ordonówna i Jej Świat* (London: Polska Fundacja Kulturalna, 1985). Additional anecdotes and descriptions of her came from conversations with Wittlin and with the late Zosia Terné, Lola and Benno Kitajewicz, Rafael Scharf, Tamara Karren-Zagórska, and Aniela Kosciółkowska, all of whom either knew Ordonówna or saw her perform.

For translations of titles of literary works from Polish to English I have relied mainly on those found in *The History of Polish Literature* by Czesław Miłosz (Berkeley: University of California Press, 1983).

Acknowledgments

I wish to thank the many people who contributed to the success of this book. (The following list is in no particular order and any omissions are accidental. I will be pleased to add names in a future edition.)

- Maryla Żuławska in London, for providing introductions to interviewees, reading the manuscript, and sharing with me her interest in cabaret.

- Maika Kwiecińska-Decker, my Warsaw colleague, who conducted interviews in Warsaw and Paris, transcribed and translated them, and provided additional information on Warsaw.

- Richard Rehl, for translations in a variety of books.

- Maria Szwede for finding out-of-print books that I needed at her bookstore, Szwede Slavic Books, in Palo Alto, and the Orbis bookstore in London.

- The Polish Arts and Culture Foundation and the Polish Memorial Library in San Francisco where I really began this book, and Wanda Tomczykowska, founder and president of these organizations, for helping me rediscover my Polish roots.

- The staff at the Polish Library in Hammersmith, London, for putting up with my numerous requests so graciously.

- Zbigniew Stańczyk at the Hoover Institution and Wojciech Zalewski at Stanford's Green Library, for helping to track down books on Warsaw.

- The Sikorski Institute in London for providing additional information.

- Maria Serenc, for translating parts of *Po Obu Stronach Oceanu*, by Zofia Arciszewska.

- Zosia Osiacka, for translating parts of Mira Zimińska's autobiography, *Nie Żyłam Samotnie*.

- Irena Narell for translating the introduction to *Jak w Przedwojennym Kabarecie*, by Ryszard Groński.

- Robin McCall, whose word processor saved me many hours of tedious typing.

- Dr. Alina Wierzbiańska, who helped me more than she realizes.

- William Brinton and Thomas Christensen at Mercury House for believing in this book from the beginning.

- Carol Christensen for doing a superb job of editing, and Zipporah Collins for coordinating the production of this book.

The following people were gracious enough to consent to be interviewed: Zosia Chądzyńska, Marceli Handelsman, Jan Merkiel, Janusz Gołaszewski, Aniela Kosciółkowska, Halina Mendelsohn, the late Feliks Topolski, the late Zosia Terne, Ludwik Łubieński, Leopold Łabędz, Stefania Kossowska, Rafael Scharf, Tamar Karren-Zagórska, Arthur Barker, Denis Hills, the late Casimir Sabbat, Count Edward Raczyński, Aniela Mieczysławska, Benno and

Lola Kitajewicz, Józef Garlinski and his late wife, Eileen, Wlada Majeska, Piotr Pałczewski, Professor George Lerski, Mieczysław Kowalski, Halina Ross, and Ludwik Żerański, who sent his tape-recorded comments. Many others replied with letters and by telephone, and I thank them all for their cooperation.

This project was not funded by grants or institutions but a number of individuals contributed to my support, and I wish to thank them publicly.

R.N.

Pronunciation Guide

The Polish alphabet is very similar to the English, except that it has two nasal vowels, some consonant combinations, and some accented letters that English does not have. What follows is a simplified guide to the sounds of Polish.

Vowel Sounds

a	as in cat	o	as in boat
ą	like the on in con	ó	as in tool
e	as in beg	u	as in tool
ę	like the en in bend	y	as in myth
i	pronounced ee		

Consonant Sounds

b	takes a softer sound when it appears at the end of a word	d	takes a softer sound when it appears at the end of a word
c	like ts	dz	like ds
ć	like the ch in chop	dź	like the j in John
cz	like the ch in chunk	dż	combined d and z

g   at the end of a word   sz   like sh
    takes a k sound   w   like v but it takes a
j   like the y in yes   softer sound when it ap-
ł   like w   pears at the end of a
ń   as in seen   word
r   always rolled   z   takes a softer sound
rz like the g in the French   when it appears at the
    gendarme   end of a word
ś   as in sure

Based on B. W. Mazur, *Colloquial Polish* (London: Routledge and Kegan Paul, 1983). © B. W. Mazur 1983.

Introduction

My obsession with Warsaw began with a song. In 1985 I saw a film — a drama about the experiences of Polish immigrants in Australia after World War II. The background music was an old record, a Polish hit song from the 1930s, "Love Forgives Everything" (*Miłość ci Wszystko Wybaczy*). It was the signature tune of the popular cabaret and film star, Hanka Ordonówna, the toast of Warsaw in the twenties and thirties.

Hanka's song stuck in my mind. It was melancholy: It had the distinctive flavor of its time. It was the song of someone whose life would end tragically. I paid a visit to a Polish foundation in San Francisco that had a collection of prewar Polish music, and I found among the albums one by Ordonówna that contained the very song I had heard in the film, the very voice I had loved. I listened to *"Miłość"* over and over, and finally the foundation's president made a tape for me from the scratchy ten-inch disk. I began to search for biographical material on Hanka Ordonówna, or Hanka Ordonka, as her friends called her. But as I prowled about in libraries, bookstores, and personal archives, I soon realized that there was almost no information about her in English. What was more surprising, descriptions and stories about Warsaw between the wars were equally hard to find. A number of personalities of the day had written their memoirs, but mostly in Polish, and few had been trans-

1

lated. I could find only a few books in English dealing with the politics of interwar Poland.

The holocaust of World War II consumed much of Polish culture. Centuries-old buildings were destroyed, museums were bombed and looted, hundreds of thousands of books and manuscripts were burned. The roster of poets, writers, and performers who perished during the war is a lengthy one. When Western observers entered Warsaw in 1945 they saw little except rubble. The artist Marek Żuławski, returning home from London, observed: "Warsaw is a living ruin, a corpse that has refused to stay in its grave, raised its bones, broken on a wheel, opened its empty eye-sockets, spread out its fingers, twisted by a hangman's tongs."[1]

Poland and her eastern neighbors tumbled into the Soviet maw and were quickly written off by the West as communist nations. Except for the occasional strike or Wajda film, one heard little from Poland for the next three decades, until Solidarity burst into the headlines in 1980. During this lull, Polish culture was languishing under Communist party domination; some artists and writers even swallowed the Party line in order to be allowed to work. Culture coming out of Poland was suspect; the Polish community in America, on the advice of the Polish-American Congress, would have nothing to do with visiting performers and writers. The popular Mazowsze Dance Troupe was picketed during an appearance in Berkeley in 1977.

Memories of the lively Warsaw of independent Poland began to fade. Postwar stagnation, along with the destruction of the interwar capital, and the deaths of many of those who had formed its society, seemed to ensure that the vibrant Warsaw that grew up during the Second Republic would be forgotten. However, I felt that the story of Warsaw in its heyday could be told, that I could discover its excitement just as writers continue to discover the excitement of Paris, Berlin, and Vienna of that same period. Poland's capital must have had a cultural life befitting its importance. So I continued to look for clues about what life had been like between the wars. Conversations with older Poles, and my discovery of a few key books, opened this world to me.

One important book, *The History of Polish Literature* by Czesław Miłosz, provided me with an exhaustive list of Polish writers between the wars.[2] Searches through cluttered bookstores finally yielded a few books about Polish and Yiddish theater (where Molly Picon acted and Joseph Green directed), some collections of cabaret reviews, copies of old newspapers, and a few other gems. Several Polish booksellers in London, Paris, and Warsaw, and one in California, suggested books, mostly in Polish, which might help me in my quest.

Eventually announcements I had placed in Polish and English newspapers turned up a few survivors, people who had actually lived in Warsaw between the wars. A man in Canada sent me, unsolicited, sheets of photo slides of Warsaw as it appeared in 1924. A woman in north London sent me a book she had written about her life as the owner of the café Art and Fashion (*Sztuka i Moda*) in central Warsaw. At London's Drian Gallery, an elderly Polish couple who barely spoke English presented me with a battered copy of a book of collected essays about one of Warsaw's best-known critics and raconteurs. Among the pieces was one by Artur Rubinstein. Another woman in London, the young widow of a Polish artist, showed me her collection of books on Polish culture and cabaret. At last I had found someone who knew about Hanka! And as a bonus she introduced me to a cabaret singer of that bygone era, a woman who had been Hanka Ordonka's understudy. In her seventies at the time I spoke to her (she died in 1987, a few months later), this woman still performed occasionally at a Polish club in Hammersmith. She was a diminutive woman named Zosia Terné; in her prime she had been known as the Nightingale of Warsaw.

One afternoon in 1986, I invited Terné to lunch at the

Ognisko Polskie club near the Albert Hall. With my friend acting as interpreter, I asked her why she had been known as the Nightingale; her response was a feigned ignorance. Unfortunately, Terné would not allow our conversation to be recorded, so much of what she said about Ordonówna, about her own work as a singer, and as Hanka's understudy ("If Hanka rejected a song, they would give it to me") had to be reconstructed from hastily scribbled notes.

Over "lunch" – she had two glasses of whiskey with water on the side – Terné regaled us with stories about celebrity affairs. She told us of her adventures as a young woman alone in Warsaw. Describing her brief imprisonment in Pawiak shortly after the German invasion of 1939, she said that the Nazi officer in charge of her case had been so charmed by her singing that he allowed her to go free. Several times she interrupted our talk by singing lines from *her* signature tune, "When the White Lilacs Bloom Again" (*Kiedy Znów Zakwitną Białe Bzy*), right there in the middle of the crowded Ognisko dining room.

Terné was not the only survivor of interwar Poland to have settled in London. I contacted dozens of members of that generation and recorded their statements, although a few, for reasons they would not disclose, refused to speak into a tape recorder. In fact, one gentleman – a writer and filmmaker – casually ran his hands over my jacket to make sure I was not "wired." The London Poles had libraries and bookstores as well as a flourishing network; information flowed quickly through their community. Whatever their political differences, the Polish émigrés I spoke with all agreed on one thing – during its brief period of independence, in the years 1918 to 1939, Warsaw was one of the liveliest cities in Europe.

It is a common conception – or perhaps misconception – that political chaos and creativity go hand in hand. One thinks of Berlin in the twenties, Paris during the Indochina and Algerian agonies, England during World War I. There is no scientific basis for this observation but it can be remarked with a certain amount of accuracy that Warsaw was at the height of its cultural achievement in the tumultuous period between the wars. The sudden burst of independence unleashed a wave of creativity that seemingly had been bottled up for over a century.

The Warsaw of 1918 to 1939 can be seen as successor to the dynamic Polish society of the late eighteenth century, when Poland was governed by King Stanisław August II Poniatowski, the last in a line of Polish kings stretching back to the tenth century. While Poniatowski was on the throne (1764–95), Polish culture took on a new life. Poniatowski's interests reflected the social change occurring in Europe at the time. The king surrounded himself with a group of intellectuals – poets, philosophers, and political theorists – who were influenced by cultural and political events taking place throughout Europe, the French Enlightenment in particular. He also invited Italian painters and architects, for example, Canaletto (Bernardo Bellotto, 1724–80; nephew of Antonio Canal, the more famous Canaletto), Domenico Merlini (1730–97), and Marcello Bacciorelli (1731–1818), to pursue their arts in Warsaw. Poniatowski commissioned many new buildings as well as paintings of Polish cities and landscapes. These paintings give us a good idea of what Warsaw looked like in the late eighteenth century – and, in fact, up to World War II, since many of the buildings survived until that time.

Poniatowski also enacted democratic reforms, establishing a constitution and proclaiming the rights of peasants. These reforms proved too threatening to the Russian empire. Empress Catherine the Great – in league with the Prussians and a number of traitorous Polish aristocrats – moved against Poniatowski, who had once been Catherine's lover. Fighting broke out in late 1792 and continued through 1794. At that time, Tadeusz Kościuszko led an army of peasants brandishing scythes in a last stand against the Russians. The peasant army was overwhelmed, and Poniatowski was forced into exile. He formally abdicated in 1795, and Poland was partitioned among Austria, Prussia, and Russia.

With the king's abdication, Poland disappeared from the maps of Europe. Throughout the nineteenth century, Poland lay obscured in a mist of political confusion. Occupied by foreign powers, its borders changed frequently, as Prussia, Austria, and Russia jockeyed for positions of dominance in Central Europe. Warsaw, on the main road from Berlin to Moscow, continued to make the news. In 1830–31 and again in 1863 Warsaw was the center of plots to overthrow the Russian oppressors. After the first defeat there was a mass exodus from Poland, as members of the officer corps and the intelligentsia sought refuge in France. Chopin and the poet Adam Mickiewicz were among those who left Poland around this time, never to return. (Neither, however, had played a major role in the uprising). The January Uprising of 1863, in which Joseph Conrad's father participated, was crushed even more brutally than the earlier rebellion. Following their victory, the Russians attempted to eliminate both the Polish culture and the Polish language from Eastern Europe.

Poland's subjugation continued into the twentieth century, though patriots like Józef Piłsudski and the renowned pianist Ignacy Jan Paderewski were covertly working on plans for an independent Polish state. The Russians were driven out of Warsaw in 1915. The country's day of deliverance finally came in 1918, after the Germans were defeated and withdrew from Poland.[3]

"Suddenly the masterly Germans had their guns taken away from them and they became *our* prisoners. There was a great air of elation, an atmosphere of fulfillment." That was how the Polish mood at the end of World War I was described to me by the artist Feliks Topolski. It was 1986 and we were in his dimly lit salon beneath London's Hungerford Bridge. Attended by three women – one Italian, one Swedish, and one Polish (or at least she spoke Polish to him) — he was sitting on a huge mattress surrounded by dozens of small pillows, and reminiscing about November 1918.

The Poles were delirious with their new freedom. People took to the streets of Warsaw in wild celebrations. The city was festooned with white-and-red Polish flags. They were raised over the Town Hall, they appeared over the Belvedere Palace, above Warsaw University and the Polytechnic Institute, and on the rooftops of hundreds of buildings. Sidewalks and cafés were packed with milling people.

As trains rumbled across the bridge overhead, Topolski sipped white wine and talked. "Warsaw was a very vigorous city, culturally and socially. Its mood, its consciousness, was *not* that of some snow-covered eastern village. Warsaw received many visitors from abroad, from England and France. People of a certain class spoke foreign languages; they had great style and elegance. The Polish aristocracy was as good as that of any other country in Europe."[4] Topolski recalled the tradition of his day: "Upper-class young men went to school in England, the girls went to France. Men had to wear only the latest styles. The snobbery was fantastic. Of course," he added, as if to illustrate his point, "there were classes and there were *classes*."[5]

By virtue of growing up in a community of immigrants I was aware that Poles were very class conscious, an attitude that perhaps had its roots in the eight hundred years when the country was ruled by royalty. I had studied Polish history as a pupil at Saint Ladislaus elementary school in Pennsylvania, and I was familiar with the stubbornness and independence of the Poles as well as with the stories of kings and queens and Polish peasants.

For its first three centuries, Poland was essentially a nation of two classes, the land-owning nobility and the peasants. Not until the thirteenth century, when King Bolesław the Chaste guaranteed the Jews civil and religious liberties, did a middle, or merchant class, begin to emerge.

Attitudes of class separation and envy of others' successes persisted into the twentieth century and were quite evident in Warsaw between the wars. In letters to his family, published privately, Topolski's contemporary, the antique dealer Stanisław Meyer, who was a prominent figure in Warsaw's social circles, wrote: "socially there existed innumerable divisions and subdivisions. People met in charitable and social work, men belonged to the same clubs, but often they remained only acquaintances, not taking any intimate part in the lives of groups outside their own set, their families, and a few friends.

"At the head of the social scale stood the aristocracy, which centered in the Hunter's Club. This very exclusive institution was definitely closed to anybody who earned his living by personal work. It was, of course, the ambition of a few snobs to be admitted to the aristocratic society."[6]

Polish journalist Zofia Chądzyńska also had vivid memories of the atmosphere in Warsaw immediately following the war. Marshal Piłsudski boarded with her family before moving into the Belvedere Palace, and she was also nearby when Poland's first president was assassinated. Now in her early eighties, living in Warsaw, she still writes and also works as a translator of Latin American literature. She defined the prevailing attitude in the interwar capital: "Snobbism—whatever one says about Warsaw before the [Second] World War, that must be stressed. Snobbism was the spirit of Warsaw—in part an intellectual snobbism. The atmosphere in Warsaw today is not as exciting as it was then."[7]

The intellectual and artistic ferment of interwar Poland was accompanied by a very unstable political situation. Except for those times when Marshal Józef Piłsudski was in control, prime ministers came and went rapidly. There were political assassinations and one dramatic coup, staged by Piłsudski himself in 1926. At the end, after his death in 1935, Poland was ruled by unelected army officers. But the political squabbling did not dampen the enthusiasm of Warsaw's artists, writers, and revelers.

An incredible number of poets and novelists burst into print between the wars. Magazines and newspapers flourished. One of them, *The Literary News* (*Wiadomości Literackie*), featured essays and reviews by Poland's leading intellectuals. It survived the war by moving first to Paris, then to London, where publication continued into 1981 under the direction of Stefania Kossowska, who still lives in London and writes for Radio Free Europe and the Polish émigré press.

Feature and experimental films were produced; theaters were packed; there were new plays and musical productions. Though there was widespread unemployment, everyone with money dressed in the latest Paris fashions. The aristocracy had lost much of its property but continued to live in the high style to which it was accustomed – and few objected. One upper-class woman spoke of 1918 as "a time of champagne!"

Numerous cabarets and clubs sprang up across the city: the Argus, the Persian Eye (*Perskie Oko*), the Black Cat (*Czarny Kot*), Oasis (*Oaza*), Qui Pro Quo, the Sphinx (*Sfinks*), the Mirage (*Miraż*), IPS (Institute for Artistic Propaganda). Every nightclub had sketches – lively, political, satirical. Warsaw cabaret was probably on a par with that of Berlin. It was original and it was daring. It differed from the cabarets of Berlin in that those in Warsaw frequently featured readings of poetry and prose and enactment of scenes from Polish literature. Old Varsovians always referred to their clubs as "literary cabaret." Many of Poland's major writers – Julian Tuwim, Antoni Słonimski, Jan Lechoń – wrote cabaret sketches between volumes of more serious work.

The talent and energy of Warsaw's artists seemed unlimited, and they moved freely from medium to medium. Ordonówna first made her mark as a cabaret performer, then made films. Tadeusz Boy-Żeleński, poet, essayist, intellectual, and translator of nearly one hundred French classics, was also well known as a cabaret and theater critic. (Before moving to Warsaw he had cofounded the Green Balloon [*Zielony Balonik*] cabaret in Kraków.) In between novels Stefan Themerson (author of the surrealistic *Mystery of the Sardine*) and his artist-wife made experimental films. Leon Chwistek gained fame as a painter and logician, and later as a philosopher. Stanisław Witkiewicz (Witkacy) started out as a portrait painter, then moved on to write philosophical tracts, plays, and futuristic novels.

Libraries had long lines of people eager to borrow the current best-sellers reviewed in *The Literary News*. Educational institutions proliferated, and despite a plethora of economic woes, a building program under President (Mayor) Stefan Starzyński was making good progress before the Nazis invaded. Even the poorest citizen could scrape together a few złotys to attend a cabaret show now and then. As Zofia Chądzyńska recalled, "Warsaw was having fun, playing and amusing herself as if she knew that life is short and disaster was approaching... I think about the Warsaw of that time with enormous pleasure, not only because I was young then, but because it was a wonderful city."[8]

By late 1918, the city was already on the move culturally. Stanisław Moniuszko's opera *Halka* was being presented at the ornate Opera House (*Teatr Wielki*), and the great Stanisław Wyspiański's play *Liberation* was on the boards at the Polish Theater (*Teatr Polski*). Numerous other theaters and cinemas had opened around the city and tickets were in short supply.[9] A group of poets who took the name Skamander had begun gathering at a café called Under the Sign of the Picador; they would become the country's leading literary movement in the coming decade.

Into this atmosphere came a sixteen-year-old blonde ballet student named Marysia Pietruszyńska, making her club debut at the

Sphinx. Shortly after arriving at the club she changed her name to Hanka Ordonówna.

By the end of the 1920s Hanka was well known throughout Poland and was beginning to gain recognition in other European capitals. In addition to performing in nightclubs, she starred onstage and made recordings, including "Love Forgives Everything"—the song that reached out and touched me across the decades.

Stories about Hanka's personal life are numerous. One correspondent described Hanka as "highly sexed and straightforward." She had affairs with many of the men in her circle, including Warsaw's favorite master of ceremonies, Fryderyk Járosy, with whom she lived for a time. There is a famous photo of them, on holiday on the Riviera, looking for all the world like American film stars. Hanka both looked and acted like a star—vivacious, blonde, dressed in the latest fashions. Pursued by adoring men, she eventually married into the Polish aristocracy.

In many ways, Hanka Ordonówna embodied the spirit of Warsaw—ambitious, attractive, talented, and very independent.

PART ONE

The Kingdom
Regained

Alive, I walk in this present and yet bygone city.

Żywy idę miastem będącym, a już tylko byłym.
Julian Przybos (1901–70)
Translated by Czesław Miłosz

CHAPTER 1

A Time of Champagne

■ 1918

The Royal Way—City Center

The tall, needlelike column of King Sigismund III in Castle Square
dominated the Warsaw skyline for centuries, before 1955 when the
Russians gave the Varsovians the "gift" of the Cultural Palace, a
monstrosity that dwarfs and demeans the city's classic architecture.

It was Sigismund who moved the capital of Poland from the
ancient city of Kraków to Warsaw at the end of the sixteenth century, after fire had destroyed his royal castle, the Wawel, which has
since been rebuilt. Thus presiding over Warsaw from his perch, the
stone likeness of Sigismund provided the link between the old and
the new Poland. The Nazis dynamited the column and damaged
the statue, but both were restored after the war.

Sigismund's column marked the beginning of what is known
as the Royal Way. This road was really three contiguous boule-

vards and the original route from Warsaw to Kraków. From the Royal Castle to Copernicus Square it was called Kraków Suburb (*Krakowskie Przedmieście*). At the Copernicus monument it became New World Avenue (*Nowy Świat*) and at Three Crosses Square (*Trzech Krzyży*) it split into three again. The main artery was the beautiful, tree-lined Ujazdowskie Avenue, which ran along the lush Łazienki Park, site of the Belvedere Palace. The palace was the summer retreat of King Poniatowski in the eighteenth century and has been the residence of Poland's presidents since Piłsudski moved into it in November 1918.

Besides having a king's residence at each end, the Royal Way was lined with palaces, small castles, and other distinguished buildings, many of which now house government bureaus. The Royal Way is redolent with memories of Chopin, for he and his family lived briefly on the grounds of the Czapski Palace at the north end of the route. In the baroque-style Church of the Nuns of the Visitation on Kraków Suburb, Chopin used to play the organ.

At the spot where Kraków Suburb becomes New World Avenue stands the Church of the Discovery of the Cross. Here, in the central pillar on the left aisle, is an urn containing the composer's heart. When he died in Paris in 1849, it was surgically removed from his body by Dr. Cruveilheir, his physician, and taken to Warsaw. During World War II the urn was hidden outside the city and only returned after the fighting was over. The Czapski Palace is now the Academy of Fine Arts.

In 1926 a monument to Frederic Chopin was unveiled in Łazieńki Park, sculpted by Wacław Szymanowski. In 1940 this same sculpture was hauled down and unceremoniously loaded onto a freight car and sent to Nazi Germany as scrap. (It has since been restored.)

Two of the city's most cosmopolitan hotels, the Bristol and the Europejski, were situated on Kraków Suburb. They were designed by an Italian father-and-son team of architects. Henryk Marconi

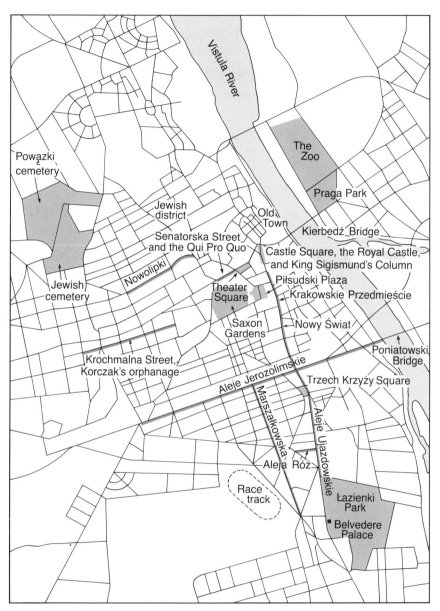

■   Notable streets and places of central Warsaw between the two
    world wars.

(1792–1863) was responsible for the Europejski, erected in 1856, in neo-Renaissance style. He also designed the city's original Central Railway station, the Zamoyski Palace, and the Society for Agriculture building. His son Władysław (1848–1915) designed the Bristol whose interiors were done by the Viennese Otto Wagner.

Before World War I, pianist Ignacy Jan Paderewski was a major shareholder in the Bristol. The German army commandeered it in 1915 and remained ensconced there until 1918. When Paderewski made his triumphant return to the city in 1919 he immediately established his headquarters at the Bristol, whose restaurant had one of the best kitchens in Warsaw.

Just beyond the Bristol at number 38 was one of Warsaw's most popular clubs, Simon and Stecki, or S and S, as it was called, where the cabaret crowd gathered on opening night much as New Yorkers used to flock to Sardi's. According to Varsovian Zofia Chądzyńska, "everyone knew that after the opening of a new show Słonimski and his friends would go to a well-known restaurant called Simon and Stecki. On that day people would reserve tables at S and S, knowing that they would be able to see the actors and hear the jokes that would be repeated all over Warsaw the next day."[1]

On the way to the Belvedere Palace one passed along New World Avenue, a lively thoroughfare that contained the British Embassy, the Hotel Savoy with its popular nightclub, and two other well-known clubs, the Paradis at number 3 and one at number 13 known simply as Café Club. In the twenties these night spots were crowded with people doing the tango, a dance craze that swept the capital. Rudolph Valentino was extremely popular in Warsaw, partly because of his association with the tango and partly because of his romance with the Polish-born film star, Pola Negri.

Besides the major hotels clustered along the avenues that made up the Royal Way, there were others on the main crosstown thoroughfare, Jerusalem Avenue (*Aleje Jerozolimskie*) and one block west, on Marszałkowska. In the hotel cafés in the Continental, the Imperial, the Metropol, the Monopol, and the Ziemiańska, on Marszałkowska, the city's intellectuals sat and took their coffee and read their newspapers.

Virtually all of the city's cultural and government buildings, its main shopping thoroughfares, the Jewish section, Old Town, the site on which the city was originally built (just behind King Sigismund's Column)—all of this is on the left bank of the Vistula. Both the Catholic and the Jewish cemeteries were—and still are—on this side of the river, just northwest of the city's center. Monumental churches and colossal synagogues dotted the center of Warsaw, dominated by the historic St. John's Cathedral in Old Town and the Great Synagogue on Tłomackie Street in the Jewish section.

The left bank was the site of the historic Royal Castle (*Zamek*), the infamous Pawiak prison, the University of Warsaw, the Polytechnic Institute, the race track at Mokotów, the city's most beautiful parks and squares, as well as its most squalid slums. At one time there were fifty palaces scattered along Krakowskie Przedmieście.

The most elegant neighborhoods were small enclaves, far outnumbered by the poorer areas. Chądzyńska, who has lived in Warsaw most of her life, said that "one of the more elegant neighborhoods was centered around Rose Lane (*Aleja Róż*), a small, tree-lined street across the Aleje Ujazdowskie from Ujazdowskie Plaza, part of a huge bosky area that includes Łazienki Park and the Belvedere Palace.

"The intellectual and cultural life of the city was concentrated in a few places, in the heart of Warsaw," Chądzyńska recalled. "Moniuszko and Aleje Ujazdowskie, Aleja Róż—it was very small and provincial. That's why all the people who were involved in the cultural life knew each other—they simply lived together in a small place. At the weekly Friday concert at the Filharmonia Concert Hall, one could meet half of Warsaw."[2]

This concert was a much-anticipated event at which music-lovers, musicians, and critics rubbed elbows. Stanisław Meyer wrote, "You could not only see everyone at a glance, but even see who was not on good terms with someone else this week, as nearly everyone occupying the first ten or fifteen rows on the left side of the hall was acquainted. No artists are more apt to quarrel than musicians, but since their feuds are mainly idealistic in character and based on differing appreciations of some new work or the performance of some virtuoso, they are not of very long duration. Still it was always wise to find out how people stood with each other at the moment in order to avoid making a 'gaffe.'"[3]

■   Aniela Mieczysławska, daughter of a rich and successful architect, was one of those fortunate enough to live on the exclusive Rose Lane. She was an eighth-generation Varsovian whose maiden name was Lilpop. Because of her family's wealth and social status their parlor was frequently visited by some of Poland's most famous cultural figures, including Artur Rubinstein and Karol Szymanowski.

Today, she lives in Lennox Gardens in London's very fashionable Knightsbridge, a few blocks from Harrod's. She has a large, well-appointed flat where she looks after Count Edward Raczyński, who was Poland's ambassador to England before and during World War II.

In speaking about her life in Warsaw she recalled: "We lived in the Aleja Róż, a short street near the Aleje Ujazdowskie, in one of the finest sections of the city. During the [Second World] War the Germans lived there. It was left untouched during the Uprising because the Nazi big shots lived there. Now, the communist big shots are living there."[4] The war left most of the area near her home devastated, including a small park across the street from it.

At Opposite Ends of the Royal Way

The two men who were to lead Poland in its first year of freedom
lived at opposite ends of the Royal Way — Piłsudski at the Belvedere
Palace and Paderewski at the Bristol Hotel. They were contrasts in
temperament as well as in appearance. The pianist was a bridge fanatic while the marshal preferred the solitary game of patience.
Piłsudski favored plain, military-style tunics except on ceremonial
occasions. His hair was close-cropped unlike Paderewski's flying
halo, his eyes glowered under bushy brows, and his upper lip bore
"bristling mustaches." He tended to brood and had an explosive
temper. Paderewski was more charming, a gentleman with old-
world manners, very popular with women. He was not a politician
in the ordinary sense of the word, but he was a true patriot.

What these two leaders had in common was that neither was
beholden to any political party. Paderewski's patriotism resembled
that of Poland's right wing, but he was never a member of the National Democratic party. Piłsudski had been a socialist in the days
of czarist domination, but once he had taken the reins of power,
he broke with his past emphatically.

After Piłsudski took office, a group of his old socialist friends
visited him at the Belvedere. When they addressed him as "comrade," he silenced them with this oft-quoted statement: "In the past
we followed the same direction and took the tramway painted red,
but I left at the station [marked] 'Poland's Independence'; you are
continuing the journey as far as the station 'Socialism.' My good
wishes accompany you, but be so good as to call me 'Sir.'"[5]

Józef Piłsudski was born and raised in Lithuania, near Wilno, and
his family was devoted to Poland. His older brother was once
imprisoned for plotting to assassinate the czar. Piłsudski himself was
exiled to Siberia at the same time, a punishment that only hardened
his patriotism. He joined the Polish Socialist Party (*Polska Partia*

Sociallistyczna), or the PPS, after his release and from then on had
a series of skirmishes with the occupying Russian forces resulting
in another arrest and imprisonment. Before World War I, he
helped form a covert army of Polish troops, the Polish Riflemen's
Association (*Strzelcy*) whose members became devoted to him. During that war they served under Austrian command against the Russians and were proudly known as the Polish Legion. But their
commander frequently led them on renegade missions, and after
the Legion followed its own initiative and seized the Polish city of
Kielce, about 125 kilometers south of Warsaw, the German high
command decided they needed to control Piłsudski. The Germans
formed a Council of State for Polish Territory and appointed
Piłsudski as one of its leaders. Although the council was designed
as a sop to the Poles, its main function was to recruit young Poles
to fight for the Germans, and Piłsudski resigned as soon as he realized that.

   The Germans then tried to integrate two brigades of the Polish
Legion into their own army, but Piłsudski encouraged the Polish
soldiers to resist an oath of loyalty to the kaiser. Most of them went
along with Piłsudski in refusing the oath and were arrested en
masse. Piłsudski and the man who later became his aide, Kazimierz
Sosnkowski, were imprisoned in 1917 and spent the remainder of
the war in Magdeburg Castle on the Elbe river.

Even before the war began Paderewski had been lobbying for a separate Polish state. Once the Allies had engaged the Germans, he began a dizzying series of concerts and lectures all over Europe and
America, donating his fees to provide food and clothing to Polish
families affected by the war.

   In America he was instrumental in raising a volunteer force of
some twenty thousand Poles, recent immigrants. They were sent
to France where they were outfitted and trained by the French military. Known as the Blue Army for the color of the uniforms sup-

plied by their French hosts, they distinguished themselves in battle against the Germans.

Paderewski also succeeded in getting the ear of President Wilson, who was so impressed with the man's sincerity that he adopted the cause of Polish independence as his own. When Wilson sent the Allies his fourteen-point peace plan, number thirteen was a plea for a free Polish state.

With their defeat assured by the autumn of 1918, the Germans anxiously sought to placate the Poles. They knew their prisoner at Magdeburg would play a key role in a resurrected Polish state, and so released him, taking him and Sosnkowski to Berlin. There, the two Poles dined with representatives of the German foreign office at the fashionable Hiller's restaurant. The Germans wanted assurances that Piłsudski would not seek retribution against them. Piłsudski gave no guarantee and demanded to be returned to Poland at once.

When he arrived at Warsaw's Vienna Station he was met by the unpopular Regency Council, formerly the Council of State. At first they awarded him the rank of commander-in-chief, with total control over military affairs. But the political situation was so uncertain that the temporary government that replaced the council named him chief of state, giving him interim control over civilian affairs as well, until such a time as a democratically elected parliament was in place.

Both the left and the right were demanding to head a more permanent government. Piłsudski chose a prime minister who lasted only a few weeks. The second prime minister he chose was a socialist, and this drew immediate fire from the right-wing National Democrats as well as more centrist parties. This prime minister too was forced to resign after a short time.

While Piłsudski was maneuvering himself into this unique position, others were also at work, seeking to secure power for themselves. As soon as the armistice was declared on November 11, Paderewski, who was in America, laid plans to return to Poland.

By the end of the war Roman Dmowski, one of the founders in 1897 of the right-wing National Democrats (*Endecja*), was already talking to Allied leaders in France. There, he had founded the Polish Information Agency, which he unilaterally declared to be Poland's official representative at the peace talks. At this point the Allies had had little direct contact with Piłsudski, but they did know that he was — or had been — a socialist and had been involved in robbing Russian banks and mail trains. With Paderewski still in America, they accepted Dmowski as the Polish representative and listened to him present Poland's case for statehood and for redrawing the country's borders, restoring territory that had been lost by the partitions.

Allied leaders were impressed with Dmowski's erudition — he had attended the University of Warsaw and spoke several languages — and his plans to industrialize the nation and move it away from its overwhelming agrarianism. But the Allies found his ethnic policy troubling — he wanted a Poland free of minorities, undiluted by other nationalities. In particular he wanted the country to be rid of its Jews, and he was very frank with the Allies on this point.

Like Piłsudski, Paderewski arrived in Warsaw to a tumultuous welcome. Though he had lived outside of Poland for many years, he was immensely popular with the Poles. When he arrived by train at the Central Station on a snowy January 2, the enthusiastic crowd seized the reins of his sleigh, unhitched the horses, and dragged the sleigh and its startled occupants all the way to the Bristol Hotel. Once settled in, Paderewski addressed the crowd from his balcony, assuring them that he belonged to no party and that he had only Poland's best interests at heart.

Even as Paderewski was speaking, a plot by right-wing dissidents was being hatched to dispose of Piłsudski. Fortunately the marshal's spies got wind of it and arrested the conspirators when they arrived at the Belvedere Palace. With that threat out of the way, Piłsudski met with Paderewski and asked him to become prime minister, replacing the interim premier. Paderewski accepted. Angered at the appointment, a contingent of socialists confronted Piłsudski, who exploded in a rage: "I care nothing about 'Rightists' or 'Leftists'; I already have them up my ass! I'm for everyone!"[6]

Paderewski also claimed the post of foreign minister for himself, and in late January set off for Paris to join the peace talks, much to the anger of Roman Dmowski. It was the pianist's pleasant demeanor and fervent patriotism that won the Allies over and swung their support behind Piłsudski.

Piłsudski and Paderewski were the nation's leaders, but they needed the cooperation of the right-wing-dominated parliament to actually govern the country. In the election that established the Sejm, or parliament, more than twenty parties had fielded candidates— socialists, various other left-wing groups, several parties representing the peasants, variations of the right-wing, Zionists, and other Jewish groups. The first Sejm had 340 deputies from all walks of life. They represented a variety of interests: "A motley assortment of morning coats, Jewish kaftans, and noblemen's traditional costumes proclaimed to the foreign observers both the remarkable unity of purpose of the nation and the differences that would later threaten it."[7]

The Center and Its Parts

In many ways the city of Warsaw resembled its government, a "motley assortment" of shifting forces rigged around Piłsudski and Paderewski, the two men at its center.

Central Warsaw was quite small in the early 1920s. Around

this powerful center lay a lively collection of small villages that were later incorporated into the city. Among them were Żoliborz, to the north, where the teachers built their first co-op housing; Wola, a working-class district west of Old Town; and Powiśle, a lower-class neighborhood, along the river, whose occupants had a reputation for producing street urchins. At this time the Jewish sector, in the northwestern part of the city, had a much larger population density than did other areas of Warsaw.

■ Warsaw sits on a high plain midway between Berlin and Moscow, a flat area that almost invites invasion, lacking mountains or rugged terrain to act as barriers. In 1939 Hitler's Panzer divisions rolled across this gentle land with relative ease; only determined resistance by the Polish army delayed their entry into Warsaw. Throughout history the city has stood as a symbolic barrier between Berlin and Moscow.

The Polish capital is divided by the Vistula (*Wisła*), a river that begins as a stream high in the Tatras, the Carpathian mountain range that forms Poland's southern border with what was once Czechoslovakia. The river passes through the ancient city of Kraków, then meanders across the Mazovian plain until it reaches Warsaw, flowing through it and cleaving the city unevenly in half. Leaving behind this upstart city, it continues its journey northward and eventually empties itself into the Bay of Gdańsk near the birthplace of the Solidarity movement.

The two banks of the Vistula were connected by several bridges, the oldest of which was the Kierbedź (*Most Kierbedza*), renamed after World War II as the Śląsko-Dąbrowski Bridge. It spans the Vistula near the Royal Palace. Designed by General Stanisław Kierbedź, the original iron structure took five years to complete (1859–64). It connected Old Town with the park and zoo, in Praga. The viaduct forming part of the structure was a popular walkway in the summer months. From atop it one could observe barges bringing goods from Danzig and boats belonging to various Warsaw rowing clubs. North of the Kierbedź Bridge was the Gdańsk Promenade, which led to the Park Traugutt, named for the leader of the 1863 rebellion against the czar. The other major crossing was the Poniatowski Bridge, just south of the Kierbedź. It connected central Warsaw with Paderewski Park and the neighborhood of Saska Kępa across the river.

In 1918 Warsaw was the capital of a predominantly rural nation. Despite Topolski's claims about vigor and Western consciousness, the Warsaw of 1918 was a city lacking in many of the amenities taken for granted in other European cities. Many of its streets were still paved with the familiar rounded paving stones called cats' heads (*kocie łby*). There were few cars; the major modes of public transportation were horse-drawn cabs (*dorożki*) and horse-drawn trams. Indoor plumbing was still the exception. The city's population was around seven hundred thousand.

■ Those who lived in Warsaw, rich and poor, Catholics and Jews, aristocrats and workers, all remember it with great fondness. Some like to recall the Warsaw of the Second Republic, the *Rzeczpospolita*, as it was known (a name restored by the Solidarity-dominated government in 1990) by describing in minute detail the landmarks of their neighborhood, the look of a street, the route they took to go to the market or to school. Some, like Stanisław Meyer, remembered the weather.

"When I think of Warsaw," he said in a letter to his family, "it is always an early winter afternoon with frost and snow. Not too much frost, just enough to keep the snow from melting when it falls in heavy starlike flakes on the road outside my nursery window. It was so white and cheerful and so nice to plod in till you came home to the hot big stove and got your hands and feet warm and dry again. As a child I often had colds and had to remain indoors, spending most of my time looking through the window at the very lively street below. We lived on the first floor of a house in a square facing a Protestant church. When there was snow the cabs changed their small victoria carriages for sledges—some of them quite beautiful. The horses wore small bells attached to their harnesses to warn pedestrians of their approach and the horses' backs were covered with large nets to protect the people in the sledge from thrown-up snow. . . ."[8]

The winter and the snow, marking the end of the old year and the beginning of the new, gave Meyer pause for a more solemn recollection: "The snow also gave a very appropriate setting for the funerals that often passed along our street. It was and still is a custom in Poland to walk through the town in a funeral procession, from the church to the cemetery. At the head of the procession went a man carrying a cross. Then followed a number of priests in white garments, then the coffin perched high on a black hearse drawn by black horses and surrounded by men in black with burning torches. The coffin was followed by a crowd of people: all the relatives, friends, and acquaintances of the deceased were expected to attend the funeral."[9]

Author and journalist Abraham Shulman and his family lived in Wola. His school was on the other side of town, and he gave a vivid description of his daily route. "I attended the Spojnia gymnasium for several years, from the fifth to the eighth and last class, which provided the student with a *matura*, the equivalent of the French baccalaureate, which opened the way to higher studies.

"I usually traveled to school by electric tramway, but I very often chose to walk instead, although walking took over an hour. My taste for walking gave me the opportunity to gain a familiarity with all the streets and squares between the distant suburb where I lived and Długa Street [where the school was located]. I knew ev-

ery house and store, the display windows and the gates, the qua-
drangular blocks of the sidewalks and the pavement cobblestones.
A few steps away from the school were such attractions as the
Kinematograf—the Municipal Cinema—and the spacious Krasiński
Square, with an imposing wrought iron fence surrounding Krasiń-
ski Park, one of the few gardens in Warsaw. It was full of Jews
dressed in traditional black clothes, reading Yiddish newspapers and
engaging in loud political debates. Farther down was Tłomackie
Street with its magnificent synagogue, the most imposing in all of
Poland.

"One end of Długa Street bordered on the beginning of
Nalewki Street, the Jewish section and the heart of Jewish life in
Warsaw—the largest Jewish community not only in Poland but of
all Europe. The other end of Długa Street ran into Freta Street, the
beginning of Warsaw's Old City, the center of which was its pic-
turesque square surrounded by ancient buildings and a maze of
winding little streets, reminders of the capital's Middle Ages."[10]
And the greatest attraction of them all: after a twenty-minute walk
through the Old City one reached the elevated viaduct that led to
the Kierbedź Bridge over the majestic Vistula River.

Among the buildings Shulman passed was a hotel that was to
figure in one of the most bizarre incidents of the Nazi occupation.[11]
For Shulman "the Hotel Polski, which I passed twice daily, was no
attraction at all. It had neither the glamour nor the mysteries I associated with a hotel. The ground-floor restaurant, announced by
a black-lettered sign over one of the windows, promised no culinary
delights. . . . Before the Second World War, the Hotel Polski was
a small, insignificant building on Długa Street, neither elegant nor
rundown." It took the atrocities of the Nazis to bring it to the public's attention.

Poor and working-class neighborhoods proliferated throughout
Warsaw. Down by the river, wrote Meyer, "there were many old

factories attracted by the water transport facilities. The main street in this part of the city, Solec, gave its name to the district. There were some flour mills and bakeries and many cabdrivers had their stables there. The people of Solec were known as the most religious in town – good, poor, and trustworthy."[12]

Helena Wasiutyńska and her mother lived in a large apartment building in New Town (*Nowe Miasto*). "It was [on] a large square beautifully situated on a high bank overlooking the Vistula. The square was bordered by late-nineteenth-century townhouses (*kamienica*), two or three stories high with large coach gates. Our house, 4 Nowe Miasto, was on the corner of a narrow, dead-end street. It was in a row of houses running parallel to the Vistula, between two beautiful churches, St. Mary's, one of Warsaw's oldest Gothic churches, and the Church of the Holy Sacrament, built by King Jan III Sobieski . . . after his victory over the Turks at Vienna in the seventeenth century. This beautiful church with its high dome was almost completely destroyed during the Warsaw Uprising. . . . In my childhood, Nowe Miasto was not a good address. This part of New Town was very much neglected. It was inhabited by small craftsmen, tradesmen, and impoverished intelligentsia like my mother."[13]

However destitute it was, Wasiutyńska's family nevertheless had a maid. She recalled: "There was a small alcove off the kitchen where our domestic help, a young maid from the village, slept. My mother was a typist with an insurance company, a widow with two girls. But in our home we always had a full-time servant."[14] It was customary, indeed, it was something of a status symbol that no matter how poor a family was, it always had a maid, usually a young, uneducated country girl, to do the heavy housework.

■ Janusz Gołaszewski, who still lives in Warsaw, was a student between the wars. His graduation was delayed for several years by the

German invasion. Later, he became the Director of Communica-
tions Ministry for all of Poland. "I was born on Czackiego Street
[near the Saxon Gardens, in the center of town], number 10, and
lived there until the Warsaw Uprising. . . . Until 1918 or 1921 one's
ancestry was very important. The status of the gentry, the nobles,
and the peasants was very different. The constitution of 1921 made
all citizens equal, at least theoretically. But people still used their
titles on calling cards and in everyday life. In referring to someone
who had a title, one would say, for example, Hrabina [Countess]
Tyszkiewicz . . . When Hanka Ordonówna, the star of Qui Pro
Quo, married a young książę [prince] whose estate was in Troki
[near Kraków], people laughed, but all the same they called her Pani
Hrabina [Mrs. Countess].

"In the first years of independence there was a serious housing
shortage in Warsaw. To some extent this was caused by the influx
of people to the capital of what was, in effect, a new country. My
parents were offered an estate of ten acres (150 hectares) in exchange for their Warsaw apartment. Their apartment was what you
would call a co-op. It was five rooms, about 130 square meters, on
the third floor of the building. In 1929 we had a bathroom remod-
eled to the modern standards of that time. It was an average, good-
enough apartment in an old building. But the best places were the
villas, in little palaces, along the fashionable streets like Aleja Ujazdowskie, Szucha, Szopena [Chopin], Aleja Róż. New buildings
went up in the Żoliborz district, the famous Warsaw Housing
Cooperative [*Warszawska Spółdzielnia Mieszkanowia*, or WSM] in
Mokotów, along Puławska Street, and Aleje Niepodległości.

"As a child I played on the streets a lot. Czackiego was a nice,
quiet street. Nearby was a little street named Dowcip, which means
'a joke.' It still exists. It was a narrow passageway to the larger and
noisier Świętokrzyska [Holy Cross]. Dowcip and Czackiego were
the streets in which I played with my closest friend, who was the
son of the building watchman. Our streets were paved with wooden

cobbles, remnants of the prewar city. The wood reduced the noise
of the horses' hooves and the horse-drawn wagons. From 1927 to
1929 the cobbles were replaced by asphalt. Things were changing
all over the city. . . .

"In the building next door to us, at number 8 Czackiego, lived
a lawyer by the name of Berson. He had a friend named Janusz
Korczak. Often, when we were playing in the street, Korczak
would come over and talk to us; he would ask about our hobbies,
our dreams, and about the financial conditions of our families and
our school. At first we were distrustful of him, but eventually he
gained our confidence. Of course we did not know at the time who
he was—to us, he was an elderly gentleman who just liked to talk
to us. Many years later, I finally found out who he really was."[15]

Gołaszewski's friend, Janusz Korczak, who had a formidable
reputation as an educator, is perhaps best known in the West as the
kindly director of an orphanage who went, unprotesting, to the
Nazi gas chamber with his children. By now most of us have seen
the famous photo of the bearded, dignified Korczak walking stoi-
cally at the head of the group of children. They were on their way,
under heavy guard, to the Umschlagplatz and from there to Treblinka.

Across from the left bank, looking east, is the working-class suburb
of Praga. Here are the zoo (*Ogród Zoologiczny*), opened after World
War I, and Praga Park. "The only thing the right bank has," said
a Polish friend contemptuously, "is flea markets." Life on this side
of the river has not been easy. During the long Russian occupation
of the nineteenth century, Praga was home for many of the officials
sent by the czar. The Russian Orthodox church on Zabkowska
Street is one of the few reminders of that era.

Praga was not originally part of the city. For decades it was
an undeveloped district with few attractions. In 1920 fierce fighting
took place just beyond Praga, where the Red Army's headlong rush

for Warsaw was finally stopped. And in 1944, perhaps as a show of revenge, Soviet troops halted there while the Nazis viciously put down the Warsaw Uprising. They could see the fighting in the center of the city quite clearly, yet waited until the Home Army had been hammered into submission before crossing over to the left bank.

Praga was also home to the *apasz*, street characters who swaggered around the Targówek section and often engaged in petty crime. They could be identified by the checkered cloth caps they wore pulled down over their eyes, hands jammed deep into their trouser pockets. (In Poland, gentlemen did not stand or walk with their hands in their pockets!) The *apasz* were the gypsies of Warsaw's streets and one could find them in a number of the city's working-class neighborhoods. Some of them played guitars and accordions. One of their group was known as Black Anna (*Czarna Anka*), the leader of the neighborhood prostitutes. These Brechtian-type men and women were romanticized in song and poem. One popular song about the *apasz* was "Barefoot with Spurs" (*Boso Ale w Ostrogach*). It was not a song you were likely to hear at the Friday night concert at Filharmonia Hall.

■ In many ways today's Warsaw is not the same city that found itself delirious with freedom in 1918. During World War II, most of the city's buildings were either destroyed or severely damaged. Deaths from battles and disease ran into the hundreds of thousands. More than four hundred streets and plazas were razed, moved, or renamed in the aftermath of the war. New streets and plazas have been added and others simply disappeared beneath the rubble. The buildings resemble those of the prewar era, but they are reconstructions and are now used for different purposes.

Since World War II, the city's acreage has increased and its population is slightly larger, but it is a somewhat different population. Warsaw was totally evacuated after the failed Uprising of 1944. Many members of the prewar population were killed, were exiled, or voluntarily moved. Adding to the few Varsovians who remained, a wave of immigrants swept into the city in 1945 with the Red Army and a contingent of Polish troops.

It was an antidote for sadness.

Zofia Chądzyńska

CHAPTER 2

Cultural Explosion

■ 1919–1923

On the Political Front

When the Second Republic took center stage in 1919 just about two-thirds of the population were predominantly Polish-speaking. More than thirteen percent were Ukrainians; almost nine percent were Yiddish-speaking Jews; and there were large enclaves of Germans and Byelorussians. Only a personality as strong as Piłsudski's could have dominated such a diverse mix of peoples.

Paderewski remained popular with the people but not with parliament. The Allies' refusal to confirm Poland's eastern borders after World War I and to settle the status of Danzig were seen as Paderewski's failures. Futhermore, he was increasingly known as an incompetent administrator. Mail went unanswered for months, and he kept no regular schedule. His wife's intrusion into affairs of state only added to his problems. Dejected, he offered his resignation to Piłsudski in November 1919.[1] He was persuaded to stay on but then several of his key ministers resigned. Unable to form a new government, he made good his resignation the following month.

After Paderewski's humiliating resignation, the country witnessed a quick succession of prime ministers. Marshal Piłsudski alone retained his position as the unelected head of state. He had enemies on both the left and the right but no one challenged his authority, and his strong presence probably prevented a complete collapse into anarchy.

With the Sejm's passage of the new constitution in March 1921, the executive branch of the government, without Piłsudski's acquiesence, was made subordinate to the Sejm (parliament). The authors of the constitution, apprehensive that Piłsudski would become president, inserted a number of provisions that would dilute his power, including one that expressly forbade the president to command the army in wartime.

The new constitution was modeled after the constitution of France's Third Republic, except that the Polish legislators paid more attention to social welfare. The March Constitution provided universal suffrage, guaranteed equal rights to all, abolished class and hereditary privileges, assured the rights of property owners, and offered free education to everyone. Like many constitutions it looked wonderful on paper, but reality was another matter.

The Catholic church was not given a prominent role by the constitution; it was recognized as the spiritual authority of the country almost as an afterthought, and perhaps its presence was taken for granted. The army meanwhile became a tool to be used by the political leaders and was to remain as such right up to the beginning of the war.

The March Constitution did not take effect immediately because one of its provisions called for new elections. These were held in 1922. Again, the right wing dominated parliament, with the centrist parties finishing second. A new political entry called the "Bloc of Nationalities" or the "minority clubs" made its appearance in this election.

Though the huge minorities—the Ukrainians, Jews, and Germans—were supposedly equal under the law, the fervor of nationalism was sweeping the country, and it soon became evident that the desires of the minorities would be subordinate to the goal of "national unity," a euphemism for Polishness. Non-Polish ethnics quickly realized they would have to band together for their own good in the face of an ever-growing demand for an all-Polish Catholic nation. This bloc managed to elect eighty-one deputies. The Sejm of 1922 also contained thirty-five Jewish deputies. The fragmented nature of the political situation is revealed by the fact that seventeen parties were represented in parliament.

The first task of the new parliament was to elect a president. Everyone assumed that Piłsudski would be selected, unchallenged. The marshal, piqued by the weakening of presidential powers, stunned the nation by announcing that he would not stand for office.

There followed a quick scramble for candidates, and out of it emerged two candidates, Maurycy Zamoyski, a wealthy landowner representing the National Democrats (*Endecja*), and Gabriel Narutowicz, a university professor and candidate of the coalition of leftist and centrist parties. The battle lines were thus drawn between nationalistic Catholic conservatives and the liberal left.

Narutowicz won, and the National Democrats immediately announced they would not support the government. Because he had received support from Jewish groups, Narutowicz was derided as "President of the Jews," and he received death threats. Five days after his inauguration he went to the Zachęta Gallery in the Society of Arts Building to open an exhibition and was shot dead by a right-wing fanatic acting on his own. The assassin, an artist and teacher, was arrested, tried, and eventually executed by a firing squad. Before dying he revealed that he had wanted to shoot Piłsudski but had settled for Narutowicz instead.

In the aftermath of the Narutowicz assassination, interim president Maciej Rataj named Władysław Sikorski, who had distinguished himself in the Polish-Soviet war and later became the Polish leader in World War II, to the post of prime minister. Sikorski, like Piłsudski, was a headstrong man. A personality clash seemed inevitable, but Piłsudski supported Sikorski's appointment.

In late December 1922, Stanisław Wojciechowski was elected to the presidency by the same coalition of leftists and centrists who had chosen Narutowicz. Wojciechowski had been a socialist and comrade of Piłsudski's in the old days, but now he was the candidate of the Peasant party. The stage was thus set for a dramatic confrontation between two friends, four years down the road.

■ Poland's economy continued to suffer under a series of finance ministers between 1919 and 1923. (In 1923 one American dollar would buy 15,000,000 Polish marks.) At least part of the fault for the failing economy lay in the deep political divisions; for example, the constitution made provisions for land reform, yet the National Democrats continued to block implementation of those provisions until 1923 when Wincenty Witos, head of the Piast Peasant party and prime minister of the day, agreed to a compromise with them. He would initiate only moderate reform in return for the National Democrats' support. It was tacitly understood that together they would oppose the left and any government supported by Piłsudski.

The biggest handicap the government faced, however, was rebuilding an economy that had been badly damaged by World War I. Both the German and the Russian armies had looted Poland. Machinery and entire factories were carted off. Food supplies were used up and many farms were destroyed while the country was occupied.

■   While Poland's first parliament was taking its seats, the Polish army was involved in a skirmish with Soviet troops in the eastern village of Bereza-Kartuska. Both Poland and the new Soviet government had sent troops to the territory separating Poland from the Soviet Union to claim it from the departing Germans. Their conflict in this little-known town was the beginning of a two-year war.

By the summer of 1919 the fighting had died down but not out. The Polish army held the upper hand, winning a series of minor victories as the fledgling Soviet leaders dealt with their more pressing domestic problems. But in the late spring of 1920 the newly formed Red Army got a new leader, the charismatic General Tukhachevsky, who announced that the path to worldwide domination lay over the dead body of "White Poland."[2] He issued his famous Order of the Day, saying "On to Wilno, Minsk, and Warsaw! March!"

Beginning in July the Red Army scored a string of victories that sent the Poles reeling back toward Warsaw. The Allies had been reluctant to support Poland, even though they—especially Great Britain—were committed to undermining the Russian Revolution. It was not until the tide turned in favor of Poland that they switched their allegiance.

France had sent a team of advisors, led by General Weygand, to assist Piłsudski, and the League of Nations sent a representative, Viscount D'Abernon, to observe the fighting. He kept a diary in which he reported the remarkable aplomb with which the Varsovians viewed the war. Not until the Red Army appeared across the river did they show any true alarm.

The war finally turned on a series of unexpected Polish victories, beginning in the village of Radzymin, about twelve miles from the center of Warsaw. After that, a combination of daring strategy and the valor of the Polish soldiers put the Red Army to flight, retreating to Moscow. The Poles pushed all the way to Kiev, which they took, and actually crossed the Soviet border.

Negotiations to end the fighting began in the summer of 1920 and went on until the fall. The Politburo was ready to accept Piłsudski's terms for peace, but Lenin insisted on control of parts of the Ukraine. Piłsudski, now accused of prolonging the fighting, was furious at Lenin and said angrily: "there's only one thing to tell them [the Bolsheviks]: *We* are a force in the world, and *you* are destined for the boneyard." In dealing with the Poles, Piłsudski said, the Soviets "ought to be humble beggars."[3]

Piłsudski may have slightly exaggerated Poland's standing in the world at the time; however, he was obviously not intimidated by the Bolsheviks or the Red Army. Unfortunately he was not present at Yalta to confront Stalin with his opinion of the problems in dealing with the Soviet government: "There can be no question of relations or diplomatic negotiations. You don't practice the former and don't recognize the latter."[4]

The war formally ended in October, and Poland resumed the business of rebuilding. This war is little known but of vast importance: If the Poles had not stopped the Red Army at the Vistula, the Soviets would have had a clear run to Berlin and perhaps on to Western Europe.

There were fewer celebrations after this war than there had been in 1918; instead, Warsaw breathed a sigh of relief. More difficult times lay ahead. Unemployment was rampant, its numbers swelled by discharged soldiers. While the city had suffered little damage compared to what lay in store on the next German visit, the economy was in shambles. The Polish mark stood at 590 to the dollar; in 1921 it would shoot up to 2,922 to the dollar.

The aristocracy, as Topolski had proudly boasted, might have been as good as any in Europe, but by now its numbers were dwin-

■ Poland during the Second Republic.

dling as fast as its resources, due to emigration during the occupation, deaths, and the break-up of estates. Though many young people were leaving the farms to come to the cities, and in fact the population of Warsaw rose to a million by 1920, Poland remained largely an agrarian nation. The capital city insisted on pretending otherwise.

The Literary Life

While the Red Army was gathering strength and preparing for a frontal assault on Warsaw, a new wave of Polish writers appeared on the literary front. They called themselves Skamander, from the name of the river Troy in Stanisław Wyspiański's poem "Acropolis." They congregated at a Warsaw café, Under the Sign of the Picador, where they read their poems to each other and to anyone else who would listen. The Skamander were the first generation of writers to experience an independent Poland in modern times, and they celebrated with enthusiasm.

In January they launched their own magazine, also called *Skamander*. The first issue of *Skamander* contained the poets' manifesto: "We believe deeply in the present, we feel we are all its children. . . . We do not wish to pretend that evil is nonexistent, but our love is stronger than evil. . . . We love the present with a strong first love."[5]

Their manifesto goes on in tones that seem to make poetry into their religion: "We have an unshakable faith in the blessed quality of good rhyme, in the divine origin of rhythm, in revelation through images born in ecstasy and through shapes chiseled by work."[6]

Skamander's exuberance was liberating. It freed writers from the romanticism and symbolism that had characterized earlier Polish poets. Skamander poets were not direct descendants of Poland's great nineteenth-century romantic poets Adam Mickiewicz, Juliusz

Słowacki, and Zygmunt Krasiński. The Young Poland poets and writers acted as godfathers to the Skamander movement.

Young Poland, whose popularity peaked in the first two decades of the twentieth century, had been influenced by the French symbolists of the late nineteenth century, especially Baudelaire and Rimbaud, and by Henrik Ibsen and Edgar Allan Poe. The Polish writers were less flamboyant and not as bizarre as the French. The movement included future Nobel Prize winner Władysław Reymont, playwright and artist Stanisław Wyspiański, the decadent poet-philosopher Stanisław Przybyszewski – poet of the "naked soul," whose scandal-ridden life was the exception among these rather staid poets – and Leopold Staff and Bolesław Leśmian. Stefan Żeromski, known as the "conscience of Polish literature," was the leading novelist of this group. His best-known work is a long, historical novel titled *Ashes* (*Popioły*).

These men continued to write and publish into the interwar period and in some cases, into the post – World War II era. But by 1920 they were already looked upon as the elder statesmen of Polish literature.

One of the Young Poland writers, the critic-essayist-translator, Tadeusz Boy-Żeleński, was among the *Skamander* founders. He and Reymont were the primary editors. Others involved in launching *Skamander* were the novelist Jarosław Iwaszkiewicz, and the poets Kazimierz Wierzyński, Jan Lechoń, Julian Tuwim, and Antoni Słonimski.

Boy-Żeleński's career revealed great intellectual versatility. Educated at the famous Jagiellonian University in Kraków, he took a degree in medicine and began a practice. According to Nobel laureate Czesław Miłosz, he was influenced toward the literary life by a meeting with Przybyszewski, and went on to write poetry and literary essays.

Boy (a name he gave himself in jest) also took an early interest in cabaret life, and at one time wrote sketches for Kraków's legendary Green Balloon. There, he poked fun at the clergy and politicians, and even questioned Poland's ability to overcome its many problems and become a great nation again. When Boy moved to Warsaw and began reviewing cabaret and theater performances, his talent for satire stood him in good stead. His daily commentary in the *Morning Courier* (*Kurier Poranny*) was eagerly read by both performers and their fans. Though he chided Poles for their sexual conservatism, it was his indignant letter to a cabaret owner that resulted in a more modest display of flesh by Warsaw's chorus girls.

Boy's greatest achievement was in translation. He made French literature more accessible to Polish readers, translating some one hundred works by Rabelais, Villon, Racine, Voltaire, Molière, Diderot, Rousseau, Balzac, and Stendhal.

Two of the more popular literary figures who began their careers with *Skamander* were Julian Tuwim and Antoni Słonimski. Tuwim, a Polish Jew who bore an uncanny resemblance to the young George Gershwin, made no attempt to assimilate into Polish society nor did he confine himself to Jewish culture. He has at various times been referred to as the Walt Whitman of Polish verse, and a leader of the country's futurist movement. He cannot, however, be firmly pegged as a member of any school of poetry. His interests were far-ranging and included demonology and collecting. The language Tuwim used in his verse also separated him from his peers, for it frequently contained slang and words that he had invented. He is said to be one of the most difficult of Polish poets to translate.

By 1918, Tuwim had already published his first volume of poetry, *Lying in Wait for God.* As the twenties progressed, Tuwim's poems became a frontal assault on the perceived reality of the day. He published two more volumes of poetry, *The Seventh Autumn* (*Siodma Jesień*) and *The Fourth Book of Poems* (*Wierszy Tom Czwarty*). Miłosz has described Tuwim as the number one Polish poet of the interwar period.[7]

In addition to writing poetry, Tuwim was a student of Russian literature and translated into Polish some of the work of Pushkin, Mayakovsky, and Pasternak. His main source of income, however, was the numerous cabaret sketches he wrote.

Tuwim's contemporary, Antoni Słonimski, had a sober mien but was in fact quite witty, as readers of his column in *The Literary News* attested. This tall, bespectacled son of a Jewish physician had studied painting in Warsaw and in Paris before World War I, but gave it up to be a writer. He was phenomenally prolific, writing novels, poetry, theater reviews, cabaret sketches, and literary criticism. Like Tuwim, he published his first volume of verse, *Sonnets*, in 1918.

The careers of Tuwim and Słonimski ran parallel to each other, and in 1921 they collaborated on a bizarre tract titled *The Busy Bee: A Farmer's Almanac*. Miłosz said it was "liable to drive any real farmer insane," and he described it as symbolic of the confusion of the times.[8]

Many critics consider Tuwim and Słonimski as Poland's finest writers. But not everyone agrees (as is the custom in Poland). A Polish writer-critic in London remarked to me that while Tuwim was certainly an outstanding poet right from the beginning, his career had no high points, that he was consistently good but never approached greatness. As for Słonimski, the same writer quipped that his fame was not entirely disconnected from his long life (1895–1976).

■ Although it was the Skamanderi who moved to center stage in Poland's literary scene at the beginning of this decade, a number of other artistic movements also surfaced at the time—futurists, dadaists (some of whom were also Marxists), and the First Vanguard.[9] As their name suggests, the futurists were artists and writers more concerned with what was to come than with what had been.

They saw themselves as more socially enlightened than their literary brethren and viewed the future of Poland through the prism of Marxism. Some of their writing extolled the virtues of the Russian revolution and they probably wished that the political ferment next door would spread to Poland.

The futurist movement itself had a short life and for all intents and purposes was moribund by the mid-1920s. Few people paid attention to its call for the overthrow of the established order in politics and in the arts.

The poet and novelist Bruno Jasieński was involved with the futurists for a time. Early in his career Jasieński wrote poems and novels with themes having to do with social reform, such as the collection of poems *Song on Hunger* (*Pieśń o Głodzie*). Perhaps the most telling of Jasieński's work was his surrealistic novel, *The Legs of Izolda Morgan* (1923), which depicted a world controlled by machines. Jasieński left Poland in 1925 seeking a more compatible environment in Paris, but in 1929 the French government expelled him as an "undesirable alien" after he wrote a novel attacking French society (*Je Brûle Paris*). Jasieński then went to the Soviet Union, where he lived until he and other Polish Communist writers were eliminated by Stalin.

A more realistic view of life in Poland was given by the journalist and author Juliusz Kaden-Bandrowski. He had begun his writing career before the war and served with Piłsudski to whom he became devoted.

His relationship with Piłsudski undoubtedly influenced his novel *General Barcz* (1923), whose protagonist is an ambitious army officer who longs to create a perfect society. Other of his novels were critical of Polish society. In the 1920s he produced half a dozen books as well as articles, essays, and short stories.

Jarosław Iwaszkiewicz, another leading literary figure in the Warsaw of the twenties, wrote poetry that had all the appearances of being anti-intellectual despite being an intellectual himself. He had a wide following because of his commercial novels, such as the autobiographical *Hilary, Son of a Bookkeeper* (*Hilary, Syn Buchaltera*).

Like many of his peers Iwaszkiewicz had successes in different genres. His accomplishments included a libretto for Karol Szymanowski and two plays, *Summer in Nohant* (*Lato w Nohant*), based on an incident in Chopin's life, and *Masquerade* (*Maskarada*), about Pushkin.

Life among Poland's Jews was a reflection of the unsettled conditions of the country itself. The Zionists were urging emigration to Palestine while other Jewish groups were equally adamant about remaining in Poland, some favoring assimilation, others advocating separatism.

In the midst of this debate, the Zionists launched their own newspaper in Warsaw in 1923, *Our Review* (*Nasz Przegląd*), edited by Jakub Apenszlak. It was written in Polish, a journalistic first in the country. Prior to this, some Jewish novelists and poets had begun to express themselves in Polish, in Zionist periodicals, when writing about personal experience, but *Our Review* was the first attempt by the Jewish press to offer its point of view to a broader audience, including those Jews who didn't speak Yiddish.

Along with *Our Review*, a number of other Polish-language Zionist newspapers began to appear in other Polish cities, and they gave the pro-immigrationists a platform from which to promote their cause. This in turn caused a shift in favor of those Jews who advocated immigration to Palestine; it simultaneously laid a foundation for a more aggressive Polish-Jewish literature heavily weighted in favor of Zionism.

Literature in all its forms flourished in Warsaw during the twenties and thirties. Thanks to Philip Roth and Jan Kott, some interwar Polish writing, like the works of Bruno Schulz (not a Varsovian) and Witold Gombrowicz, underwent a revival in the United States in the 1980s. Anthologies of Polish writing contain works by the outstanding writers of the time – Jarosław Iwaszkiewicz, Konstanty Ildefons Gałczyński, Jan Lechoń, Kazimierz Wierzyński, and the women novelists Zofia Nałkowska (Schulz's mentor and alleged lover), Maria Kuncewicz, and Maria Dąbrowska.

The Club Scene

April 1919 was memorable for two events, one military, the other cultural. On Easter Sunday, Polish troops recaptured Piłsudski's beloved Wilno. And back in Warsaw a new cabaret, Qui Pro Quo, opened in the Luxemburg Gallery on Senatorska Street, near the Saxon Gardens. It was to become a legend in its time. For those who lived in Warsaw between the wars, Qui Pro Quo was the sine qua non of cabarets.

A new form of entertainment for the masses, cabaret, had begun in Paris, spread to Berlin and Munich, and made its first appearance in Warsaw just before World War I. The impresario Arnold Szyfman, who is best known for founding the Polish Theater, opened the first club, Momusa. It was followed in quick succession by the Mirage, the Sphinx, and the Black Cat. If theater and opera were considered high culture for the upper classes and the educated, cabaret became the most significant form of entertainment for the less cultured. But, like white Americans who ventured into Harlem in the Roaring Twenties, Warsaw's elite eventually discovered the forbidden joys of cabaret life.

Warsaw cabaret had much in common with its Berlin cousin; both were bawdy and politically cynical. Often shows featured poetry readings and topless showgirls on the same bill. An evening's program in a Warsaw cabaret might combine a reading of Polish literature, scantily clad dancing girls, monologuists or stand-up comics, and original humorous skits, usually skewering some popular personality of the day. There was a small orchestra to provide the music and a master of ceremonies to preside over the evening.

The early cabaret shows were performed in noisy, smoke-filled theaters. Their owners came from the world of commerce — one man had owned a highly successful shoe repair shop — and not infrequently from the underworld. Nevertheless, some of Poland's best writers, including Tuwim and Słonimski, honed their skills by writing sketches for these clubs.

Performers sometimes recited poetry as part of a night's program, but the language of Warsaw's cabarets was a far cry from the romantic verse of Adam Mickiewicz. It was less formal, reflected contemporary usage, and contained German and Russian expressions, leftovers from a century of occupation.

Cabaret was more democratic than Polish theater (and cheaper), and it rivaled the theater for attendance. Speaking of the cabarets, Zofia Chądzyńska recalled, "People might have been poor but they always found the money to go there."

For Polish entertainers, Qui Pro Quo represented the pinnacle of success. For cabaret-goers it was the pinnacle of entertainment.

It had opened its doors on April 4, 1919, in a space that had formerly been a roller skating rink. Tadeusz Wittlin noted that the renovation took about three months, but the acoustics were then found to be inadequate until the floor of the orchestra pit was raised and rebuilt atop a layer of Clicquot Club bottles. When completed, Qui Pro Quo could seat an audience of about five hundred.

Jerzy Boczkowski, a former songwriter, was hired as its manager. Until then he had been best known for his 1920 hit tune "Echoes of the Café." The club's directing and writing was handled by a top-notch team of Tuwim, the actor Konrad Tom, and Andrzej Włast, who turned out to be more successful as a director-lyricist than as a poet.[10]

From its opening day Qui Pro Quo was a smash hit. In fact, it was so popular that legitimate theaters, including the respected Polish Theater, avoided scheduling premieres when Qui Pro Quo was opening a new show. On those nights the cream of Warsaw society swarmed to the basement of the Luxemburg Gallery to watch the latest revue. All of Warsaw's best comics, dancers, singers, and actors eventually appeared on the club's tiny stage.

Though she was just a young girl when Qui Pro Quo opened, Chądzyńska later attended shows there. She described it as "a cabaret frequented by the intelligentsia—especially the Skamander group of poets and it had wonderful scripts and actors. All the Skamander wrote for Qui Pro Quo—each opening night was a party, a celebration."

In the club's heyday, "the MC at Qui Pro Quo was a Hungarian, Fryderyk Járosy. He spoke Polish poorly, but his mistakes and his asides to the audience became part of the everyday speech of Varsovians. In fact, part of the bon ton of the day was to know all the Yiddish jokes, the *szmoncesy*, of comedians like Krukowski or Lawiński, and to weave them into one's conversations."

Chądzyńska was wistful: "Never again in my life have I encountered such a sense of humor, and such joy, as at Qui Pro Quo. It was an antidote for sadness."[11]

■ Despite frequently being on the brink of financial disaster, Warsaw's cabarets seemed to flourish. For a time another new club, Mirage, provided Qui Pro Quo's main competition. This situation was resolved when one of the Mirage staff left a lighted cigarette in a dressing room. The building was severely damaged, and the club had to find a new home. Its director, Seweryn Majde, moved his company to a nearby restaurant; unfortunately, his fickle audience did not follow, and Mirage was forced to close. Majde and some of his cast were then hired by Qui Pro Quo.

■ One of the major cabaret events of the decade did not take place at a major nightclub. Before Qui Pro Quo came into being, its future star Hanka Ordonówna was just beginning her career. While a sixteen-year-old student at the Warsaw Opera and Ballet School, Hanka and several of her friends were offered jobs dancing in the chorus line of another cabaret, Sphinx. At that time she was still known by her real name, Marysia Pietruszyńska. When it came time to feature her as a solo artist, her director had misgivings about that name, feeling that perhaps it was too ordinary. After running through several combinations of names, she and he settled on Hanka Ordonówna and then set about launching her glamorous career.

Her first career move turned out to be a minor disaster: She moved from the Sphinx to the ill-starred Mirage. After the fire she was offered a job in Lwów, where she sang and danced in a run-down theater, the Bagatelle. Like the other members of the cast, she was poorly paid. Hanka then left the Bagatelle and went on the road, performing in Kraków and Wilno before returning to her beloved Warsaw.[12]

Though she had begun her career as a dancer, Hanka had a more-than-adequate voice – low-pitched and throaty – and it was as a singer that she had her greatest success.

Cinemas and Cafés

That the capital and the nation were opening up to new ideas was evidenced by the dramatic increase in film production. Film as an art form was relatively new, even though the Poles had begun experimenting with the medium in the late 1890s. Their early experiments, although little known, kept them in step with the international film community. In 1893, for example, before the Lumieres publicly unveiled their movie camera, a Polish scientist had constructed a crude camera of his own. By the turn of the century another Pole had invented the pleograph, and Jan Szczepanik had received a British patent for color film. Despite these mechanical strides, Poland produced only four films in 1914 and only fifteen in 1922. Most of these films were based on themes from contemporary Polish literature, such as *The Shriek* (*Krzyk*), from the novel by Stanisław Przybyszewski, *On the Bright Shore* (*Na Jasnym Brzegu*), based on a story by Henryk Sienkiewicz, and *The Beauty of Life* (*Uroda Życia*) and *The Year 1863*, both adapted from the fiction of Stefan Żeromski. Even the work of the national poet-hero, Adam Mickiewicz, was plumbed for possible movie plots. In 1920 a film based on his ballad "The Watch" (*Czaty*), was made. And in 1928 one enterprising director produced a wonderful cinematic version of Mickiewicz's great narrative poem, *Pan Tadeusz*. Other films were based on more contemporary novels, such as *The Peasants* (*Chłopi*), Władysław Reymont's monumental trilogy.[13]

In general Polish film of this era was mediocre. To rectify this situation a small group of directors founded START, an association for the advancement of artistic films. But it wasn't until the late 1930s that Poland began to develop a respected body of cinematic work, and that was largely the result of the efforts of Aleksander Ford, who made *Street Legion* (*Legion Ulicy*) in 1932.

Poland's actors of those early days were not particularly distinguished either. Among the early film actors only Pola Negri (née Apolonia Chałupiec) achieved international success. Negri was born in 1896 and at the age of eight was enrolled in the Warsaw Opera's ballet school. She made her acting debut in 1912 in a stage production of Aleksander Fredro's *Vows of the Virgins* at Warsaw's Little Theater (*Teatr Mały*). Her appearance—thin as a reed, with dark blue eyes set in a pale face—caused a minor sensation.

Negri first appeared on screen during the first year of the war in *The Prisoner of the Senses* (*Niewolnica Zmysłów*). Her second film,

The Wife (*Żona*), a tragedy, really launched her international career. The Sphinx film studio in 1916 immediately signed the young actress to a two-year contract during which she appeared in *The Students, Beasts, The Secret of Aleje Ujazdowskie, Arabella,* and *Her Last Act.*

Negri left the Sphinx studio before her contract expired (and was promptly sued) to go to Berlin, where she continued acting in films. She made a brief return to Warsaw after World War I to make the movie *Madame DuBarry*; however, Negri played almost no role in the growth of the Polish film industry.

In 1922, in the company of Ernst Lubitsch, she left Poland permanently for the bright lights of Hollywood. During the era of silent films she was a top star and made a fortune before sound put an end to her acting days.

Foreign films (mostly American) had a larger impact on the city's populace than did the homegrown product. Aniela Mieczysławska remarked, as she served me tea in a London flat filled with mementos of old Poland, that as English became more popular than French, American films became correspondingly more popular. There can be little doubt that the popularity of American and foreign films reflected the Poles' desire for modernity, for a break with the heavy traditions of the past.

The large number of American film imports fueled a huge growth in the number of cinemas in Warsaw. By one account Warsaw had fifty-nine cinemas by the time of the German invasion.[14] Many of those cinemas were to be found on Marszałkowska, the boulevard that was Warsaw's equivalent of Broadway. Marszałkowska was a busy commercial street running parallel to the Royal Way. Interwar photos of Marszałkowska show it bustling with crowds of pedestrians spilling out of cinemas, clubs, and cafés into a street where trams, dorożkis, and automobiles came together in a collision of the old and the new.

Looking at the cinema marquees, one saw names reflecting the dreamlike world of film: Atlantic, Casino, Colosseum, Elite, Fame, Florida, Hollywood, Love, Mars, Metro, Rialto, Riviera, Rome, Sphinx—and many others. As Halina Mendelsohn—who worked as a cashier in one of her family's four theaters—said, "It was just like Hollywood" (which she imagined was crowded with cinemas).

Varsovians went to these movie houses looking for a romanticized version of life in faraway America and then tried to prolong the illusion by stopping for a coffee or aperitif at the Belle-Vue or the Satyr or at one of the many other bars and cafés dotting this tree-lined avenue.

In that era movie-going was not a family experience, even though the movie houses were owned by families, not corporations. In their early days Polish cinemas were forbidden to children. There was no rating system and all films were "unacceptable" for them. In Warsaw, the authorities kept a close check on whether cinema owners were obeying the law. Inspectors would visit the movie houses looking for underage persons. Those who violated the law were first given a warning; if a theater persisted in admitting children, it was shut down.

Witkacy and the Legitimate Theater

Warsaw's legitimate theater presented Varsovians with a wide variety of plays, including many Western imports, as the more progressive wing sought to enlarge its repertoire beyond traditional Polish drama. Some of the highlights of the 1924 season included a version of Dickens's *Cricket on the Hearth* (*Świerszcz za Kominem*) in four acts at the Little Theater; *The Eaglet* (*Orlę*) by Edmond Rostand at the Variety; *The Red Mill* (*Czerwony Młyn*) by Ferenc Molnar (later titled *Mima* when it premiered in New York in 1928) at the Polish Theater; *Knock, or the Triumph of Medicine* (*Knock, Czyli Triumf Medycyny*), a farce by Julian Romains; and *Danton*, a drama about the French Revolution, by Romain Rolland. (Several years later

Stanisława Przybyszewska, daughter of the notorious Stanisław Przybyszewski, would write her own stage version of *Danton*. She read the Rolland version as well as *Danton Tods* by Georg Büchner, in 1924. She disagreed with their portrayals of the French revolutionary but was definitely influenced by Büchner's version, which she studied intensely.)[15]

These imports added to a full plate of dramas and comedies by Polish authors such as Juliusz Słowacki and Zygmont Nowakowski. Warsaw theater also saw a very popular play by the great novelist Stefan Żeromski, titled *My Little Quail Has Run Away* (*Uciekła Mi Przepióreczka*), written the year before his death. This is one of the few plays Żeromski wrote. *My Little Quail* began rehearsing in 1924, and its first performance by the National Theater took place in February 1925. The opening was a great success, and Żeromski was called to the stage several times by the audience. Juliusz Osterwa enhanced his reputation as both an actor and a director with this play. *My Little Quail* has continued to be popular in Poland, and during World War II it was even performed in Polish prisoner-of-war camps.

■ When one reads a list of Polish playwrights who came to the fore during this period, the name of Stanisław Ignacy Witkiewicz stands out; Witkacy, as he was universally known, always occupies a chapter of his own. Independent-minded, bizarre, with a taste for adventure, Witkacy led a fascinating, peripatetic existence that was envied by many of his peers. Although he was admired by writers and critics, he remained aloof from the literary crowd. Unlike many of his contemporaries, he was not a habitué of Warsaw's cabarets nor did he ever write for them.

Witkacy was born in Warsaw in 1885 when it was still a part of the Russian empire. While he was quite young the family moved to the resort area of Zakopane in Poland's southwest corner, where

he spent much of his time. His godmother was the famed Polish actress, Helena Modjeska (Modrzejewska). His father was an artist,
and so the son began painting while still quite young – his nickname
derives from the manner in which he signed his canvases. At the age
of eight he wrote his first play, but painting remained his main interest. In his midteens Witkacy began exhibiting his work, making
his debut with a one-man show in Zakopane. By the time he
reached the age of twenty he had begun writing philosophical trea-
tises.

By 1918 Witkacy had already experienced a lifetime of adventure and accomplishment. He had met and traveled with the composer Karol Szymanowski and the anthropologist Bronisław
Malinowski, with whom he allegedly had an affair. Their relationship, whatever it was, did not last long and ended with bitterness
on both sides. Meanwhile, Witkacy continued to paint and exhibit
his work. He also traveled around Europe where he saw exhibits
by Gauguin, the Fauvists, and the cubists in Paris, all of which influenced his painting as well as his writing.

At age twenty-three he had an affair with the actress Irena
Solska, described by one critic as "neurotic and . . . impressionable
in her reactions to the world," but who nevertheless "set the audiences aquiver."[16] Witkacy wrote a novel about their affair titled
The 622 Downfalls of Bungo, or the Demonic Woman.

Before World War I broke out, Witkacy had been psychoana-
lyzed and been engaged to a young woman who had committed suicide. When World War I started, Witkacy went to St. Petersburg
and enrolled in the officers' training school, despite the fierce objec-
tions of his father, whose sympathies lay with the anti-czarists. He
fought and was wounded in 1915 and was elected commissar by
the members of his regiment. While recuperating from his wounds
Witkacy was introduced to morphine. Later, he incorporated that
experience and other drug experiments into a long essay, "Nicotine,
Alcohol, Cocaine, Peyote, Morphine, and Ether."

After the war he returned to Poland and continued to pursue his dual careers of painting and writing. Witkacy's first plays were produced just after World War I. Both actors and directors frequently complained that they did not understand his scripts. That did not deter him. In one year—1920—he wrote ten plays, including *The Pragmatists*, in which he attempted to illustrate his theory of Pure Form. (He wrote thirty plays altogether but only seven were ever produced.) Witkacy strongly believed that art and life should be entirely separated and that certain art forms, such as novels, could not be pure because their influences came from life experience. As far as he was concerned, only music truly represented pure form.

The Pragmatists was published in Warsaw in 1920 and performed the following year, causing controversy among the critics. It was not a box-office success. That same year, another play, titled *Tumor Mózgowicz* (the name of the main character), opened in Kraków, where the critics tore it to shreds. One of them wrote: "It seems we are watching and hearing the ravings of a syphilitic in the last stages of creeping paralysis. . . . Witkiewicz's play is a total absurdity from which nothing can ever arise. It is an unnatural clinical abortion. It should be put in alcohol and studied by psychopathologists."[17]

Witkacy's artwork occasionally set off similar outbursts. Of his own painting he once remarked: "My paintings were not painted in cold blood, but quite the contrary, in the state of total unconsciousness."[18]

In 1923 Witkacy married and shuttled back and forth between his wife in Warsaw and his mother in Zakopane. Daniel Gerould, Witkacy's biographer, once met his subject in Warsaw. He described some of Witkacy's idiosyncrasies in the foreword to *The Madman and the Nun, and Other Stories.* "He had the habit of keeping a numbered list of his acquaintances, and whenever he lowered the position of one of them, he would inform him about it in

an 'official' letter."[19] Witkacy invited the young Gerould to his
home, where he displayed his collection of canes, including one that
had belonged to Madame Curie, and an umbrella that had once belonged to Paderewski.

In 1925 Witkacy wrote his last drama before turning to writing novels. His *Beelzebub Sonata* was based on the Faust legend.
Witkacy's theme was that all artists must break bread with the devil
if they are to succeed. Unlike other dramatists who used the Faust
legend in their plots, Witkacy viewed the artist's dilemma in a
sardonic way so that his version was more farce than tragedy.[20]

The play's central character, a composer (said to be modeled
after Arnold Schönberg), reflected yet another of Witkacy's seemingly unlimited interests, music. At age five, under the tutelage of
his mother, Witkacy had begun to play the piano. He developed
that talent throughout his younger years but as he grew older his
interests in painting and writing became dominant. Nevertheless,
he remained interested in music, particularly in new schools and
techniques, virtually all his life.

Witkacy's friendships helped him stay current with the music
scene. Among his friends were Artur Rubinstein and the composer
Karol Szymanowski, whose opera *King Roger* was completed in
1924. Witkacy had known Szymanowski, his Zakopane neighbor,
since his youth. Witkacy was keenly aware that the new develop-
ments in modern music, embodied in Schönberg's works, paralleled
breakthrough movements in art.

Witkacy's modern temperament and the nature of his thought
are signaled by the titles of his plays and other works: *Miss Tootli-
Pootli* (an operetta), *The Independence of Triangles, Metaphysics of a
Two-Headed Calf, Dainty Shapes and Hairy Apes, The Madman and
the Nun, The Beelzebub Sonata.*

"A mad eccentric artist." That is how he is remembered by Feliks Topolski, his contemporary. Topolski also commented that
Witkacy "really was the first one in Europe with the concept of the

theater of the absurd, a theater of anger and absurdity. He created fantastic plays which now . . . are being played everywhere. He was an outstanding personality."[21]

By the end of the twenties Witkacy's absurdist work would look prescient, full of predictions that would prove to be horribly true.

Yiddish Literature and Theater

Polish Jews have always played an important role in Poland's cultural life. This is especially true in the interwar period. Antoni Słonimski, Ludwik Lawiński, Julian Tuwim, Janusz Korczak, Marian Hemar, Mieczysław Grydzewski, the conductor Grzegorz Fitelberg, the theater entrepreneur Arnold Szyfman – these are but a few of the Jews who contributed greatly to the city's reputation as the center of contemporary Polish culture.

But there was also in Warsaw – and throughout Poland – a Jewish cultural life completely separate from the larger community. This was not accidental. The General Charter, drawn up in 1263 at Jewish insistence, gave Jews the right to establish their own quarters within Polish cities; it also established their right to practice their own religion and to establish schools in which to educate their children in Jewish cultural and linguistic traditions. These rights were extended in the fourteenth century by another Polish king, Casimir III Wielki (the Great) when he offered the Jews sanctuary from persecution in other countries.

It was not until the Enlightenment, however, that Yiddish first made its appearance as a vehicle for Jewish literature and theater. Until then the language of educated Jews had been Hebrew, an effective barrier between the upper- and middle-class Jews and their peasant and working-stock brethren.

Yiddish sprang from the same Old German roots as does English, hence the similarity of some words. It developed in Central and

Eastern Europe and was the language in which many legends and myths of the Jewish people were passed along. In the nineteenth century, plays written in Yiddish by educated Jews gradually evolved out of the folk stories connected with the sometimes raucous celebrations of Purim, a Jewish festival that commemorates the deliverance of the Jews in ancient Persia from destruction. From then on the use of Yiddish in literature and theater grew rapidly, and by the early twentieth century it was the common mode of expression in novels, plays, and poetry, especially in America. One of the foremost (and perhaps the last) practitioners of Yiddish writing was the former Varsovian, Isaac Bashevis Singer.

His older brother, Isaac Joshua, was the first of the Singer brothers to establish a literary reputation. Joshua had come to Warsaw in 1921 with several published stories under his belt. His play, *Earth-Cry* (*Erd Vey*) was first published in Poland and also brought him fame abroad when it was produced in New York in 1923. He followed that triumph with two books of stories, *The Pearl and Other Tales* (*Perl un Andere Dertailungen*) and *Oh, Strange World* (*Oy Fremder Erd*). That led to an assignment as a correspondent in the Soviet Union for the New York-based *Jewish Daily Forward*. His novel *Shtol un Azyn* appeared in Yiddish in 1927; it was translated into English as *Blood Harvest* and published by Alfred A. Knopf in 1935, and revived by Funk and Wagnalls in 1969 as *Steel and Iron*. In 1923 Joshua was hired as an editor in Warsaw for the magazine *Literary Pages* (*Literarishe Bletter*). He then wrote to his younger brother, Isaac Bashevis, still living in the village of Dzików, offering him a proofreading job.

Isaac Bashevis was only too happy to move to Warsaw. He had already tried and discarded the idea of becoming a rabbi, having spent an unhappy term at Warsaw's Tachkemoni Rabbinical Institute. At this stage of his life he was more concerned with the pleasures of the flesh. He was eighteen and desperate to have his first love affair. Nevertheless, Singer began to spend long hours at the

Writers' Club soon after his arrival in Warsaw. The club was a hangout for ambitious, unpublished writers, and for the older, established writers who were objects of their scorn. Debates about communism and socialism were continuous and heated, along with talk of literature, poetry, and philosophy.

Of his visits to the club, Singer wrote: "Nearly everyone at the Writers' Club bore some passion and was blinded by it. The young writers all aspired to become literary geniuses and many of them were convinced they already were, except that other people refused to acknowledge the fact. The Communists all waited patiently for the social revolution to begin so that they could exact revenge upon all the bourgeois, Zionists, socialists, petit bourgeois, the lumpen proletariat, the clergy, and most of all the editors who refused to publish them. The few women members were convinced that they were the victims of male contempt for the female sex."[22]

■   Poland has a long and honorable tradition of Yiddish theater. There were several centers of Yiddish theater in Poland—Kraków, Łódż, Białystok, Wilno, and Warsaw. The largest of these was Wilno, known to the Jewish world as the Jerusalem of Lithuania. The Lithuanian capital, however, lacked Warsaw's comparative sophistication and was not nearly the attraction for talent that the Polish capital was.

Though space for commercial theaters became scarce in Warsaw between the wars due to the combination of a depressed construction industry and the rapid spread of movie houses, one could still see Yiddish actors and actresses performing in the Kaminsky Theater, and at the Eliseum, the Central, the Eldorado, the Venus, the Scala, and later the innovative and grand Nowości.

The performers recited their lines in Yiddish, but their material was frequently contemporary in nature. It was not limited to the traditional Yiddishkayt—plays only about Yiddish culture—but included Shakespeare, Strindberg, and the European avant-garde. Although few non-Jews would admit to patronizing Yiddish theater—there was a language problem, of course—there seemed to be no lack of interest in the other direction. The Jews of Warsaw not only attended Yiddish theater, but also went outside their district to attend plays performed in Polish.

Despite the constitution of 1921, which guaranteed everyone equal rights, many Jews felt uncomfortable with the rising tide of Polish nationalism. Jews who resisted the call to emigrate were divided between assimilationists and those loyal to Jewish culture and religious traditions, who wished to remain in Poland but separate from the Christian population.

The assimilationists, however, were poised on the horns of a dilemma—they were not quite accepted by Polish Catholics and were treated with disdain by other Jews. Their quandary was best summed up by the songwriter Marian Hemar, himself a convert to Catholicism: "That I'm hobbling with grace seems true / alas, I remember I'm a Jew."[23]

Warsaw is a bewitching city, the great capital of
Eastern Europe, the Paris of that region, the intellectual and artistic center radiating a Polish Sla-
vism sharpened and heightened by occidental and
Latin culture.

M. and L. Barat-Forlière
Notre Sœur – La Pologne (Paris, 1928)

CHAPTER 3

Welcome to Cabaret!

■ 1924-1925

On the Political Front

Although President Wojciechowski remained in power for several
years immediately following Narutowicz's assassination, General
Sikorski's prime ministry enjoyed popular support for only about
six months. By the late spring of 1923, his government was sunk,
indirectly torpedoed by the issue of land reform.

Soon after Sikorski took office, Wincenty Witos, leader of the
Piast Peasant party, had begun quietly negotiating with the right
wing to produce a moderate land-reform program. The coalition
of these two opposing groups forced Sikorski to resign as prime
minister. Witos succeeded him and immediately appointed a number of National Democrats to cabinet posts, a payoff for their
cooperation on limited land reform. Piłsudski, still seething at the
right's involvement in Narutowicz's murder, resigned as chief of the

general staff rather than serve in the same cabinet with them. Several months later he quit his last remaining post, head of the Inner War Council.[1] Parliament awarded him a lifelong pension and adopted a resolution of gratitude for his service to the nation.

Witos's political manuevering fed into the economic collapse of 1923. The undercapitalized banks that had proliferated after the war began to fail. The independent government proved inept at collecting taxes. The Germans gave Witos a shove by increasing duties on Polish exports while shipping many of their own goods elsewhere. The National Democratic party reneged on its pledge to support land reform. Numerous strikes in the winter of 1923 sounded the death knell for the Witos government.

An economist, Władysław Grabski, became the new prime minister. Before taking the post, he demanded President Wojciechowski give him total control over the economy. Under Grabski's leadership, Poland enjoyed a brief and illusory period of economic stability. Grabski quickly reduced the huge government ministerial staffs, established new procedures for collecting duties and taxes, and initiated a monthly budget review. Grabski also established the Bank of Poland (Bank Polski) and created the złoty, the currency that replaced the Polish mark.

Prime Minister Grabski's term was due to expire at the end of 1924 and until then he staved off serious financial problems by obtaining loans from Italy and by renegotiating the country's debts with the United States and Great Britain. He was also not above giving bribes to keep the ship of state sailing smoothly. Politically, he kept the peace by shuffling ministers so that every faction was represented in the government at some point.

Grabski's juggling act ran into trouble when inflation began to rise at the same time that his estimate of collectible taxes proved wrong. A fall in world agricultural prices affected Poland's agricultural exports, which were already small due to widespread crop failure. Grabski was forced to devalue the złoty and the Bank of Poland halted the sale of its gold reserves.

In 1925 Germany added to Poland's economic woes by initiating the Tariff Wars. In June, without any advance notice, Germany stopped buying coal, at a time when Poles were shipping half their coal exports to the Germans. Poland retaliated by limiting the amount of goods imported from Germany, but this gambit failed since the Poles were more dependent on their neighbor than vice versa. This economic tit-for-tat continued until a trade agreement was reached in the 1930s.

The prime minister who replaced Grabski, Count Aleksander Skrzyński, fared just as badly as his predecessor. Economic conditions continued to deteriorate, and in the spring of 1926 a number of strikes and riots occurred throughout the country, resulting in several deaths. The army had to be called out to control the mobs. The stage was now set for Marshal Piłsudski to reenter the government.

The Troupes in High Gear

Warsaw's cabarets moved into high gear in the midtwenties. This is not to say that all of them were commercially successful; on the contrary, they opened, closed, and changed names and owners regularly. The Black Cat (*Czarny Kot*) and the Argus, for example, declared bankruptcy soon after they opened. Almost without exception the clubs had financial problems, even though some of them, like Qui Pro Quo and the Persian Eye, were quite popular. The Bat (*Nietoperz*) rose on the site of the burnt-out Mirage and mounted successful productions, but it too had to struggle financially.

Undeterred by disaster, the owner of the old Mirage opened another venue called the New Theater (*Teatr Nowy*), which featured operetta.

Many of these clubs were gone before the next war. And yet it was a heady time for cabaret performers and their audiences, and certainly exciting, if not financially rewarding, for the owners.

■   In 1924 the Russian cabaret troupe Blue Bird (*Niebieski Ptak*) came to Warsaw on tour. Its productions were to have a profound influence on Polish cabarets.

Blue Bird's cast members were Russian émigrés who had fled to Berlin at the start of World War I, during the upheavals in their own country. The group's leader was a balding actor named Ivan Juzny, or Jushnij. The actors were multilingual and loaded with talent. Their fantastic productions stunned Warsaw, and their entire week's shows were sold out immediately.

Blue Bird's sketches were usually a blend of music and pantomime. Its fantastic set designs, influenced by cubism and constructivism, could suggest ethnic fairy tales as well as the dehumanizing aspects of modern life. The actors were sometimes positioned behind life-size cutouts and at other times appeared as puppets and even robots.

Blue Bird's productions blended German influences with aspects of Russian folklore. But its revues were not limited to European themes. In one sketch, titled "Time Is Money," the American obsession with work and money was brutally mocked. The group's material, like the best of European cabaret, was provocative and sometimes downright confrontational.[2]

The artistry of the Russians' innovative programs opened up an entirely new set of possibilities for Warsaw's actors, directors, and set designers.

Among Blue Bird's cast was a man who was to become one of the most celebrated personalities of interwar Poland, Fryderyk Járosy. By 1924 the thirty-four-year-old Járosy was a well-traveled actor.

Born in Hungary, he had at one time been the Austro-Hungarian cultural attaché to St. Petersburg. Járosy was an attractive master of ceremonies, of average height, with dark hair, black eyes, and an engaging smile.

Járosy knew only a few Polish expressions when Blue Bird opened its Warsaw engagement. One of those was the common phrase *Proszę Państwa*, which simply means Ladies and Gentlemen. But he said it in such a grand manner that *Proszę Państwa* soon became a popular catchphrase. When you uttered that phrase, you marked yourself as a habitué of the liveliest club in town. Járosy never did learn to speak Polish properly, but his sincere attempts to do so and occasional mispronunciations endeared him to the Varsovians, who adopted him as one of their own.

Járosy quickly became one of the bright lights on the city's cabaret circuit. Socially, he was frequently seen with Antoni Słonimski and Julian Tuwim, as well as with Mieczysław Grydzewski, publisher of *The Literary News*.

Járosy led a storybook existence, but his life was tragic as well as romantic when World War II intervened.

Another Varsovian who was interested in Járosy—or Fritz as he came to be known—was none other than Hanka Ordonówna. At a party given to honor the Blue Bird cast, she was introduced to Járosy and immediately fell in love with him. The feeling seemed mutual, and the couple embarked on an affair, ensconced in a pension on New World Avenue. When Blue Bird ended its week-long run, it left town without Járosy.

The couple lived in unwedded bliss, adding one more note to the city's gossip columns, which were already abuzz about celebrities Zula Pogorzelska and Konrad Tom, who had set up housekeeping together. The public may have been titillated but professed to be appalled. After all, such living arrangements were—and still are—frowned upon in this predominantly Catholic nation. But then, the cabaret crowd was expected to shock. To add to the scandal, Járosy was already married to an actress who lived in Berlin.[3]

Before she met Járosy, Ordonówna's career had been off to a slow start. A tour of Polish cities had not gone well, and she returned to Warsaw. Her affair with an actor ended when he told her that he had become engaged to another woman. Hanka then made a botched suicide attempt. She was badly in need of a friend and found one in the more worldly Zofia Bajkowska.

Bajkowska was a well-known cabaret lyricist of the day. Her scripts — and her casual conversation — were notoriously rude. After she had become a celebrity of sorts, she would purposely cause public scenes, especially in restaurants, telling off the people around her with a shouted "Kiss my ass!" (*Pocałuj mnie w dupa!*)[4]

Over tea one afternoon the veteran songwriter shared the gossip of the day with her young friend and offered her some friendly but frank advice. "You picked up some bad habits on your tour. Those mannerisms — the way you wave your hand under your nose and roll your eyes, those provincial expressions. You pucker your lips like a chicken's ass! And that hat — it's so old-fashioned — it's definitely not Warsaw."

The bewildered Hanka stammered, "But what can I do?"

"For the time being, nothing," replied her older companion, "just don't show yourself to any directors right now. Tonight we'll have a good dinner, then get some rest, and we'll start in the morning."[5]

The very next day the pair began work to improve Hanka's stage presence. It was only then that Hanka realized she had had absolutely no serious direction during the course of her career. After several weeks' work, Bajkowska suggested that her young charge first audition for a job at Qui Pro Quo and, if that did not work, apply to a new club a called the Jester (*Stańczyk*).

Boczkowski of Qui Pro Quo felt that Hanka's talent was not polished enough for a Warsaw audience. But the director of the

Jester remembered Hanka from her early work at the Mirage and signed her on.

Cabaret programs at the Jester and elsewhere were heavy on political satire, yet the nation's politicians and high-ranking officers frequented it and other cabarets, sitting politely through the shows, laughing even though they were often the butt of the jokes. The Polish government never attempted to censor the cabarets. Some government officials and army officers, such as Colonel Józef Beck and Colonel Wieniawa-Długoszowski, genuinely enjoyed the cabarets and mixed freely with the entertainers in their off-hours.

Some of Warsaw's outstanding talents performed at the Jester, including Halina Szmolcówna, the opera's prima ballerina; the actress Irena Solska who recited the poetry of Bolesław Prus, Julian Tuwim, and others; and the comics Ludwik Sempoliński (who confessed to having a terrible crush on the teenaged Ordonówna) and Ludwik Lawiński. Hanka was in distinguished company.

Bajkowska also helped Hanka get her big break. She kept pestering Boczkowski until he finally went to a show at the Jester and saw Ordonówna's performance. What he saw so impressed him that he went backstage and offered her a job in the Qui Pro Quo lineup.[6]

It was the beginning of an extraordinary career.

By the time Hanka joined Qui Pro Quo, the company already had two outstanding female stars, Zula Pogorzelska and Mira Zimińska. The two were close friends offstage and occasionally performed together.

Zula was a very attractive woman whose round face and big dark eyes were framed by severely cut bangs. She could sing and dance and was famous for her beautiful legs. She was frequently compared to the French cabaret star Mistinguette.

Zula and Konrad Tom were also having an affair and were one of the city's most-liked show-business couples. They were seen in the finest restaurants and could be found at the Bristol after almost every show. After a late supper at the hotel's dining room, they usually went to a gambling club called the Resource so that Konrad could indulge his favorite addiction.

Mira Zimińska had wanted to be a singer at an early age and was encouraged by her father, who would play the piano while his daughter sang songs that were popular at the time. Mira was not blessed with a great voice, and to improve upon it she studied voice with two of Warsaw's better-known teachers, the Misses Dietz and Szymanowska.

By the midtwenties Zimińska had become a featured performer at Qui Pro Quo while Hanka Ordonówna was still struggling with her career. As Zimińska tells it, she had two great rivals who were also her friends offstage: Hanka Ordonówna and Zula Pogorzelska. Mira respected Hanka's talent, her perfect memory, and her hard work. But she felt that perhaps Hanka got more attention because of her good looks and because she was Járosy's lover for a time.

"Ordonówna," Zimińska wrote, "was like a chameleon. She constantly changed her clothes, behavior, mood, humor, etc. One never knew if she was going to be a girl from the Polish countryside or a countess, a lady, a femme fatale, a demon, or an angel. . . . I had the upper class behind me. She was worshipped by all of Poland."[7]

Mira Zimińska was better known for her zany sense of humor than for her looks, although at the height of her career she was a very handsome woman. She was the star at Qui Pro Quo before Ordonówna came along, but even after Hanka became the star Mira's popularity was not diminished, as she appeared in numerous cabaret acts, films, and stage productions. She specialized in playing silly young wives who betray their husbands.

"As a star I performed before . . . Józef Piłsudski. It was shortly before the tragic day in May [1926]. I don't remember who put this concert together but I do remember the fact that everyone was very nervous. It had been announced that Qui Pro Quo was to be included in the celebration of the marshal's nameday (St. Joseph's Day). There were some doubts if the ceremony would take place at all, since that year Piłsudski was in Sulejówek, in 'voluntary exile.' These doubts were dispersed at the last moment, so we didn't have much time to prepare a special program. . . . I don't remember much, only ballrooms, late evenings, government and diplomatic figures, people from the artistic world, and stage fright.

"The marshal was sitting in an armchair, pushed forward before the others, and he was holding a *maciejówka* [a kind of vizored cap originally worn by Polish peasants and later adopted by the military]. The performers included Járosy, Dymsza, Krukowski, Ordonówna, and Pogorzelska. Hanka sang a pretty song, 'Mimosa.' I had the task of presenting the marshal with versified greetings, preceded by the 'Song with Medals' (*Piosenka z Orderami*). I circled the auditorium, with a basket in my hand, singing and at the same time presenting 'medals.' I don't remember anymore to whom I presented them: Wieniawa-Długoszowski, a silver bottle; a big red heart to a womanizing dignitary; the figure of a stork to someone who didn't want to be a father; a duck to a naughty journalist [in Polish journalism the duck symbolizes a typographical error that makes nonsense of the original text]. There was a lot of laughter around. The versified greetings had a tune, but I don't remember who wrote the music:

A happy day we have today
And we're really jolly because
It's St. Joseph's Day here.
We love him a lot
And we all know why—
These rhymes are imperfect
But our hearts are sincere.
Instead of medals, accept these roses

And may happiness be always with you,
Dear Marshal Józef Piłsudski

"I gave him the roses. One fell and he picked it up, stood, and thanked us with a military salute. . . . Did we have illusions then!"[8]

The actors who formed the nucleus of the Qui Pro Quo company throughout the twenties numbered about sixteen. According to Tadeusz Wittlin, a playwright and author who now lives in Washington, D.C., they got along well. They were "one big happy family" with no jealousy, no backbiting, and no intrigues.

Well, almost none. Wittlin himself described the one "sour apple" in the Qui Pro Quo family, an actor named Romuald Gierasiński. A favorite "Gieras" story circulated in Warsaw—at least according to Wittlin—was that when one of the troupe's actors was taking his curtain calls, Gieras would rush to the lavatory where he would flush the toilet repeatedly to drown out the noise of the applause.[9]

The comedian Adolf Dymsza was the leading practical joker in the group. Once, he snuck into Mira Zimińska's dressing room and nailed her slippers to the floor. When Zimińska dashed in to change between skits, her slippers stopped her in her tracks. On another occasion, when Zimińska was recovering from a hangover after a late-night party, Dymsza showed up outside her apartment with a brass band that played loudly until she staggered to the window and begged them to stop.[10]

The cabaret people thought such pranks were great fun. Their behavior was a reaction to the times, an era that saw a tremendous explosion of talent in an atmosphere of political uncertainty. There may have been, as one observer put it, a collective subconscious feeling that disaster waited in the wings.

Onstage as well as off, the humor of the times had an edge of cruelty. Jokes about Jews not only were common but often were told by Jewish comedians such as Kazimierz Krukowski. The lyrics of the songs were bittersweet and tough, for example:

Where were you tonight
You old bum
With whom and where?
You've fallen in love again
with some dame,
I know you.
Where were you tonight
you creep,
Tell me —
Who bit you on the lips,
you devil,
You're bleeding...[11]

Warsaw's cabaret world really was an ensemble group. Its members wrote songs for one another, appeared in each other's sketches, dined and drank together, sometimes slept together, and for the better part of two decades provided Warsaw with top-rate entertainment and copious amounts of gossip.

Even after the cabaret era ended, the lives of the stars were still the subject of speculation. For example, a Polish gentleman from that era, now living in San Francisco, told me on two separate occasions that Zula Pogorzelska had abruptly retired from the stage in 1939 and had disappeared, only to resurface, years later in Moscow, the wife of a Red Army officer. He insisted on this version despite eyewitness accounts of Zula's death by her best friend, Mira Zimińska, and by Hanka Ordonówna's biographer. Other people I interviewed told me that Ordonówna died of cancer or of a heart attack and was buried in Warsaw. Neither story is true; in fact, she died of typhus while abroad and lay buried far from Poland, until very recently.

The cabaret people inspired so much gossip because they were so well loved. Stefania Kossowska was one of their enthusiastic fans. "The cabaret people were the best in the world." Polish cabaret, she said, "could be compared to prewar French. Even now, after almost sixty years, when you read the sketches and the songs, they seem so good. The proof of it is that they are still performed in Poland, even today. I remember several years ago some young people came [to London] from Poland and went to see a show composed mostly of the songs of Marian Hemar, at the Ognisko Polskie club on Exhibition Road. They were so amazed—they couldn't believe their ears—they thought these songs were written after the war. . . . I can't say the same about Polish theater because after seeing plays here [in London], where the actors are the best in the world, I had second thoughts about Polish theater."[12]

Stanisław Meyer disagreed with her judgment of the theaters, relating them to a wide range of Warsaw performance art. "A specialty of Warsaw was the small variety show consisting of a series of separate production numbers: singing, dancing, and recitation, plus short sketches and a few very good comedians.

"This kind of entertainment developed from the 'Cabaret of Artistes' popular on the Continent at the beginning of the twentieth century. In Warsaw it became a specialty of the small theaters; the acting in them was always excellent and the songs and sketches were written by real poets, men of great talent. The most promising young writers worked for these shows—the programs always contained the names of many prominent literary figures.

"Sometimes the shows were given in cafés, in particular the Ziemiańska on Mazowiecka Street—for a few years it was a meeting place of the younger poets. The humor and wit were exquisite, very much in keeping with the local character, and the performances roused a lively interest. A close understanding existed between the town and these small shows; quotations from the stage were often dropped into ordinary conversation and again the authors drew freely on the local slang and dialect for their own purposes.

"A variation of these shows used political marionettes, in shows based on the traditional Warsaw 'Punch and Judy' [plays. They] were performed in cafés, using marionettes that caricatured famous people, and their songs and dialogue were invariably full of fun and biting satire. All Warsaw loved the small shows and the political marionettes that were a true expression of their genius."[13]

Of course, Warsaw cabaret had many songwriters, but the premier composer-lyricist of this period was Marian Hemar, regarded by many Poles as the embodiment of Polish cabaret. Hemar was born in 1900 in Lwów, birthplace of so many of the stars of this era. His parents were well-to-do Jews who exposed their son to all forms of culture at an early age.

Hemar did not arrive in Warsaw until 1924 but by then he had already done some traveling. From 1919 to 1920 he served in Piłsudski's Legions and fought against the Red Army. Afterward he visited Berlin and Vienna where he saw the Blue Bird cabaret at the Goldstrasse theater.

Hemar acknowledged a debt to German cabaret and to German composer Friedrich Hollander who wrote "Falling in Love Again," sung by Marlene Dietrich in the film *The Blue Angel.* From the Berlin cabarets Hemar picked up a cynical, sophisticated tone and a mature understanding of what audiences wanted. He could see the potential for humor in any situation.

Prior to Hemar's arrival, Julian Tuwim and Konrad Tom had written most of the club's material. But once the young Hemar arrived at Qui Pro Quo he eclipsed all the other songwriters to become the club's primary composer and lyricist. Along the way Hemar formed close relationships with Mira Zimińska and Tuwim, friendships that later ran afoul of politics. Hemar's scripts occasionally contained double entendres and he played games with the audience, challenging them to decipher his hidden meanings. Zofia Chądzyńska claimed that in this way he sometimes sent public love notes to actress Maria Modzelewska, later his wife.

Hemar's first revue, *Seven Fat Cows*, opened at Qui Pro Quo on January 21, 1925, and ran through May for a record 156 performances. He quickly became a celebrity in cabaret circles and during his career wrote hundreds of songs.

The Literary Scene

The year 1924 was a high-water mark for Poland's literary life. *The Literary News* (*Wiadomości Literackie*) made its debut in the spring of that year. For the next five decades it would remain one of Poland's most influential periodicals. Its founder, Dr. Mieczysław Grydzewski, was a well-educated Polish Jew who refused to accept the idea that the Poles were anti-Semitic. His magazine led a popular and charmed life, surviving the war although it was forced to move its offices from Warsaw to Paris and finally to London.

The Literary News was the voice of Poland's intelligentsia. Zofia Chądzyńska contended that "the notion of an intelligentsia is a very Middle or Eastern European notion – it has nothing to do with academic degrees but rather with one's interests and concerns." She thought this "snobbish division . . . was positive, since the result of it was better education, more literacy, etc." Intellectualism was so fashionable that "people would line up at some libraries to get books that were reviewed in *Wiadomości Literackie*, or to which allusions were made in a show at Qui Pro Quo."[14]

This interest in literary news developed, in part, because "Grydzewski had a natural gift – he created a magazine that became a classic. On Thursdays, when *The Literary News* appeared, people queued up to buy it. At home I had to fight with my father to read it because the next day in class we would discuss the articles that appeared in the *News*. It set a level beneath which one could not descend if one wanted to be a member of the intelligentsia."

New issues of the *News* were displayed in the magazine's office at 11 Holy Cross Street (*Świętokrzyszka*). There, a passerby could glance at the front page and see how Grydzewski had chosen to stimulate his audience that month. A typical issue of *The Literary News* contained a front-page essay on Immanual Kant plus a sidebar on him by the noted historian Marceli Handelsman; essays on Balzac, Erik Satie, Eleanora Duse; a piece on theater in Berlin; and an article on G. K. Chesterton's visit to Poland. Other features included excerpts from novels; a column titled "Russian Chronicles" (*Kronika Rosyjska*); Antoni Słonimski's column; editorials and articles by Julian Tuwim, Tadeusz Boy-Żeleński, and other leading intellectuals, plus reviews of films, books, and musical events. The *News* also ran a popular cartoon strip called "Mr. Gryps" (in Polish *gryps* are notes smuggled in or out of prison). The strip was drawn by Marian Eile who was also the magazine's publicist. To drum up subscribers the *News* had a contest that required readers to deduce what Gryps was up to, based on clues in the strip. The youthful Zofia Chądzyńska once won the contest, a fact she still relates with pride.

Słonimski wrote a column for *The Literary News* called "The Weekly Chronicle." He "borrowed" the title from the poet Bolesław Prus, a Słonimski family friend and one of the foremost novelists of the Young Poland movement. Słonimski was given the freedom to write about whatever he chose, and his subjects included theater, commentary on the other Warsaw newspapers, and whatever else struck his fancy.

Słonimski, himself a Jew, once published an essay in the *News* titled "On the Oversensitivity of the Jews." But the *News* also printed an article defending Julian Tuwim, who had come under attack from a right-wing journalist because of his "Jewishness."

The Literary News also discussed important political issues of the day; for example, in the early 1930s, it supported the opening of a Warsaw maternity clinic that advocated birth control, performed abortions, and gave medical advice to pregnant women, something previously unheard of in this church-dominated country. Catholics, led by their clergy, were highly critical of the clinic, but it remained open nevertheless.

The Literary News was always subscriber-supported, but it did carry advertising. In the early days advertising revenue was sparse and supplied mainly by supporters of the magazine. Later the magazine carried more substantial ads from clients such as Fiat cars, Chanel No. 5, Clicquot Club seltzer water, other popular interwar products, publishers, men's clothing stores, dress shops, films, well-known cafés and restaurants, such as the Adria, the Florida, and the Ziemiańska café.

The Literary News was always a progressive magazine, but even members of the Polish right wing grudgingly gave *The News* its due. Helena Wasiutyńska wrote, "In old Warsaw there were two influential literary weeklies: *The Literary News* on the left and the right-wing *Prosto z Mostu.*" Still she claims that "the best writers and poets of my generation, born just before the First World War, made their debuts in *Prosto z Mostu* [Straight from the Shoulder]."[15]

In London the magazine's last editor, Stefania Kossowska, reminisced about the *News.* In her memory there was no partisan division. "*The Literary News* was one of the most important accomplishments of interwar culture in Warsaw and Poland. Founded by Dr. Grydzewski, *The Literary News* was tremendously influential. Dr. Grydzewski had a genius for editorship, [creating] a very eclectic paper. It was not partisan. Grydzewski printed articles from every shade of opinion, as long as the articles were well written. He was completely unbiased and had a great knack for surrounding himself with good writers.

"Before founding *The Literary News* Grydzewski had edited a very elitest magazine, a monthly I think it was, called *Skamander*, just for poets. The Skamander group of poets who started this paper had a great influence on Polish poets and literature. There were five leading figures—Słonimski, Tuwim, Kazimierz Wierzyński, Jarosław Iwaszkiewicz, and Jan Lechoń. And later on there were others, like Baliński and Pawlikowska, who pretended to be part of this group but really weren't.

"*Skamander* was so powerful, in a literary sense, their poetry, their writing had a strong influence . . . particularly on the younger Polish writers. They're the ones who really made *The Literary News* famous.

"*The Literary News* was distributed only in Poland and was purely a Polish paper. From time to time there were special numbers, for example, a special issue on French literature. There was also a special edition in French, a supplement called *Pologne litteraire*. Before the war the main influence on Poland was French. Very little was known—I exaggerate—about England and America. There was not half as much interest in them as there was in France. But France was the most important.

"After the Nazis attacked, all these people from *The Literary News* and *Skamander* found themselves abroad. Grydzewski started to publish in Paris but couldn't continue because France collapsed in a few months' time, in 1940. He then came to London and continued to edit and publish his magazine for more than twenty-eight years. Then he was taken ill. He was sick off and on, for about three years before he died. Another man took over briefly, then I had to take over. I edited the paper for a while, but not all the time, just whenever Grydzewski had to go to the hospital.

"I edited *The Literary News* for ten years and finally had to stop publishing it in 1981—it was just too difficult financially. I couldn't do it myself. You know, it's incredible, I had no staff at all. There was one person who would come in occasionally to do corrections and so forth, and one person to do the administrative work. At that time this paper was going to fifty-two countries, although there weren't that many subscribers, two or three subscribers here and there, because the Poles were scattered all over the place. And the postage was so expensive!

"The last issue published in Poland was dated September 3, 1939. When the magazine resumed publication in Paris, in 1940, its name was changed to *Polish News* (*Wiadomości Polskie*). After some political upheavals while in London, *The Literary News* had to cease publication because its vital supply of paper was withdrawn by the British government in retaliation for the paper's anti-Russian policy.[16] In February 1944, when the paper reappeared after a two-year absence, its name was shortened to *The News* (*Wiadomości*) and it existed under this name from then until 1981. The last issue was dated March/April 1981."[17]

The Polish diaspora and the devastating loss of life during World War II robbed *The Literary News* of its core support. Considering the lack of financing and the peripatetic existence, it is something of a miracle that it survived for more than half a century.

The archives for its fifty years of publication are controlled by Stefania Kossowska, who is the sole trustee. They are stored at the Lanckoroński Foundation on Eardley Crescent in London. Everything is there, she said, inviting my interest: back issues, correspondence, photographs, even some of the furniture. Today, in this quiet corner of London, copies of this once-influential magazine sit unread—except by an occasional researcher—in an office that receives few visitors. (Copies of *The Literary News* can also be found at the Polish Library in the London borough of Hammersmith, and in the United States at the Library of Congress and the New York Public Library on Fifth Avenue.)

Speaking with Mrs. Kossowska in London, I once suggested that we revive the magazine as a bilingual Polish-English periodical. She refused. She was probably right. Many of the magazine's subscribers are no longer alive, and those who are would not tolerate a contemporary substitute.

■ Warsaw's cabaret life and its literary milieu were closely linked by a group of writers working both sides of the street, so to speak. In the twenties, a number of the poets who wrote lyrics and dialogue for Qui Pro Quo and other cabarets, met frequently at the Ziemiańska café, which was to Warsaw writers what the Deux Magots was to writers in Paris in the twenties. Later, this group of writers moved to the Café IPS (*Instytut Propagandy Sztuki*, at the National Institute of Art), which changed its name to the Zodiac just before the war.

Zofia Chądzyńska was one of the admirers who followed the lives of prominent writers. She said, "The literary personalities had their own cafés. For a long time the favorite was the Ziemiańska. Well-known writers like Antoni Słonimski, Julian Tuwim, and Jan Lechoń sat at tables in the mezzanine (called *na pięterku*) and anyone who was invited to join them was extremely proud of it."

Years later, Mrs. Chądzyńska was still gushing about her own experiences in the Ziemiańska, where she met "all those great writers. . . . When it happened to me, I was reluctant to wash my hands afterwards. It was a holy place."

Stanisław Meyer's memoirs provide an explanation for this reverent attitude. He notes, "In the days of political slavery, books and their authors had a great mission to fulfill: they kept alive the national spirit, gave hope, and formed social and political opinions. Writers were often looked upon as the spiritual leaders of the nation and some of them were treated as national prophets. This spirit still prevailed for some time after the reestablishment of independence and lent a special distinction to the literary profession."[18]

Meyer describes literary hangers-on as "lay assistants" in the café ceremony, pointing out that "the coffeehouse life had its advantages, both to the writers who exchanged ideas and formed convictions and to their lay assistants who had an opportunity of spending some time in stimulating and interesting society."[19]

Besides café sitting, Warsaw's writers were busy publishing in 1924. Antoni Słonimski published a book of poetry, *Road to the East* (*Droga na Wschód*), which reflected his recent travels to the Middle East and Brazil. Jan Lechoń brought out his poems in a volume titled *The Silver and the Black* (*Srebne i Czarne*), to much critical praise.

Adam Ważyk, who is usually bracketed with Poland's Second Vanguard of literature (those published after 1930), also published his verses, *Semaphores* (*Semafory*) in 1924. Ważyk was a Warsaw Jew whose poetry clearly revealed the influence of French cubism. He was also known for his translations of Guillaume Apollinaire, the French poet whose mother was Polish.

Among the novels of 1924, perhaps the best known is *The Moon Rises* (*Księżyc Wschodzi*) by another original Skamander, Jarosław Iwaszkiewicz. The action of this novel takes place in the turbulent Ukraine during one of that territory's many political crises.

The Nobel Prize was big news in Poland in 1924. Władysław Reymont, who had been a leading member of the Young Poland movement before World War I, was awarded the Nobel Prize for Literature for his great work, *The Peasants*. As was to be expected, Stanisław Meyer had a story about Reymont also. He and Reymont had mutual friends, and it was in their home that Meyer says he "used to meet Władysław Reymont, the author of that great epic novel *The Peasants*. He seemed a pleasant gentleman, with a charming manner." Although Reymont seemed rather ordinary, Meyer says, "he had one peculiarity: every time he started to write a new book he bought a new writing desk; just as one needs fresh paper he had to start on a fresh table."[20]

Coincidentally it was in 1924 that the body of Poland's first Nobel Prize winner, Henryk Sienkiewicz, was finally laid to rest in Warsaw. The author, who had won the prize in 1905 for *Quo Vadis?* and other remarkable books of Polish fiction, had been buried in Vevey, Switzerland, where he died in 1916. With the war on and Warsaw occupied by the Germans, it was not possible to have Sienkiewicz brought home for burial. Eight years later his remains were brought to Poland and interred in the crypt of St. John's Cathedral.

■   Stefan Żeromski, the "country's conscience," and one of Poland's great novelists, died in 1925, bringing to an end an illustrious career that had begun at the turn of the century. Żeromski was one of the outstanding figures of the Young Poland movement, and he continued to turn out important work even after that group had been surpassed by Skamander.

As Stanisław Meyer describes him, "Stefan Żeromski was a master of Polish prose and a writer who had a very great influence on my generation. We awaited with excitement every new book of his and read it with almost religious zeal. The names of some of the characters in his books were used in conversations to describe a certain type of man or a particular state of mind. Some problems raised by him were topics of permanent debates among the young people.

"I met him in later years and found him a striking personality, difficult to approach, and usually hidden behind a screen of his own thoughts. When I read his works again after his death I felt disappointed; my youthful enthusiasms found little justification in my more mature opinion. This was probably my own fault; it's possible that a decline in direct perception and the growth of a critical attitude are symptoms of middle age that affect one's response to a work of art."[21]

Żeromski was not a native of Warsaw but came to the city to study veterinary medicine. He supported himself as a private tutor and, like many beginning writers, faced financial problems while trying to launch his writing career. Though he published his first novel, *Sisyphian Labors* (*Syzyfowe Prace*), in 1898, it was not until 1904 with the publication of his major novel, *Ashes* (*Popioły*) – later made into a film – that he achieved serious recognition.

Ashes is set in the Napoleonic era; it touched the Polish soul because it dwelt upon the struggle for independence and the radical ideas that were being voiced in the early nineteenth century. The novel is both heroic and tragic in its portrayal of Polish soldiers who leave their homeland to fight in Napoleon's armies, hoping desperately that his victories will lead to the restoration of the Polish nation. Reality proved to be even more tragic than Żeromski's novel.

Żeromski's plots turned on great moral issues and frequently showed a deep compassion for society's underdogs. In his novels and short stories Żeromski focused on the changing consciousness at some levels of Polish society as well as on important topics such as the Russian attempt to obliterate Polish culture. He went on challenging traditional thinking even after the country had become independent in 1918. His novel of that year, *Before the Spring* (*Przedwiośnie*), is outspoken in its criticism of Poland's backwardness and conservatism in the face of its new freedom.

Like any progressive writer of the interwar era, Żeromski had his detractors, mainly among the conservative right wing. But he achieved an exalted status among the Poles by virtue of his lofty subject matter and serious tone. Many Poles felt that Żeromski, not Reymont, should have won the Nobel Prize.

Formism and Beyond

Warsaw's artists were also struggling to break from the past with its emphasis on traditional and nationalistic themes. Immediately after World War I, a group known as the formists emerged from the Polish expressionist movement, which had its first and only major group show in Kraków in 1917. The Polish expressionists were influenced by movements from abroad, mainly cubism and futurism, and while forging ahead with their own brand of expressionism they also wished to retain a national identity.

Formist art was in a way a protest, an attempt to breathe life into what this group saw as an undistinguished and even timid society of artists. The group's name had no hidden meaning—the emphasis in their painting and sculpture was on form, not content.

In Poznań a group of artists there, also formists, called themselves Revolt (*Bunt*). They included among their number writers who worked for the literary magazine *Source* (*Zdrój*). With their proximity to Germany they found it easy to make contact with German expressionists, and a number of the group produced woodcuts of the kind usually associated with Käthe Kollwitz.

Among the Warsaw artists who shared the formists' beliefs were the future novelist and playwright Witkacy, the talented Pronaszko brothers who would later become star set designers for cabaret shows, and the mathematician Leon Chwistek. Both he and Witkacy applied their theories of logic and philosophy to painting, and in that sense their works were manifestations of those theories.

Zbigniew Pronaszko was one of Poland's earliest cubist painters. He began experimenting with this form even before World War I. His many studies of nudes are good examples of elemental cubism.

Unlike his French counterparts, Pronaszko did not progress beyond this stage. He was also a quite talented sculptor. Unfortunately, his huge (twelve-meter-high) wooden cast for a concrete statue of Adam Mickiewicz no longer exists, but examples of his cubist paintings are available in Polish museums.

His brother Andrzej painted in a softer cubist style, without the sharp angularity usually associated with cubism. His talent flowed over onto the stage, and he developed a reputation as one of the country's best set designers.

Though he is known to the West for his novels and plays, Witkacy also maintains a prominent place in the study of modern Polish art. He was an early expressionist and formist, but, unlike those of his fellow artists, Witkacy's canvasses exploited grotesque figures, bringing to art the fears that lie hidden within us all. His painting *Composition: Satan* (1920) is typical of this sort of work.

The formists represented a transition from a classic to a modern style, which eventually led to avant-garde art in Poland. But the formist movement was short-lived, to be replaced by several movements, or schools of art, in major cities—Blok and Praesens in Warsaw, Artes in Lwów, and a.r. (*artistes revolutionnaires*) in Łódż.

A group show in Wilno in 1923 marked the break with old art forms. The artists, many from Warsaw, who participated in the Wilno Exhibition of New Art displayed a new form of Polish art, one that emphasized creativity for its own sake, that did not pay homage to any ideal of the past, but sought a place in contemporary Polish society. Out of this exhibit emerged a group of Warsaw artists who called themselves Blok.

Blok placed a great deal of emphasis on economy of material and utility rather than individuality, and it proclaimed that art and social responsibility were inseparable. Its program as well as its graphic design ideas were made explicit in the group's magazine, also called *Blok*, which published about a dozen issues beginning in 1924.

Blok's major exhibition was held in the Warsaw showroom of a Czech auto manufacturer, Laurin and Klemont, which seemed to symbolize the connection between the group's art and modernity.

One of the best known of the Blok group, Mieczysław Szczuka, began his career as an expressionist, had a brief period of painting biblical themes in contemporary settings, and then began experimenting with a variety of other forms. He also wrote articles in the magazine *Blok*, as well as in the Communist magazine *Nowa Kultura*. In 1924 Szczuka mounted an exhibit that featured the poems of the Communist poets Bruno Jasieński and Anatol Stern, demonstrating that even Polish artists had joined the battle between the left and right wings.

In 1926 differences of opinion developed within the Blok group, and some of the artists split off from Blok and formed another group known as Praesens.

Henryk Berlewi was one of the artists who defied Blok. Not a member of any group, he had his own vision. Having lived in Berlin for a time, Berlewi had mingled with artists of the German avant-garde. When he returned to Poland, he brought with him a bizarre formulation of art that he called mechanofacture. It featured geometric forms, blocks of red and black paint, and an obvious fascination with machinery. Berlewi had his own one-man show the night before the Blok show, also in an auto showroom, this one belonging to Austro-Daimler—creating a modern-art showdown.[22]

Radio Warsaw

As Poland continued to absorb innovations from the West, Warsaw radio went on the air in February 1925, the result of a cooperative effort between military engineers, technicians, and a small group of investors. Experiments with this new medium had been conducted several years prior to this by the Polish Radiotechnical Association (PTR), but it took many months before the association was able to produce a live broadcast. This was not bad, considering that in the United States the first major radio station (KDKA in Pittsburgh) had begun broadcasting in only 1920.

The offerings of the PTR consisted mainly of classical music and readings from Polish literary works, interrupted occasionally by news and weather reports. The talent for the live musical concerts was provided by musicians and singers from Warsaw's Symphony and Conservatory, directed by Emil Młynarski. Faculty from the University of Warsaw gave lectures on a multitude of subjects. All participants served on a voluntary basis.

The PTR had little money of its own and needed government subsidies to keep up with increasing production costs. The government meanwhile was wrestling with the problem of how to control the airwaves. In the summer it granted a broadcasting concession but not to PTR. Funding went to a new group called Polish Radio, whose wealthy backers had influence with government officials. Polish Radio had to start completely from scratch since, aside from backers' connections, it had no facilities, no equipment, and no trained staff.

As a sop to PTR, the government provided funds to it in April 1926 but only until Polish Radio was ready to begin operations.

Once it was operational, Polish Radio expanded its rival's format beyond live concerts and lectures to include children's programs, information features, and weather. The station was on the air forty-four hours per week.

Warsaw was the first Polish city to have a radio station, and its signal reached many parts of the country. Those who wished to listen to it had to obtain a license to own a set, much as citizens in the United Kingdom must obtain a permit to have a television set. Nevertheless, the number of radios purchased in the late 1920s grew astronomically, reaching more than 200,000 by the end of the decade.

Affiliates of Polish Radio were later established in other major cities, mainly Poznań, Kraków, Katowice, and Wilno, but the Warsaw operation was the only station until the late 1930s.[23]

Author and pediatrician Janusz Korczak, incidentally, was one of the early enthusiasts of radio. He thought it had great potential for educating both adults and children and predicted, "The radio will change the very nature of man."[24]

If Europe be the nymph, Naples
be her blue eyes, and Warsaw her heart.

Jeśli Europa jest nimfa — Neapol
Jest nimfy okiem błękitnem — Warszawa Sercem.
Juliusz Słowacki
"Quiescence" (*Uspokajenie*)

CHAPTER 4

A Box at the Opera

■ 1925–Spring 1927

On the Political Front

Between 1926 and 1928 Marshal Piłsudski's political fortunes
changed dramatically. In the spring of 1926 Piłsudski, disgusted
with rumors of high-level corruption, took on the government in
three days of fierce street battles in central Warsaw. Earlier in the
year the Sejm had taken advantage of Piłsudski's retirement to reduce executive powers. When it also proposed drastic cuts in the
officer corps, which included many of Piłsudski's friends and supporters, he responded by attacking government corruption. On
May 11, 1926, Piłsudski gave an interview at his home in
Sulejówek to the *Morning Courier* in which he openly criticized the
government. President Wojciechowski had the edition suppressed
and warned the marshal of the consequences of any further inflam-
matory remarks. Poles took to the streets in protest.

The following day, May 12, Piłsudski and his loyal supporters headed toward the Poniatowski Bridge, where he was to meet with the president. Wojciechowski had already stationed troops on his side of the bridge. The two men, once comrades in arms, met at center span with their supporters watching anxiously. They had a brief, heated discussion: Piłsudski demanded that the president withdraw his nomination of Wincenty Witos, who was supported by the marshal's perennial enemies, the National Democrats; Wojciechowski refused this demand, and the meeting was abruptly terminated.

That evening, without waiting for Piłsudski's orders, a brigade of his troops crossed the Kierbedź Bridge. After defeating government soldiers there, the marshal's men entered the center of Warsaw, and full-scale fighting erupted on the streets.

For a time it looked as though government troops might prevail. But gradually more soldiers began defecting to Piłsudski's side. When the railway workers, socialist to the core, called a nationwide strike, they effectively cut off government reinforcements.

With the Piłsudski troops drawing nearer to the Belvedere Palace, President Wojciechowski and his cabinet fled to the Wilanów Palace, several kilometers to the south, and soon he and his ministers surrendered. They were put under house arrest and later pardoned.

The three days of fighting had left more than three hundred dead and about a thousand wounded. An interim government was formed with Maciej Rataj, the head of parliament, as acting president. Piłsudski demanded that his man, Kazimierz Bartel, be appointed prime minister until elections could be held. Piłsudski himself was named to the newly created post of minister of war, thereby removing control of the military from civilian hands.

After some semblance of normalcy had returned to the city, presidential elections were held. Piłsudski was nominated for the presidency, and, in a runoff against the National Democratic candidate, he polled the most votes, winning support from both left and center parties. But he startled everyone by refusing to serve, and new elections had to be hastily called. In June, Ignacy Mościcki, a former socialist and a chemist of some renown, was elected with Piłsudski's backing. He would serve until 1939.

A new cabinet headed by Bartel forced upon parliament changes that reversed those pushed through while the marshal was in retirement. The Act Conferring Full Powers gave the president sweeping authority, including the right to adjourn the Sejm for thirty days and to govern by decree; it also gave his cabinet the authority to pass a budget without parliament's approval.

Bartel turned out to be a competent premier, and Poland enjoyed a brief period of economic growth, aided in no small part by the British miners' strike, which brought coal buyers to Poland. In 1927 Poland even had a trade and budget surplus. In the meantime the nation entered an era known as *sanacja*, or cleansing, during which all traces of corruption were to be eliminated.

Prime Minister Bartel was unable to secure the cooperation of the National Democrats on the budget and was forced out of office. He was reappointed by President Mościcki but resigned when his budget was slashed even more.

Mościcki decided that only Piłsudski himself could bring calm to the parliament and appointed the marshal prime minister. Once in office Piłsudski wisely chose a cabinet that included men from a variety of political backgrounds, which silenced the opposition briefly.

It was a short honeymoon. Interparty squabbling soon resumed. Piłsudski tried to pass legislation that would greatly curtail freedom of the press, but he was defeated on this important measure.

Marshal Piłsudski lacked a political power base, and he now moved to rectify this. He asked his close friend Colonel Walery

Sławek to form a party composed of people from all walks of life. It was to include people who opposed the marshal, as long as their ideals matched his: unquestioned patriotism, morality in public life, and unselfish public service. This party was henceforth known as the Nonpolitical Party Bloc for Cooperation with the Government (*Bezpartyjny Blok Współpracy z Rządem*), known by its Polish initials, BBWR.

The new party was fairly representative of the Polish people as a whole – it included landowners, industrialists, some socialists, defectors from the Piast Peasant party, even some people who had opposed the 1926 coup. Some of the people who joined claimed to have fought in Piłsudski's Legion, even though they had not. They were jokingly called the Fourth Brigade (Piłsudski had once had three brigades under his command).

Relations with the Soviet Union took a dramatic turn for the worse in 1927. The Soviets now began a campaign of accusations against the Poles including charges that Piłsudski's coup was aided by the British Secret Service. This campaign seemed to be a smoke screen to divert attention from the Soviets' domestic problems.

Relations worsened when the Soviet ambassador to Poland, Pavel Voikov, was shot to death in June at Warsaw's Central Station. He was known to have many enemies outside the Soviet Union, primarily because of his role in the murder of Czar Nicholas II and his family.

In fact, Voikov's assassin turned out to be the son of a Russian monarchist family residing in Warsaw. Despite his quick arrest and conviction and apologies from Poland, the Soviets continued their anti-Polish propaganda. Finally, when Piłsudski warned that their actions might have serious consequences, the Soviets backed off.

Poland was having its own domestic problems and was in great need of financing. This they obtained from the Americans in the form of a $62 million loan, arranged by officials of the Bank of Poland. The agreement contained one embarrassing clause – it required the American banker Charles Dewey to come to Poland to supervise expenditure of the funds. The Poles had no choice but to agree.

Regularly scheduled elections were due to be held in 1928, and Piłsudski and President Mościcki campaigned vigorously to make the newly created BBWR the big winner. Tax bills for wealthy landowners were ignored, rallies of the National Democrats were broken up by the police, and ND newspapers were temporarily shut down. Most blatantly, on Piłsudski's orders, eight thousand złotys from the Polish treasury were funneled into the BBWR campaign. The period of moral cleansing was not off to an auspicious start.

In spite of all its efforts the BBWR fell short of majorities in both the Sejm and the Senate, the less powerful upper house of the legislature. Piłsudski was now openly jeered by his opponents, and some former supporters on the left deserted him.

In April Marshal Piłsudski collapsed, probably from a stroke. He recovered, but his health began to deteriorate. This sudden threat to his life caused him to reconsider his role in government and led to his eventual retirement from public life.

White Tie and Tails

On a chilly day in November 1986, I arrived at the London flat of Count Edward Raczyński. Former ambassador to the Court of St. James and one-time president of the Polish government-in-exile, Raczyński had a long and sometimes troubled association with the British. He was still the Polish president when the British recognized the Soviet puppet government in Lublin in 1945. Many years later, *Observer* columnist Neal Ascherson poignantly summed up Raczyński's diplomatic relationship with Britain: "He received the blow, as he had received the sword, with the polite bow of a grand diplomat."[1]

Scion of an aristocratic and wealthy family, Raczyński had begun his diplomatic career in 1919 when he was appointed secretary
to the Polish legation in Copenhagen. He was transferred to London in 1922 and posted to Warsaw in 1925. (In the labyrinthian
network of the Polish aristocracy, Raczyński was related to Hanka
Ordonówna by virtue of her marriage to the youngest son of Raczyński's half-sister.)

Between the wars Raczyński had "lived and worked in my
own house," the family's palace near Krasiński Square, at 7 Długa
Street.[2] This "house" was originally known as the Brühl Palace,
built in the eighteenth century by Count Brühl, a German who was
a minister in the cabinet of Augustus III, Poniatowski's predecessor
on the Polish throne. The palace was one of several baroque-style
buildings erected in this period, and was designed by Tylman van
Gameren. His original design underwent several renovations from
successive inhabitants — it housed the Ministry of Justice at one time
and the American ambassador at another; during the Warsaw Uprising of 1944 it was used as a hospital for the insurgent forces and
was heavily damaged. Ironically it was destroyed by another generation of Germans — the Nazis — less than 150 years after its construction. All that remains of the original palace today is part of the
colonnade, which guards Warsaw's Tomb of the Unknown Soldier. The rebuilt structure is now the Central Archive.

When I visited Raczyński in the autumn of 1986, he was living
in a large flat on a quiet street in Knightsbridge, a few blocks from
the Sikorski Institute where I spent many hours doing research.
Raczyński's close friend, Aniela Mieczysławska, a tall, attractive
woman in her late seventies, greeted me at the door. The walls of
the flat were covered with paintings, sketches, photos, and icons,
representing a thousand years of Polish culture. She led me to the
sitting room and introduced me to Count Raczyński, who sat
dressed in a formal business suit. He excused himself for not being
able to rise.

At the time Raczyński had just celebrated his ninety-third birthday. Frail and nearly blind, he nevertheless spoke forcefully and emotionally of the Warsaw of his youth. "It was a gay city," he recalled, "in a country that was making good progress . . . it had a good symphony, theaters, an opera—on the whole the amusements were of a high class. For instance, thanks to the British Embassy, the members of the diplomatic corps in Warsaw had boxes reserved for them at the opera house on Thursday nights. On these evenings the corps were decked out in evening dress, dinner jackets, white tie and tails. So, on that evening at least, diplomacy honored the opera.

"The Warsaw opera was on a par with the opera in any major city. The conductor was Emil Młynarski, whose daughter married Artur Rubinstein. She now lives in Paris, Spain, and America."[3]

The year 1926 opened with productions of two tragedies—the operas *Othello* at Warsaw's State Theater in Theater Plaza and *Faust* at the National Theater over on Karasia Street. Writing in *The Literary News*, Antoni Słonimski reviewed both productions favorably.

Besides standard international fare, Raczyński said, Warsaw also "had Polish operas, *The Haunted Manor* (*Straszny Dwór*) written by Stanisław Moniuszko [1819–72] and *King Roger* by [Karol] Szymanowski," who was in some ways the logical successor to the nineteenth-century Moniuszko.[4]

■ Karol Szymanowski (1882–1937) came into his own as a composer during the twenties. Early in his career he had been influenced by the music of Chopin and the symphonic elements in Wagner and Richard Strauss. Later his interests broadened to include impressionism. Though he sometimes incorporated Polish folk music into his compositions, they showed a definite tendency toward progressive ideas and away from traditional Polish music, which drew the hostility of Warsaw's conservative element toward him. That he was allegedly homosexual did not help matters either. Fortunately his work was powerful enough to overcome some of the prejudice held against him.

The indefatigable Stanisław Meyer knew Szymanowski and described him as a great talent and a humble person. "Karol Szymanowski . . . was the most outstanding personality among my musical friends. His musical work is known all over the world and it is not for me to write about it; it belongs to the treasury of human achievements. Szymanowski was a man of very great culture, who read and digested everything that was worth reading in all spheres of thought and activity. He was interested in very many topics: music, philosophy, literature, history, sociology, politics, poetry, sculpture, theater, all of the arts. I do not think that I have ever known intimately anyone more intelligent than Szymanowski, with his fresh, courteous, considered approach to any subject, so characteristic of the deep thinker. There was nothing in him of the naive student who discovers things long known to others, nothing of the intellectual parvenu. He was a splendid talker, always interesting, who knew how to express his ideas without being too insistent, to discuss without dictating or preaching. You could talk for hours with Szymanowski and never hear a word about music and it was just chance that he was a great musician—he could as easily have been a man of letters, his writing in prose was excellent.

"Szymanowski had a most attractive way with everybody. Fairly tall, thin, slightly lame, loosely built, and of a truly aristocratic appearance, he was good-looking, with fair hair, deep-set blue eyes, and beautiful hands. There was something very distinguished about his quiet and modest manner, which revealed the importance of his inner life. Under this image of the well-bred, slightly bored *homme-du-monde*, Szymanowski concealed a very strong will, a great capacity for work, and a definite purpose. He had radical social views and luxurious tastes. He was indolent but did a great deal of work. He went straight toward a definite goal but appeared not to care about it. He was bored with music but went on composing and living for it. He despised money but was in constant need of it. These contradictions, these apparent inconsistencies were, I think, the source of his very great charm. I see Karol, sitting in his usual attitude with the lame leg out, resting his chin on the palm of his hand, holding a lighted cigarette between two fingers, and telling us how boring music was and what a really good concert he had heard last Friday. . . .

"Szymanowski was never really physically well. He suffered from tuberculosis, which cut short his fruitful life, and he often had to spend long months in the mountains and in different sanatoriums. He never married, but was very much attached to his family: his mother, an older brother [Feliks, a distinguished pianist and composer who wrote operettas and popular music], and his sisters. One of his sisters, Stanisława, was a brilliant concert singer and a perfect interpreter of her brother's songs, which often were composed for her. For a time he was director of the Warsaw Conservatory, which, thanks to his efforts, rose to full academic status, and for years he was professor of composition. Under his guidance, a whole generation of young Polish composers grew up, some of them outstanding, and his influence on them was great.

"In short, Szymanowski's work both as teacher and leader of Polish musicians was tremendous."[5]

Two of Szymanowski's most successful works, *King Roger* and his Stabat Mater, were completed in the twenties. The Stabat Mater was written while Szymanowski was living in Paris in 1926 but did not have its Warsaw debut until 1929. The idea for the Stabat Mater came after the deaths of two people close to the composer. It was reminiscent of a medieval Lenten lament and contained parts for a choir, solo voices, and orchestra.

Szymanowski's opera, *King Roger*, written in 1924, had its

first performance at the opera house on June 19, 1926, with Emil
Młynarski conducting. It tells the story of Roger II, a descendant
of the Normans, who ruled the island kingdom of Sicily. Both Szymanowski and his collaborator, the poet-novelist Jarosław Iwaszkiewicz, were fascinated by the history of this island with its blend
of Christian, Greek and Roman, and Oriental elements.

King Roger was not an immediate success. The critic for the
Musical Review (*Przegląd Muzyczny*) wrote: "This work will certainly hold a prominent place in our relatively modest operatic
literature – but this will only happen after some time, when the evo-
lution of public taste will have progressed to the point of understanding its beauties and appreciating its true worth."[6]

Szymanowski was disappointed by the Warsaw public's reaction to his early works. The composer wrote: "there is no real contact between myself and the Polish (or at any rate Warsaw) public.
I seem strange, incomprehensible to them. . . . The European climate of my art does not suit this local provincialism. I am an embarrassment, because I unmask and debunk." Szymanowski knew his
Warsaw audience. While composing the music for his ballet *Har-
nasie*, he explained to his scenarist, Iwaszkiewicz, why he would
limit the number of scene changes: "the whole thing should not be
too long, or the Warsaw public would walk out in droves."[7]

Szymanowski, who was born in the Ukraine, had ambivalent
feelings about Warsaw, even though he maintained a residence at
47 New World Avenue. He felt much more at home in Zakopane
with a close circle of friends that included Witkacy. The young
composer had established a penchant for travel while he was a student in Berlin, a city he visited numerous times. After that he traveled often, performing throughout Europe and in the United States,
where he mingled with internationally known musicians.

Film director Ryszard Ordyński knew Karol Szymanowski in
Paris: "the endless days and nights we spent together in Paris, where
there was for many years the traditional congregation for the sea-

son, bringing the Kochańskis [violinist Paul Kochański and his wife] from America and their innumerable friends rambling after them from all over the world. Karol adored Kochański as an artist and as a man, and his wife Zosia as a loyal and wise friend. The group, which also included Stanisława Szymanowska, [Grzegorz] Fitelberg, [Jan] Lechoń, and Piotr Perkowski, had Rubinstein as a charter member. They were surrounded by a swarm of friends from all over Europe, North and South America, and God knows from where else."[8]

The poor reception Szymanowski's music received in Warsaw did not endear the city to him. He complained, "The concert was in the Conservatory Hall, which holds about six hundred people. Despite the presence of Paul Kochański . . . and my sister [Stanisława], it was not completely filled. This means that there were not six hundred people in Warsaw who cared what I had been doing for the past five years! . . . At the first opportunity I will leave Warsaw again and go west or south, to Italy. . . ."[9]

Despite his dissatisfaction with Warsaw, Szymanowski passed up offers outside Poland, including one from Egypt, to accept a position as director of the Warsaw Conservatory. Many Varsovians, including his friend Iwaszkiewicz, expressed surprise at this move. Everyone knew that the conservatory's board was dominated by conservatives; Szymanowski referred to them as "musical reactionaries." He hoped to get rid of some of them, but he was not influential enough to revamp the entire board, which at one time included both Paderewski and Młynarski. As a result, his tenure was marked by a series of confrontations, which began almost as soon as he took office. The conservatives wanted a program of traditional music; their ears were not attuned to the new sounds emanating from the various musical capitals of the world.

The rivalry between the conservatives and the progressives at the conservatory was a reflection of the struggle within Polish society itself. After 1918 the winds of change swept across Europe and were felt in the arts as well as in politics. Innovations in music, poetry, art, and architecture filtered into Poland from the West but were met by strong opposition in this traditionally conservative, Catholic nation. Politically, the status quo was being challenged by communism and socialism.

The response to these ideologies was a stiffening of the Polish spine and a drift toward an authoritarianism that relied more and more on the military to resolve conflicts. But in the creative performing arts it became impossible to suppress the talents of Witkacy, Tuwim, Schulz, Wat, Schiller, Szymanowski, and others like them.

As composer and conservatory director, Szymanowski played an important role in modernizing Polish classical music. He may have recognized the need for tradition, but he was also aware that changes were taking place on the international music scene, and he wanted Poland to be included in the forefront of more enlightened countries.

Unfortunately the battle he was forced to fight as conservatory director along with the job's heavy administrative duties wore Szymanowski down. Never a very robust man, he was soon exhausted by the stress. He went to a spa to rest in late 1928, and by early 1929 his condition had been been diagnosed as pulmonary tuberculosis. He entered a sanatorium in Davos, Switzerland, where he remained for the rest of the year.

The Press Corps Cometh

Almost as soon as Piłsudski launched his May 1926 coup, journalists from the international media headed for Warsaw to cover the story. Among them was the American Dorothy Thompson. One story has it that she was attending the opera in Vienna when she heard the news. Thompson, then a foreign correspondent for the *Philadelphia Public Ledger,* wanted to leave for Warsaw immediately, but because of the late hour, she could not draw money from a bank for the trip. Never one to stand on ceremony, she rushed to the home of Sigmund Freud, whom she had recently interviewed for a magazine article, and borrowed enough cash from him to leave for Poland. She boarded a train still dressed in her evening gown and eventually reached the Warsaw suburbs traveling by train, bus, and horse-drawn cart. Because rail lines into the city had been damaged, she had to walk the final distance. Her coverage of the coup appeared in the *New York Post.*[10]

After the coup d'etat, a kind of calm settled over Warsaw. Perhaps Varsovians—or at least a large percentage of them—felt that with Marshal Piłsudski in control there would be better times ahead. Arthur Barker became the *London Times* correspondent to Warsaw that autumn and took a generous sampling of the city's social life. "There were various occasions on which the foreign press, among others, were invited to great receptions, or 'routs' as they called them, at the Zamek [Royal Castle]. At these occasions one had the opportunity to see Piłsudski at close quarters.

"I first met Count Raczyński and his then English wife at a party in his palace, in the Krakowskie Przedmieście. It was one of the few great palaces in Warsaw that was fully occupied and fully active. Others had been converted into embassies and the like.

"When I arrived in the capital there were no ambassadors, only ministers. These were eventually promoted by their respective governments to the rank of ambassador; for example, the British minister became the ambassador while I was in Warsaw. I wrote an article about him for the *Times,* to coincide with an article on the history of British-Polish relations, which dated back to the sixteenth century. My main source of information in those days was a Szymon Ashkenazy, a professor of history and a leading intellectual in Warsaw.

"The British ambassador was William Max-Müllar who was just ending his career. His wife was a Scandinavian, and she was one of the leading ladies of Warsaw society in those days, a very impressive blonde woman. Max was the son of a great scholar, also named Max-Müllar. They occupied a rather small palace in the Nowy Świat. . . . The leading diplomatic figures were the French ambassador, [Jules] Laroche, and the Germans, who were in a very delicate position at that time. There was one haughty character, Uli Rauscher, who was a German socialist."[11]

After Piłsudski's coup ended, there were only a few other foreign journalists in the capital. There were no Americans that Barker could remember. "There was one other Britisher," Barker said, "Darcy Gilly, a very distinguished foreign correspondent . . . who was with the *Morning Post*. . . . The rest were predominantly Germans, and interestingly enough, predominantly Jewish Germans. . . . The great cabaret was the Oaza. . . . We spent quite a lot of fun evenings there. . . . I also belonged to the Warsaw Rowing Club [*Warszawskie Towarzystwo Wioslarskie*]."[12]

Barker traveled in Yugoslavia as a student but had never lived in Eastern Europe before. "I found Warsaw a great deal more civilized and Western than I'd expected. . . . I had a season's subscription at the Teatr Polski, I was there for every first night. I was there for the world premier of Shaw's *The Apple Cart*, which he had promised to his Polish translator, Florian Sobieniowski, to whom he was very devoted. The manager of Teatr Polski was Arnold Szyfman, who was one of the prominent figures in Eastern and Central European theater. There were some very fine actors and actresses [in Poland] in that period."[13]

Barker's experiences as a journalist reveal just how underdeveloped Poland was in the 1920s. "I did a great deal of traveling throughout Poland with Frank Savory, who was the [British] consul. I did two tours with him. He hired a car and we toured the eastern provinces in which we were both interested. There was a good paved road in eastern Poland. I believe it had once been the Warsaw–Moscow road. It had obviously been a great military road at one time. But the roads were often just dirt tracks. We hired a large American car and a chauffeur. . . . Luckily we were never stranded on these dirt roads, which were just great wide stretches with peasants, horses and wagons, and bands of Orthodox pilgrims tramping along."[14]

When asked how he managed to file his stories with London, Barker replied, "*The Times* had invented a system of filing by telephone, placing full-time telephonists in Brussels, Paris, Berlin, and Milan. Wherever you were, you could reckon on getting a line to one of those telephonists, and you might get to London by ringing Milan who would ring Berlin, and so on."[15]

Warsaw society not only enjoyed "routs" at the Royal Castle and "fun evenings" at the clubs, but also entertaining at home. Zofia Chądzyńska recalled the parties that she and her friends shared in their parents' homes. "The soirees at our house were quite formal – full dress, dancing the mazurka, etc. The party would begin around 6:00 P.M. and last until 6 A.M. Around 11:00 P.M. we had supper, then about 2:00 A.M. we were served *bigos*, or hunter's stew. If the family could afford a musician, we had a piano player, frequently a blind musician. For the party the furniture would be moved to another room so we had room to dance.

"We began with slow dances, then later *obereks*, the *kujawiak*, and by morning, the obligatory *mazurka*. The neighbors each took turns hosting such a soiree at least once a year.

"Our school also held such parties, but these lasted only until 11:00 P.M. We were each allowed to invite a friend. These parties usually took place during Carnival [which begins on New Year's Eve and ends on Shrove Tuesday, the day before Ash Wednesday, called *Zapusty* in Poland]. There was no orchestra so we played records.

"After graduation we went to more fashionable dances. One that I remember well was held in a place that used to be a fish market, on Jerusalem Avenue. During the war a German officer was killed there, and the Nazis detroyed the place.

"These dance halls were similar to today's discos. The dancing began around 10:30 P.M., and the girls always had a partner. The dance floor was rather dark and the lights projected shadows on the walls. These places only closed between two and four in the morning. We also danced at the Bristol Hotel, at the Paradis Club on New World Avenue, and at the Adria at 4 Moniuszki Street.

"For the adults there were several balls during Carnival, like the Fashion Ball (*Bal Młody*); the White Ball (*Bal Białych Łóżeczek*); the Beaux Arts Ball (*Bal Akademi*); and the Architects Ball (*Bal Arkitektów*). The women who attended these balls were dressed so elegantly, so fashionably, that they could have been attending any high society ball in Europe. . . . I think Warsaw was like a young girl who wants to enjoy herself at any price, emotionally as well as intellectually, and to be fashionable. To achieve this goal without money, people had to be very creative."[16]

British author G. K. Chesterton also visited and wrote about Poland in the twenties, although not in his capacity as a journalist. One of the country's staunchest supporters, he was attracted to Poland because of its unyielding Catholic faith and its ability to resurrect itself after national tragedies that would have undone lesser nations.

Chesterton visited Warsaw in late April of 1927 as the guest of the Polish writers' PEN Club. A large gathering of Polish writers, reporters, and curiosity-seekers were on hand to greet the Chestertons when they arrived at the Central Station from Berlin. Piłsudski had sent several officers to represent him. In a theatrical display of faith, one of his hosts said "he could not call Chesterton the chief friend of Poland, because the chief friend of Poland was God."[17]

The British author, his wife, Frances, and his secretary, Dorothy Collins, were given rooms at the Hotel Europejski in Kraków Suburb. The weather in Warsaw was still rather chilly; Chesterton remarked that it reminded him of "England on a nasty day of east wind." The hotel did not have central heating so they were provided with electric heaters.

The British visitors were both amused and impressed by Polish customs. In particular they found it difficult to survive the long social evenings, which included dinners lasting until 2 A.M. Stanisław Meyer, a veteran of such occasions, describes the scene: "You were usually invited 'about nine o'clock,' but you were not really expected before eleven. To arrive later than twelve without an acceptable excuse was bad form. The dance, interrupted by supper, lasted until the morning, and no hostess was satisfied if her guests left before 6 A.M., but I remember parties that went on until 8 A.M. That we managed to go to such parties for several nights in succession seems incredible now."[18] The Poles entertaining Chesterton were familiar with his books, and at one banquet several of them made speeches in English. Their guest responded appreciatively, drawing the applause of the assembled diners.

The Chesterton entourage was escorted about the city and observed the National Festival on May 3, to commemorate the constitution of 1791. They were also guests at a tea hosted by the vaunted Chevaux-Légers, a much-decorated cavalry regiment. This was followed by a reception given by President Mościcki at the Royal Castle.

Chesterton was overwhelmed by the friendly welcome he was accorded. "Everybody in Warsaw was there, at least, so I was told and I think it must be true, because the crowd was enormous. . . . the old Royal Palace [Castle] [was] filled with lights and color. . . . One Polish lady said to me, 'It is like a dream that we Poles should be able to use our own beautiful [castle] ourselves. Until now no Pole was allowed in the [castle] except under escort; and even now, though it is still beautiful, the Russians have taken away and the

Germans have destroyed all the things, such as pictures and decorations and furniture we valued so much."[19]

The famous author was also treated to a visit to a Warsaw landmark, the Fukier wine cellar in Old Town. The building is reputed to date back to the fifteenth century, and it became a winery in the sixteenth. It then was used as a restaurant and had a wine museum. There, Chesterton enjoyed an evening of military and old folk songs, climaxed by the familiar refrain, *Sto lat!* (May you live for a hundred years!), traditionally sung at dinners and receptions as a tribute to the honored guest.

Chesterton and Poland were absolutely compatible in their religious fervor. At the PEN Club, Chesterton wrote in the guest book: "If Poland had not been born again, all the Christian nations would have died."[20] This was a sentiment shared by many European Catholics, including Chesterton's contemporary, Hilaire Belloc, also a staunch member of the faith. "The determination to save Poland, which is a determination not only to defeat Prussia but to oust the vile and murderous Communism of Moscow, is the moral condition of victory. If we waver we are lost."[21]

Back home in England Chesterton continued to praise the Poles. At Essex Hall in London he gave a lecture about his tour in which he declared that he could not define Poland "because nothing can be so living as a thing that has risen from the dead."[22] He went on to describe the country as "a sane, well-ordered, humorous, well-balanced . . . society, where the people joked with him, talked to him, and treated him exactly as they did in this country [England] or any other civilized country."[23]

Chesterton saw Poland through the misty eyes of the traveler. He saw the Poland of the old aristocracy whose customs and way of life ignored the passage of time. He does not seem to have met with Witkacy or Schiller or Tuwim, the vanguard of a new society. Nevertheless, he valued Polish friendship, even if he had to play second fiddle to God.

Intellectuals and the Theater

Arthur Barker's tour of duty in Warsaw coincided with the rise to celebrity status of Leon Schiller (1887–1954), Poland's leading theater director of that time, perhaps of all time. Schiller studied under the legendary British director Gordon Craig but developed his own unique approach to directing. Like Bertolt Brecht and Max Reinhardt, Schiller totally dominated any production he worked on. In 1924 he founded his own theater group, the Bogusławski Theater, named after Wojciech Bogusławski (1757–1829), sometimes called the father of Polish theater. In the new group Schiller put his ideas into practice, staging traditional plays in untraditional settings and inserting his own attitudes about social realism into the text. He also designed the settings for many of the plays he directed. In this he was assisted by the remarkable set designer Andrzej Pronaszko, an artist who had been influenced by the leading movements of the day, formism and cubism. Pronaszko was as individualistic in his stage set decoration as Schiller was in his directing techniques.

Because of his avant-garde approach to theater, Schiller soon became the darling of Warsaw's intellectual circles; however, he also made enemies among the more conservative theatergoers and the government. The Communist party had been banned now for several years, and the various Polish administrations were suspicious of anything that smacked of rebellion. Schiller inevitably managed to inject into his direction some revolutionary message, and this did not sit well with the authorities, who were still in the early stages of rebuilding the foundations of a Polish society and were keeping a watchful eye on the arts.

Schiller and Aleksander Wat (1900–1967), a poet and novelist, were part of a group of nonviolent radicals who were attracted to socialism because they saw in it, perhaps naively, the possibility for justice for all mankind. Their outlook on the world extended beyond Warsaw and Poland and was at odds with much of Polish society. Wat has said that the members of his group were not really politically motivated, in the sense that they were actually ideologues.

In a talk with Czesław Miłosz, Wat described Schiller as "a fine specimen of the salon communist."[24] One might compare him to the conductor Leonard Bernstein, one of the American "limousine liberals" who briefly took up the cause of the Black Panthers in the 1960s. Wat and Schiller were part of Warsaw's café society in the late 1920s and mingled easily with such opposite political figures as Colonel Józef Beck, the future foreign minister; Stanisław Pieracki of the right-wing journal *Prosto z Mostu* (*Straight from the Shoulder*); and Colonel Wieniawa-Długoszowski, the Piłsudski stalwart, all of whom met frequently at the Café Ziemiańska.

Many of Schiller's productions reflected his socialist beliefs. Although his repertory was not limited to purely political dramas, much of his work reflected the desire for dramatic political and economic change. In addition to directing the standard Polish theater fare (in which he sometimes changed the text to suit his own purposes), Schiller also brought to Warsaw works such as *Roar, China* by Piotr Tretyakov (1930), *The Brave Soldier*, adapted from the novel by Jaroslav Hasek (1923), and *The Case of Sergeant Grischa*, from Arnold Zweig's novel (1927). Besides work by these contemporary European writers, he produced plays by Shakespeare and the French dramatists and familiar Polish plays by Stefan Żeromski, Juliusz Słowacki, and others.

One of his most exciting ventures was his staging of Zygmunt Krasiński's (1812–58) *Undivine Comedy* (*Nie-Boska Komedia*). It starred Irena Solska, Witkacy's onetime lover. The play used a three-level set, with actors separated from one another in cubicles from which they did not move as they spoke their lines. The starkness of the production was something Warsaw audiences had not encountered before. The text, as edited by Schiller, spoke with an obvious revolutionary sentiment.

After his dramatic presentation of *Undivine Comedy*, Schiller staged a production of Żeromski's originally pseudonymous play *The Rose* (*Róża*), which dealt with the rebellion against Czar Nicholas II in 1905.

Schiller's revolutionary zeal was not accepted by Warsaw officials; they closed the Bogusławski Theater just two years after it had opened.

Leon Schiller was not only a director but also a writer and teacher. He created a directing department at the State Theater Institute, and many of his pupils went on to become top directors. He refined his ideas in the more than two hundred articles and essays he wrote on theater, and at one time he edited three magazines, *The Polish Stage* (*Scena Polska*), *Theater* (*Teatr*), and *Theater Chronicle* (*Pamiętnik Teatralny*). Wherever he worked, he never abandoned his belief in socialism.

■ Throughout the 1920s Warsaw's theaters were heavily dependent on city and state subsidies. Their funding was an on-again, off-again proposition and was for some time a political issue. Even so, there was sufficient support to enable them to produce a variety of dramas. Antoni Słonimski, who had established himself as one of the city's leading critics, reviewed plays at many of Warsaw's theaters, but spent most of his time at the National, which produced a wide range of plays, including *Politics and Love* (*Polityka i Miłość*) by Józef Raczkowski, a comedy in four acts; Ibsen's *Enemy of the People* (*Wróg Ludu*); *The Tempest* (*Burza*) by William Shakespeare; *Maids of the Nobility* (*Śluby Panieńskie*), a comedy by the nineteenth-century Polish humorist Aleksander Fredro; *The Silver Dreams of Salome* (*Sen Srebrny Salomei*) by Juliusz Słowacki; *The Candlestick* (*Świecznik*), a three-act comedy by Alfred de Musset, translated into Polish by Tadeusz Boy-Żeleński; and *The Barber of Seville* (*Cyrulik Sewilski*) by Pierre Beaumarchais.

There were also a number of independent theaters where one could see more avant-garde works. At least one, the Atheneum, was known for presenting works by leftist playwrights, such as Bertolt Brecht. The Atheneum, according to Zofia Chądzyńska, "was the workers' theater, organized and supported by the workers' money. It was the only theater that had (and still has today) hard chairs instead of upholstered ones, and it was much cheaper than the others."[25]

In contrast to the Atheneum's austerity was the plush Nowości, one of the most attractive theaters, on Bielańska Street near the Jewish section. It opened in 1926, primarily as a showcase for Yiddish theater. It had the most modern trappings, including state-of-the-art lighting equipment, two balconies and a buffet, and seating for two thousand. Until its demise during the Nazi invasion some of the greatest Jewish actors and actresses, including Ida Kamińska and Molly Picon, appeared on its stage.

The Little Theater (*Teatr Mały*) and the Polish Theater were considered by Varsovians to be the city's two major theaters. At the Polish Theater, in 1926, Schiller directed and did the set for Dumas's *Lady of the Camelias* (*Dama Kameliowa*), translated into Polish by Tadeusz Boy-Żeleński.

Among other plays the Little Theater produced in 1926 were Pirandello's *Each in His Own Way* (*Tak Jest, Jak Się Wam Wyduję*) and Witkacy's *The Madman and the Nun* (*Wariat i Zakonicca*), subtitled *There Is Nothing Bad That Could Not Turn into Something Worse*, perhaps an inadvertent comment on Polish politics.

Witkacy's play, which is set in a madhouse, reveals the author's hostility toward repressive social customs, as well as his anger at the Varsovians who treated him as an eccentric. The protagonist, Walpurg (from Walpurgisnacht?), is both a drug addict and a decadent poet. He is imprisoned in the asylum, confined in a straitjacket. He breaks free of his restraints by seducing a nun employed at the hospital, and then murders one of the psychiatrists.

He escapes the asylum, in a manner of speaking, by hanging himself. In this Witkacy foretold his own death. The climax comes with the appearance of the spirit of Walpurg, dressed as a dandy. He takes the nun shopping, leaving behind the spirit of the murdered doctor, his Freudian analyst, who goes mad and attacks the guards.

The Madman and the Nun contains no direct criticism of the government, but there is little doubt the author held the government responsible for his feelings of repression. In fact, the play can be seen as a metaphor for Polish politics of this period.

The Madman and the Nun continues exploration of the theme of artist-lunatic first developed by Witkacy in his 1911 play, *Bungo*, in which the second lead (said to be modeled after Witkacy's former friend, Bronisław Malinowski) is a madman-genius confined to an asylum. The theme of artist-lunatic reappears in a later novel, *Farewell to Autumn* (*Pożeganie Jesieni*) (1927), in which Witkacy predicted a totally conformist society where individuals are treated as lunatics.[26]

Witkacy and Schiller were just two of the avant-garde Polish artists who wanted to break the pattern of social conservatism and authoritarian government so characteristic of Polish society.

■   The turbulence created by Piłsudski's return to power only provoked greater activity in Warsaw's literary community. The prolific Słonimski produced a volume of optimistic poems titled *From a Long Journey* (*Z Dalękiej Podróży*). His colleague, the irrepressible Tuwim, by contrast, published a more biting volume titled *Words in Blood* (*Słowa we Krwi*), in which he mocked the reality of the new Poland.

During the period of independence a number of women novelists became popular mainly on the strength of the romantic stories they wrote. Never accorded the same recognition as their male counterparts, they nevertheless produced novels that were, by all accounts, fairly accurate depictions of life – and love – in Poland, and in Warsaw, during these twenty years.

Maria Kuncewicz was born in Russia of Polish parents but educated in Kraków and at the Warsaw Conservatory. During her long career – she died in 1989 at the age of ninety – she wrote books exploring such subjects as motherhood and the female ego. In the twenties she published two books in quick succession, *Alliance with the Child* (*Przymierze z Dzieckim*) (1926) and *Face of the Man* (*Twarz Mężczyzny*) (1927).

Zofia Nałkowska was a native Varsovian who published her first novel, *Women,* at the age of twenty-one. Nałkowska was an exceptionally bright person with an abiding positive attitude about the prospects for a better world. She was a student of psychology, philosophy, and economics, among other subjects, and produced a large body of works reflecting these interests. In the middle twenties and thirties she published several novels, including *The Jackdaw* (1927).

A much better-known writer, Bruno Schulz, credited Nałkowska for being his mentor. The two may also have been lovers.[27] In the 1930s, when Schulz visited Warsaw on vacation or on publishing business, he stayed with Nałkowska. His published letters hint at an affair, but in keeping with the modesty of his style, he never revealed any details. Nałkowska was rumored to be fairly promiscuous when she was younger. At the age of fifteen she attended one of the illegal "flying universities" in vogue when Warsaw was under Russian domination – classes and tutorials where Polish language and history were taught in defiance of the czar's ban. Indeed, even the revered Janusz Korczak remarked that, before her marriage [to Leon Rygier], while the students were having a drinking party, Nałkowska "drank wódka from a bottle, kissed the mistress of the laundry owner and enjoyed flirting with the poet [Ludwik] Liciński who was hopelessly in love with her."[28]

The third woman novelist, and perhaps the one most favored

by Polish critics, was Maria Dąbrowska. She too was born in Russia, of a Polish family that had lost its holdings. Nevertheless, she was well educated abroad and had a deep-rooted interest in Poland's problems. Dąbrowska began her writing career by producing children's stories. The first, in 1922, was *Branch of a Cherry Tree and Other Stories (Gałąż Czereśni i Inne Opowiadania)*. She followed that in 1923 with *A Smile of Childhood: Recollections (Uśmiech Dziecinstwa: Wspomnienia)*. Her best-known work is *Nights and Days (Noce i Dnie)*, a generational work in four volumes, which deals with the members of a family named Kalisz and their lives as they attempt to adjust to an ever-changing world.

Aleksander Wat, who had previously published just one volume of poetry, produced his only book of stories in 1927. The collection was titled *Lucifer Unemployed (Bezrobotny Lucyfer)*. Of this book he said, "what I put together in *Lucifer* was a confrontation of humanity's basic ideas — morality, religion, even love. It's especially paradoxical and interesting that just then I was going through the second year of a great love. But that cerebral questioning and discrediting of love was thorough, taken right to the end. The discrediting of the very idea of personality . . . everything is brought into question. Nothing. Period. Finished. *Nihil.*"[29] One of the oddest stories in *Lucifer* describes a futuristic world in which everyone has been converted to Catholicism. Anti-Semites study cabala and speak Hebrew.

Wat could be described as a literary agitator; he was opposed to the policies of both the Polish left and the Polish right. Though he had close ties with the Communists and has been called a Marxist, Wat avowed that he never joined the Party and, in a book-length interview with Czesław Miłosz, even denied that he was a true believer in Marxism.[30] The Communists nevertheless asked him to be their candidate for the Sejm in the 1928 elections, and in 1929 he became the editor of the controversial communist magazine, *The Literary Monthly.*

■ Janusz Korczak, then in his forties, continued his phenomenal out-pouring of writing. Much of it grew out of his work with children, which he had begun as early as 1905.

Korczak was born Henryk Goldszmit in Warsaw, in 1878, to a family of wealthy, educated Jews. By the time Poland achieved its independence, Korczak had already established a formidable reputation as a pediatrician, educator, and novelist. His articles also frequently appeared in education and medical journals. Early on in his career Korczak realized the interconnectedness of affection, good nutrition, independence, and learning, a regime that some of the so-called free schools attempted to emulate in the United States in the 1960s.

For the first forty years of his life Korczak lived in Warsaw un-der Russian jurisdiction. He enrolled in the czarist university as a medical student and also taught in the city's "flying universities." It was during this time, on one of his many excursions around the city, that he became interested in the lives of the poor, especially their children.

His first attempts at writing consisted of articles on the sad state of the health of these children, and their need for care and edu-cation. He took his medical degree in 1905 and immediately began pursuing his multiple careers: medicine and childhood education.

Korczak was probably one of the few Varsovians to serve in three wars—the Russo-Japanese war (1905), World War I, and the Polish-Russian war. He saw service as a physician in all three, and continued to write. During the Russo-Japanese war a collection of his feuilletons, *Stuff and Nonsense* (*Koszałki i Pałki*), was published. In the following year, 1906, his book *The Drawing-Room Child* ap-peared and became an immediate success.

Between 1906 and the beginning of World War I Korczak continued to work with children and formulated his theories of child care that ran counter to the traditional methods of education.

Several years before World War I he joined the Orphans' Aid Society and two years later became its director. In the meantime he was instrumental in building the Orphans' Home on Krochmalna Street.

World War I did not stop his writing career; he continued to publish books on pedagogy and education through the end of that war and into the next. While Korczak was recovering from typhus in 1920, one of his most important books, the three-volume *How to Love Children*, appeared.

After leaving military service for the last time, Korczak realized a long-cherished dream by establishing a summer camp for his orphans away from the city. His life continued in this manner—teaching, writing, caring for children, publishing medical papers—through the interwar period. In 1923 two of his best-known children's stories, *King Matt I* (*Król Macius Pierwszy*) and *King Matt on a Desert Island* (*Król Macius na Bezludniej Wispiej*), were published. The former was translated into English and published in America by Farrar, Straus and Giroux in 1986.

In 1926 he convinced the Jewish weekly *Our Review* to add a children's supplement to its pages, which he edited. He also published another book, *Shamelessly Brief: Humoresque.*[31]

From Lepers to Eaglets

The major film hit of 1926 was *The Leper* (*Trędowata*), starring the popular actress Jadwiga Smosarska. It was based on a contemporary romantic novel by Helena Mniszkówna. The story, subtitled *A Song of Love*, was so popular that it had three movie versions, the last one filmed after World War II. Film critics agree that this first, silent version was the best literal interpretation of the book. Smosarska, a dark-haired beauty, called it a fairy tale without a happy ending. The book received mixed reviews but nevertheless sold thousands of copies.

Large amounts of money were expended to assemble a top-notch cast and crew in a time when films were usually made with exceedingly low budgets. *The Leper* was produced by the Sphinx production studio. The film was shot at the country estates of various members of the aristocracy and in Warsaw. The major male character is a matinee idol who bears a striking resemblance to Rudolph Valentino.

One reviewer who did not like the film was Antoni Słonimski. He attacked it and the studio that produced it, calling the movie "a relay race run in reverse. *Trędowata* falls below the usual level of quality of the films produced by Sphinx and its owner, Mr. Hertz. One cannot deny Mr. Hertz his business acumen; he appealed to the lowest common denominator in human values.... The very idea of filming *Trędowata* is a classical example of cynical thieving management. The main character is the goddess of cooks and seamstresses...."[32]

Unfortunately, we cannot judge *The Leper* for ourselves. The original negative, the copies, and even the screenplay have all been lost, probably destroyed in the war. All that remains of *The Leper* are some well-preserved programs, which fortunately are very detailed in their narration and profusely illustrated.

■   Hanka Ordonówna made her film debut in 1926, in an unmemorable short film titled *The Eaglet (Orlę)*, directed by Viktor Biegański. It was perhaps one of the earliest docudramas, for it was based on the successful round-trip flight from Warsaw to Tokyo by Lieutenant Bolesław Orliński. Much was made of the film's opening. It premiered at the Apollo Lejman cinema on Marszałkowska, the Broadway of Warsaw, and was attended by a number of dignitaries, including President Ignacy Mościcki, Deputy Foreign Minister Józef Beck, and the ubiquitous Colonel Wieniawa-Długoszowski, by now a familiar figure in the city's night life.[33]

Despite all the hoopla, *The Eaglet* did not measure up to Biegański's earlier success, *Vampires of Warsaw* (*Wampiry Warszawy*).
That 1925 thriller caught the imagination of Polish audiences. As
for Ordonówna, *The Eaglet* was an exciting distraction from cabaret
life, not the beginning of film stardom. Zosia Terne remembered
that Hanka tackled her role with her usual zest, rehearsing at Qui
Pro Quo in the mornings, appearing before the cameras in the afternoon, then doing two shows at the club in the evening. Her career
was now beginning to take off.

PART TWO

Summertime

I don't know why God ordered me to live in
Poland...

Józef Piłsudski

CHAPTER 5

Presentiments of Catastrophe

■ Summer 1927-1931

Politics and the Economy

Summer arrived in Warsaw and found few changes in the political
climate. Marshal Piłsudski was still at odds with the Sejm, and
Kazimierz Bartel was again the prime minister. Before making way
for Bartel, Piłsudski had delivered a blistering attack on the deputies
(members of parliament), carrying on at length about how impossible it was for any prime minister to get cooperation from them. His
reason for resigning, he said, had more to do with ill health than
with the difficulties of governing. Later he contradicted himself in
a newspaper interview, where he confessed that the combination
of conflicts with the Sejm and all the details a prime minister had
to deal with were too much for him. He believed that his role was
to intervene in times of great crises; let others worry about the daily
affairs of state.

Before leaving office he permitted the Kellogg-Briand Pact to be ratified. Piłsudski generally opposed multination pacts and initially opposed signing this one, but he relented after the Soviets agreed to include Rumania and the Baltic states. The pact, drawn up by the Allies, guaranteed the newly defined borders of Poland and the Soviet Union and helped to reduce the tensions that had arisen the year before.

When the Sejm demanded an explanation from the prime minister and cabinet on budget overspending in early 1929, it discovered that much of the spending had been legitimate. Construction of Poland's first port on the Baltic, at Gdynia, had cost a large sum. Still, there remained the question of a missing eight thousand złotys, which had financed the BBWR campaign, and the spotlight was turned on the treasurer, Gabriel Czechowicz.

Piłsudski came to his man's defense by accepting responsibility for the transfer of funds from the treasury to the BBWR coffers, but the deputies were determined to bring Czechowicz to trial. He resigned his post in March and Piłsudski lambasted the Sejm for daring to try a minister of state. Kazimierz Bartel, now in poor health, decided to resign also. Over Piłsudski's protests, Czechowicz was examined by the deputies who, after days of deliberation, exonerated the treasurer and let the matter drop.

Bartel's successor lasted less than a year. He was ousted by a vote of no-confidence spearheaded by members of the Centrolew, a coalition of the Polish Socialist Party and other left and center groups furious at Piłsudski's arrogant behavior. The reliable Bartel was once more brought in as premier. By this time the effects of the worldwide economic depression were beginning to be felt in the Polish economy. Orders for coal, steel, and textiles slowed to a trickle, causing mass unemployment. To make matters worse, many of the unemployed returned to their villages, which themselves were suffering from a drop in demand for agricultural products. The government's reaction was to protect the złoty, and to do this it immediately made significant cuts in public expenditures.

The brief period of prosperity and growth came to an abrupt end just after receipt of the American loan. In the late 1920s things had been looking up for the Poles in spite of the conflicts between the government and the Sejm. A reorganized public school system had helped reduce the nation's illiteracy rate, and university enrollments were up. There was a noticeable increase in attendance at the opera and at the theaters. The cafés were crowded with poets, artists, and assorted intellectuals, and for the price of a złoty one could buy a coffee and spend hours poring over the newspapers. The middle class in particular enjoyed a period of nearly full employment, aided by the availability of more civil service jobs.

But, like the Western nations, Poland was hit hard by the depression. Once-prosperous clerks could be seen begging on the streets alongside common laborers. Many small businesses went under, swelling the numbers of the unemployed.

Bartel's return to the post of premier did not last long. He clashed almost immediately with the deputies over the issue of presidential authority. They responded by giving two of his ministers no-confidence votes, and he then resigned for the fifth and last time.

President Mościcki again turned to Piłsudski. The marshal declined to serve, but his loyal friend Walery Sławek accepted the invitation to form the next government. He walked into an ambush led by the Centrolew, which was demanding a special session of the Sejm to iron out its differences with the president and his cabinet. Mościcki twice postponed this session, and the Centrolew went to the people. It organized a major rally in June 1930 in Kraków, but the BBWR countered by holding one in Galicia. The Catholic church, not previously supportive of Piłsudski, gave the government its support by convoking the first Polish Eucharistic Congress on the same day.

The Centrolew rally was disappointingly small, but those who attended heard the speakers call Piłsudski a dictator, deride Mościcki as his accomplice, and demand the president's resignation. They also urged the people to refuse to pay their taxes.

The accused retaliated swiftly. Sławek agreed to step down as prime minister and Piłsudski succeeded him. Mościcki then dissolved parliament and scheduled elections for November.

As prime minister, Piłsudski ordered the arrests of the Centrolew leaders, including former prime minister Wincenty Witos. They were carted off to a military prison instead of a civilian jail and while incarcerated were badly mistreated.

Elections went ahead in November 1930, and the BBWR gained majorities in both the Sejm and the Senate. As was expected, the Centrolew lost seats, but the National Democrats made gains. Having defused the opposition movement, Piłsudski again decided to resign, and Sławek was reappointed in his place.

Though retired from active politics, the marshal still held the twin posts of Minister of War and Inspector General. At a time when a military threat always seemed to be looming from some quarter, these posts gave him a lot of power, and as long as he remained in the public eye Piłsudski would continue to dominate Polish politics. But perhaps the worst part of his legacy is that he had unwittingly laid the foundation for the coming rule of the "colonels."

Literary Laurels

Summer in Warsaw: The Sejm was in recess and the Qui Pro Quo troupe was about to make its regular summer tour of Polish cities. There was a lull in both the social and the political lives of the capital. Many of its citizens spent the summer months, or at least August, in the countryside. Professor and scholar Wacław Lednicki was one of the few who did not. For him, the Polish summer was a time to have the city all to himself, to retreat to a café, have a simple meal, and read his newspapers in peace. In his memoirs, he conveyed the pace of a Warsaw summer:

"I liked Warsaw at that time of year. The city was quieter than in winter, and its population was different. The permanent residents were away; theaters, restaurants, and streets were populated by visitors, by people from the country, from provincial towns. . . . It was pleasant to walk along the streets of the city, which were still the same but looked quite different. They seemed to acquire an entirely new significance. I liked to wander after work in some secret, beautiful section of old Warsaw under the golden sky of the Warsaw summer evenings. . . . In those days I occasionally took my meals in a modest coffee shop called the Parliament [*Sejmowa*] Coffee Shop. It was located on the Three Crosses Square not far from the parliament and one of the most beautiful avenues, the Warsaw Champs-Élysées—the Aleje Ujazdowskie. The small dining room of the shop was humble, it sold no liquor, the meals were simple, healthy, country-style: Polish cold soup, cucumber salad in cream, buttermilk, cottage cheese, pork chops, braised beef with boiled potatoes and braised beets in a cream sauce. The people who ate there were small officials, high school teachers, librarians, dispossessed landowners, university professors, and among them from time to time appeared the face of a newcomer."[1]

Not all Varsovians who left the capital went to the country that summer. Some journeyed instead to Amsterdam to watch the Ninth Olympic Games. Among the athletes competing that year were the great Finnish runner, Paavo Nurmi (10,000-meter race) and Johnny (Tarzan) Weismuller, who won the 100-meter freestyle swimming meet.

The industrious Poles had taken up sports with a passion in the twenties. Warsaw had three sports complexes that drew large crowds for track and field events and soccer: Legia, Polonia, and Warszawianka. Legia was frequently the scene of international matches, and the Poles particularly enjoyed playing and beating the Germans in soccer. Legia also had a fifty-meter swimming pool and a diving board available to the public. The Warsaw Cyclists Society staged bicycle races on the track at Dynasy, and wrestling had become a popular feature at the Stanislaus Circus (*Cyrk Stanisław-skich*).

In the winter young and old flocked to the Swiss Valley (*Dolina Szwajcarskiej*) skating rink to skate to popular music and eat lunch at the rink's restaurant. In the summer months, those who could afford it joined one of the city's rowing clubs like the Vistula (*Wisła*), or the more socially prominent Yacht Club (*Wał Miedrzeszyński*), which hosted very elegant balls.

All this participation in sports enhanced Polish interest in the Olympic Games. Two Poles returned with gold medals from the Ninth Olympic Games. One medal went to Helena Konopacka, who took first in the discus throw (129 feet, 11 ⅞ inches). The other gold medal was won by the poet Kazimierz Wierzyński. Poetry and sport may seem exact opposites – one features brain and the other brawn. But in those days, it was not considered too effete to have a literary contest to complement the athletic events in Amsterdam.

Wierzyński was one of the rare contemporary poets who successfully incorporated sports into his poetry, and he walked off with the first prize for his volume *Olympic Laurel* (*Laur Olympijski*). Like so many other writers and politicians, Wierzyński had been a Piłsudski legionnaire during World War I. Afterward, he, Reymont, Tuwim, and several other poets began to meet at the café Under the Sign of the Picador to compare notes on their poetry. In 1920 he was involved in the founding of *Skamander* magazine.

■ Marszałkowska, the boulevard that was the commercial center of Warsaw. (Courtesy of the Polish Library, London.)

■ View of Krakowskie Przedmieście and Senatorska Street from Castle Square, at the turn of the century. In the center is King Sigismund's Column. (Courtesy of the Historic Museum of Warsaw.)

■ The Copernicus Monument, where Krakowskie Przedmieście becomes Nowy Świat. (Courtesy of the Historic Museum of Warsaw.)

■ Unveiling of the Adam Mickiewicz monument on Krakowskie Przedmieście in 1898. (Courtesy of the Historic Museum of Warsaw.)

■ Town Hall on Theater Square. (Courtesy of Wydawnictwo Książka i Wiedza.)

■ The Brühl Palace, which later became the Raczyński Palace and then the Ministry of Foreign Affairs. It was destroyed during World War II. (Courtesy of the Polish Library, London.)

■ Theater on the Island in Łazienki Park. (Courtesy of the Historic Museum of Warsaw.)

■ *Above:* A second-hand-book seller (*bukinista*), 1927. (Courtesy of Wydawnictwo Książka i Wiedza.)

■ *Left:* Crowds in front of an army post on Mokotów Street during the coup of May 1926. (Courtesy of Wydawnictwo Książka i Wiedza.)

■ A street in the Jewish district. (Courtesy of the Polish Library, London.)

■ *Above:* Interior of the café Art and Fashion (*Sztuka i Moda*, or SiM). (From *Po Obu Stronach Oceanu* by Zofia Arciszewska. © Polska Fundacja Kulturalna 1976.)

■ *Right:* Actress Lena Żelichowska on the cover of the magazine *Cinema.* She spent the last half of her life in San Francisco. (From *W Starym Polskim Kinie* (At the Old Polish Cinema) by Stanisław Janicki. © Krajowa Agencja Wydawnicza 1985.)

■ *Left:* Hanka Ordonówna in the popular film *The Masked Spy* (*Szpieg w Masce*). (From *W Starym Polskim Kinie* (At the Old Polish Cinema) by Stanisław Janicki. © Krajowa Agencja Wydawnicza 1985.) *Below:* Ordonówna in a bedroom scene from the film, with costar Bogusław Samborski. (From Archiwum Dokumentacji Mechanicznej.)

■ *Left:* Actress and comedienne Mira Zimińska in the musical comedy *Soldier of the Queen of Madagascar* (*W Zolnierz Królowej Madagaskaru*), 1936. (From *Nie Żyłam Samotnie* by Mira Zimińska-Sygietyńska. © Wydawnictwa Artystyczne i Filmowe 1985.) *Right:* Zimińska at home in Warsaw, 1928. (From Archiwum Dokumentacji Mechanicznej.)

■ At the opening of the Artists' Resource Club (*Resursa Artystyczna*) in Warsaw, 1930, Antoni Słonimski (seated left), Zula Pogorzelska, and General Wieniawa-Długoszowski (right) celebrate. The man standing at the left is unidentified. (From Archiwum Dokumentacji Mechanicznej.)

■ *Left:* Zula Pogorzelska, one of Warsaw's most popular cabaret stars. She died at the height of her career. (From Archiwum Dokumentacji Mechanicznej.) *Below, left:* Julian Tuwim, Poland's foremost poet of the interwar years. (From Archiwum Dokumentacji Mechanicznej.) *Below, right:* Lyricist and poet Marian Hemar in a postwar portrait. (Courtesy of Wlada Majeska.)

■ Celebration in honor of Konrad Tom (left), on the occasion of his twenty-fifth year as an actor, in Warsaw, 1938. Director Jerzy Boczkowski is next to Tom. (From Archiwum Dokumentacji Mechanicznej.)

■ *Right:* Tadeusz Boy-Żeleński, the critic and reviewer who translated virtually all the French classics into Polish. (From Archiwum Dokumentacji Mechanicznej.)

■ Composer Karol Szymanowski. (From *Szymanowski* by Teresa
Chylinska. © PWM-Edition, Polski Wydawnictwo Muzyczne, 1981.)

Wierzyński remained a prolific poet throughout his long career (1894–1969).

Wierzyński's early poems were full of enthusiasm for nature as well as for sports. "Spring and Wine" (*Wiosna i Wino*) (1919) and "Sparrows on the Roof" (*Wroble na Dachu*) (1921) brought him to prominence in Poland while he was still a young man.

Wierzyński once worked as the editor of *The Sports Review,* located in the modern Polish Press building. The press building housed the satirical magazine *The Barber of Warsaw* (*Cyrulik Warszawski*), the magazine *The Movies* (*W Kinie*), and the newpapers *Morning Express* (*Kurier Poranny*), *Red Courier* (*Kurier Czerwony*), and *Good Evening* (*Dobry Wieczór*).

The offices of these periodicals were separated from one another by glass partitions so that one could observe the goings-on at the other periodicals. Tadeusz Wittlin worked on the staff of the *The Barber of Warsaw* next to the editorial office of *The Sports Review,* where Wierzyński directed his staff. He recalled Wierzyński as "that fabulous poet, from the immortal Skamander group . . . handsome, tall, full of charm and young at heart. He runs his office with enthusiasm and verve and the group that he has gathered is excellent."[2]

I met Wierzyński in 1964, in New York, long before any thought of writing about Warsaw had entered my mind. He was living at the Kościuszko Foundation on Fifth Avenue and I had gone there to see an exhibit. I remember him as a tall and courtly gentleman. During our conversation he suggested that I come to the foundation to study Polish with him, but I was still in self-imposed exile from the Polish language and declined his offer. Before I left the foundation he gave me a signed copy of his *Collected Poems* (*Poezje Zebrane*). The inscription, in Polish, read: "Welcome back to the Polish language."

■ Witold Gombrowicz, one of the few Polish writers of this era
known to Americans in translation, now made his first appearance
in Warsaw literary circles with the publication of four stories:
"Kraykowski's Dancer," "The Memoir of Stefan Czarniecki," "Pre-
meditated Murder," and "Virginity."

Gombrowicz's family owned an estate in southeast Poland,
where he was born in 1904. During World War I the family moved
to Warsaw, and Gombrowicz was educated at an exclusive private
school there. He entered the University of Warsaw in 1923 as a law
student and, upon receiving his diploma in 1928, went to work in
the city's municipal court.

Gombrowicz continued to write short stories, including
"Symposium at Countess Kotłubaj's," but he was then a relative unknown compared to Warsaw's more established writers. Tuwim,
for example, published a new volume, *Czarnola's Speech*, at about
the same time, and Jarosław Iwaszkiewicz published *The Book of
Day and the Book of Night (Księga Dnia i Księga Nocy)*, an exploration
of cultural myths in the form of verse. Kazimierz Wierzyński followed up his Olympic triumph with another book of poems, *Fanat-
ical Songs (Pieśni Fanatyczne)*.

One of Warsaw's more enigmatic poets, Konstanty Ildefons
Gałczyński, wrote poetry that included elements of classical
mythology, outrageous humor, and contemporary slang. The title
of his lengthy poem, *The End of the World: Visions of St. Ildefonse,
or a Satire on the Universe*, published in 1929, gives some sense of
his style and thought.

Gałczyński was a native of Warsaw and a brilliant but cynical
student. Because of his linguistic abilities, he was able to read the
work of poets of other European nations in the original. Judging
from the content of his poetry, one would have thought him to be
a member of Poland's liberal element, yet he was in conflict with
those poets. As his career progressed he expressed more interest in

Polish folklore and nationalism, and eventually began to publish in the right-wing periodical *Prosto z Mostu*.

His attitude toward Jews was ambivalent. His writing sometimes contained attacks on Jews, but at the same time he sought out the friendship of Julian Tuwim. This feeling of ambivalence is typical of his thought, extending even to a description of his own role in Polish society, in his poem "The Intelligentsia":

We always run away, from town to town
we – intellectuals:
small and shivering, a tribe without a tribe,
a class of ineffectuals

From country to country, we shift about with our families:
we each have a gramophone,
millions of us. But it's no use. They keep asking:
"Which country is your own?"

And since we don't know, we can only weep
oceans of salt oblations.
Beneath fake palms we write artificial letters
and post them in dirty stations.[3]

Gałczyński's long poem, *The End of the World (Koniec Świata)*, was published in the outsider literary magazine *Quadriga (Kwadriga)*, which appeared in 1926 but survived for only five years. *Quadriga's* editors were concerned with social causes and were at odds with the Skamander poets, whose verse they considered self-centered. But the magazine's policies were not all that clearly defined, and none of its poets achieved the status of Tuwim, Słonimski, or Wierzyński. One of *Quadriga's* better-known poets, Władysław Sebyła, later became a Polish officer and was one of those murdered by the Russians in the Katyn Forest massacre of 1940.

The Literary Monthly, which began publication in 1929, was a magazine with more clearly defined policies. It was started by a small circle of leftists, including the director Leon Schiller and the poet Władysław Broniewski, who decided they needed a forum in which to express not only their ideology but also their ideas in poetry, literature, and criticism. Its editors were Aleksander Wat and Jan Hempel.

Those involved with *The Literary Monthly* usually met in one another's apartments—Schiller's or Wat's—or at the Café Ziemiańska where Colonel Wieniawa-Długoszowski and several cabinet ministers occasionally joined the conversation. For the time being, their friendship and their interest in exploring ideas overcame ideology. On these occasions, according to Wat, Schiller would play the piano; someone would give a talk; and always there were the discussions and the arguments. Wat claimed that the police spied on his apartment for years while the *Monthly* was in operation.[4]

The first issue of *The Literary Monthly* appeared in early 1929. It was iconoclastic, intellectual, and well written, and it drew strong response both from the supporters and the opponents of communism.

The Literary Monthly stirred up more controversy in its short life than did *The Literary News*. Among Wat's more memorable essays were his criticisms of Erich Maria Remarque's alleged pacifism, his attack on Polish futurism and other avant-garde movements, and his obituary for Vladimir Mayakovsky in an issue devoted entirely to the Russian poet who died by his own hand in 1930.

The Jewish novelist Sholem Asch was the subject of one particularly vicious essay (not by Wat) for his supposed fascist tendencies. There were also attacks upon attacks, for example, Słonimski's rebuttal to Wat's article criticizing Remarque was also a broadside against both Wat and his magazine. In fact it was a fairly emotional one since Słonimski was not at all sympathetic to the Communists, whose forum in *The Literary Monthly* particularly raised his hackles.

In the early aftermath of the Bolshevik revolution there were power struggles within the Party in Poland as well as in Russia, and these were reflected in rivalries within *The Literary Monthly*. The magazine's content may sometimes have been difficult to comprehend for those with little education, but nevertheless it served as a rallying stage for Polish workers as well as intellectuals during its brief existence.

The Warsaw police watched the comings and goings at the *Monthly* quite closely and finally moved to shut it down in the autumn of 1930. The Communist party was outlawed in Poland, and the police issued several warnings concerning the radical nature of the magazine's writing, before confiscating an entire issue in October 1930. Still, the magazine continued to be published until the arrest of Wat and his staff in 1931.

Aleksander Wat later reminisced with Czesław Miłosz about his 1931 arrest. Even before being apprehended Wat had become disenchanted with communism and had begun to devote his energies to writing purely literary essays.

In the period before the arrest the staff of *The Literary Monthly* had been badly demoralized. The magazine had failed to build a substantial following, and the masses had not picked up on its political message. The conflicts within the Communist party itself and between the Polish and Russian parties were discouraging. The Piłsudski government had begun a crackdown on radical activities throughout Poland, and the government decided to close the magazine.

Wat and his staff were holding a meeting at a relative's apartment when the police broke in and arrested them. The editorial office, however, was in Wat's own flat in another part of the city, and the police took him along when they went to search it.

"I was taken by car to Hoża Street, where they were planning to search my apartment. We rang the bell. A commotion. Our maid answered the door, her name was Genia, a very pretty girl, very intelligent, very charming, very promiscuous. She had a fiancé who worked at Borman's as an electrical engineer and visited her in the evening. It was midnight. There was some guy in our bed, very good-looking. A dress coat and dress shirt were hanging in the closet. It turned out he was a footman from the Italian fascist embassy, a Pole; apparently he was her sister's fiancé. He was terrified of losing his job. The plainclothesman wanted to take him along with me. He explained that he worked in the embassy, but the plainclothesman didn't believe him. Finally, we all started laughing because the situation was so ridiculous.

"The plainclothesman called the embassy to find out if he worked there and then handed him the receiver. He took it and we heard him explain that he had dropped by an apartment and the Communist who lived there was being arrested. And clearly the people on the other end of the line asked him, 'Who is the guy getting arrested?' to which he replied, 'How should I know?' *That* I found irritating. He sleeps with my maid in my bed and, to top it off, talks about me like that. And so I said to the plainclothesman, only half in jest, 'You know, maybe we should be brought in together.' But of course they let him go."[5]

The arrests occurred during Jewish holidays. "They packed us into the cellars of the Security Division, which was housed in the cellars of Central Prison on Danilowiczowska Street, where we were imprisoned later. The investigating officers were upstairs, and the Security Division was down below in the cellars. The cells were quite clean but covered with graffiti. Plank beds. And they pushed us into a large cell, which at the time was occcupied by Jewish bakers. That was a very Communist union. I don't know if they had been planning a strike, but they had all been picked up during the holidays and jailed in the Security Division. There was plenty of food in those cells. Jewish bakers were arrested during the holidays, and so of course they had all their treats with them."[6]

Later, Wat took part in a short hunger strike and was placed in solitary confinement. He was released after two months, his freedom secured by a ruse: Wat's wife, Ola, arrranged for Dr. Stefanowski, Piłsudski's personal physician, to examine her husband. Prior to that, Wat was given a medication that dramatically increased his pulse rate. Dr. Stefanowski declared that Wat was quite ill and should be released. No one challenged the doctor's findings, and Wat was let go.

The odd relationship between the Polish Communists and the government is illustrated by what happened upon his release:

"I had the melancholy of a creature who is two-dimensional, but there was a certain joy as well—that it was autumn, the golden Polish autumn. It was a very beautiful day on Krakowskie Przedmieście; there were a great many women in the street that day, lightly dressed, wearing summer dresses. The street was like a garden. The policeman escorting me was very friendly. I met my sister, and she gave me some money and a couple of packs of cigarettes, which I, of course, gave to him. He was a pleasant lad, entirely without malice, and he even went into a bar with me on the way back. We drank beer—he didn't want any more than that; he was afraid of being seen. Those were idyllic times."[7]

Wat's imprisonment was an eye-opening experience, not least because he was confined with people from the working class. Up until then his associations had been with other intellectuals and poets who could only theorize about how the masses lived.

The Literary Monthly was closed down, and later attempts to revive it were unsuccessful.

Seasons in the Theater

The year 1928 saw demonstrations of patriotism in Warsaw streets and theaters. On November 11, all Poland celebrated the tenth anniversary of independence. There were festivities and Masses said throughout the country. Paul Super—one of two foreigners to receive the Ten Years Medal, a medal given to non-Poles who had served the Polish nation for at least five years since it had regained its freedom—witnessed the celebration in Warsaw: "One long remembered the endless line of men, women, and the children of all classes parading past Marshal Piłsudski as he stood in the front of the reviewing stand receiving the spontaneous cheers of civilians, soldiers, and war-crippled veterans, an infinitely deserved tribute of love and devotion."[8]

Perhaps inspired by the mood of the day, dramas with parallels to Polish politics began to appear, mainly in the Polish Theater, and under the direction of Leon Schiller. In successive months, beginning in February, he directed adaptations of Shakespeare's *Julius Caesar* (*Juliusz Cezar*); Shaw's *Man and Superman* (*Człowiek i Nadczłowiek*), translated by the faithful Florian Sobieniowski; and an operetta based on the legend of Don Quixote, in which dancers from Madame Tatiana Wysocka's School of Theatrical Dance took part. Madame Wysocka's school taught modern or interpretive dancing, such as the Delacroze style and the expressionistic movements pioneered by Isadora Duncan.

In May the New Theater (*Teatr Nowy*) produced its version of Ibsen's *The Master Builder* (*Budowiczny Solness*). The following month the versatile Schiller switched to comedy and mounted a production of the George Abbott—Phillip Dunning play, *Broadway*. The artist Stefan Norblin was engaged to do the costumes and Madame Wysocka's pupils provided the chorus line. This play marked the appearance of something new in Warsaw—a jazz score by the Polish musician Rajznera.

The balance of the theater season consisted of homegrown comedies and revivals of Polish classics, with notable productions of *Wanda*, written by the nineteenth-century poet Cyprian Kamil Norwid, and *Lelewel* by Stanisław Wyspiański. The season concluded, appropriately enough, with the world premiere of Paul

Claudel's play *On the Seventh Day He Rested* (*Odpoczynek Dnia Siódmego*).

In 1929 Leon Schiller produced *The Threepenny Opera* (*Opera z Trzy Grosze*) at the Polish Theater. The authorities did not look kindly on this Brechtian drama, with its revolutionary message. The play was closed down, and Schiller was dismissed from his job at the theater.

The year 1930 was a good one for traditional plays. Three George Bernard Shaw plays were produced in Warsaw, all translated by Florian Sobieniowski, who enjoyed a long, warm relationship with the Irish playwright. *Misalliance* (*Związek Niedobrany*), directed by Arnold Szyfman, the theater entrepreneur, opened in March at the Little Theater. *Heartbreak House* (*Dom Serc Złamanych*) was performed in May at the New Theater, directed by Leon Schiller. And in November the New Theater mounted a production of *Getting Married* (*Nowa Umowa Malzenska*), directed by the actress Irena Solska. Shaw's work had a strong appeal for Warsaw audiences.

In March the Polish Theater performed *The House of Women* (*Dom Kobiet*), directed by Marie Przybyłko-Potocki and written by novelist Zofia Nałkowska, whose work was starting to gain more recognition. The New Theater performed *Don Juan*, with direction by Juliusz Osterwa in March. The Polish Theater produced Ben Jonson's *Volpone* in May, adapted by Stefan Zweig and translated into Polish by the poet Kazimierz Wierzyński. Two Wyspiański plays were seen that year: *Legion* at the Great Theater in April and *Varsovienne* (*Warszawianka*) at the New Theater in December.

Rehearsals were scheduled to start in March 1930 for Stanisława Przybyszewska's *The Danton Case*. The author wanted Schiller to direct it, but memory of his run-in with the government over *The Threepenny Opera* was still fresh in his mind, and he declined. Another director acceptable to Przybyszewska was found, and the play went into rehearsal in March 1931.

Przybyszewska was not an easy person to deal with. Devoted to the French Revolution and to Robespierre, she would not allow her text to be altered. Other theaters, including the prestigious Staatliches Schauspielhaus in Berlin, wanted to produce *The Danton Case*, but the play ran to five hours, and the author balked at any attempts to edit it. After tedious negotiations the play was finally produced in Lwów at the Grand Theater in March 1931. Two years later it was staged in Warsaw at the Polish Theater.

Despite the play's revolutionary fervor, the government permitted its production, choosing to view it as a call for strong government. Przybyszewska, however, refused to travel from Gdańsk to see it. By then the author was seriously addicted to morphine, having been introduced to the drug by her poet-father. She was also suffering from malnutrition and was at times mentally unbalanced. Her aunt, who was virtually Przybyszewska's only contact with the outside world, went to Gdańsk and offered to take her niece to Warsaw for treatment, but Przybyszewska's pride would not allow her to appear in the capital in her present condition. She never saw the play performed in her lifetime. It was not staged again until 1967, when it was revived by Jerzy Krasowski in Wrocław. Much later Andrzej Wajda made his film based on the play.

By 1931 the dramatic theaters of Warsaw were in trouble, as actors, directors, and virtually everyone connected with the stage went on strike. All the theaters in the capital were shut down while management and artists engaged in a bitter conflict. The issue was money, for the performing arts were also feeling the effects of the Great Depression. Everyone working in theater—actors, directors, stagehands—was seriously underpaid. Ticket sales could not sustain the theaters, and both city and federal governments refused to entertain the possibility of subsidies. Pressured by members of the cultural community, mainly the writers Juliusz Kaden-Bandrowski and Wojciech Zawistowski, the federal government became involved in the dispute. Zawistowski came up with the idea of establishing a State Institute for the Theatrical Arts. It was to be a quasi-official body that would oversee all types of theater activities, plus organize competitions and hold seminars and workshops.

In 1933 the new prime minister, Janusz Jędzejewicz, and his brother Wacław, minister of education, were sympathetic to the proposed institute and gave government support. Arnold Szyfman also lent his support – he had considerable influence as a man of finance and a man of the theater. He was appointed director of the government-sponsored Association for the Promulgation of Theatrical Culture (*Towarzystwo Krzewienia Kultury Teatralnej*), or TKKT. Under his leadership the Polish Theater and the Little Theater were the first to get government subsidies. By 1934 most of the municipal theaters were under some form of government control and were receiving financial assistance.

After the turmoil of the strike, Warsaw's theaters came back to life with a wide variety of dramas and entertainments. In July Janusz Korczak's play, *A Senate of Madmen* (*Senat Szaleńców*) was performed at the Atheneum, starring the popular veteran actor-director Stefan Jaracz and directed by Stanisława Perzanowska. One critic described it as a "grotesque farce."

In the two seasons following the strike, the invasion of Western drama continued. Staged in Warsaw were two Shaw plays – *The Doctor's Dilemma* (*Lekarz na Rozdrożu*) and *Pygmalion*, both translated by Florian Sobieniowski; *Of Human Bondage* (*Mam Prawo Odejść*) by Somerset Maugham; *Marietta, or How to Write History* (*Marieta, Czyli Jak się Pisze Historie*) by Sacha Guitry; *Dove's Heart* (*Gołębie Serce*) by John Galsworthy, directed by Stefan Jaracz; *Once, Twice, Three Times* (*Raz, Dwa, Trzy*), a one-act play by Ferenc Molnár; Vicki Baum's *Grand Hotel* (*Ludzie w Hotelu*); *Romeo and Juliet* (*Romeo-Julia*); Dickens's *Cricket on the Hearth* (*Świerszcz za*

Kominem); *School of Hypocrisy* (*Szkoła Obłudy*) by Jules Romain; *The Dreyfus Affair* (*Sprawa Dreyfusa*), by Hans Joseph Rehfisch and Wilhelm Herzog; *Black Ghetto* (*Czarne Getto*) by Eugene O'Neill; Rostand's *Cyrano de Bergerac;* Carl Zuckmayer's *The Captain from Kopenick* (*Kapitan z Koepenick*); and *Die Fledermaus* (*Nietoperz*) by Johann Strauss, with set designs by Max Reinhardt and program notes by Julian Tuwim.

End of the Chorus Line

There was no hint of the coming demise of the Qui Pro Quo club during its last few exciting seasons. In 1926 the QPQ troupe made its regular summer tour of major Polish cities. Upon returning to Warsaw it began the autumn season. Hanka Ordonówna presented a new long poem by Tuwim that drew critical praise from Boy-Żeleński in the *Morning Courier*. Not all her performances drew such rave reviews, but she was gradually becoming a favorite of the cabaret crowd.

In September 1927, Qui Pro Quo opened its season with a new member, Zosia Terné, a singer from Lwów. I met Terné while scouring London for survivors of the Second Republic. She was a small woman, and her physique reminded me of photos I had seen of Edith Piaf. Terné, however, was much more attractive and very well dressed.

Terné had studied music and voice at the Royal Academy in Lwów. She wanted a career in the theater, but her teachers suggested that young Zosia study for the opera. Indeed, she once sang the role of Adela in *Die Fledermaus* and had appeared in a production of *Così Fan Tutte.*

In the summer of 1927 the Qui Pro Quo company performed in Lwów as part of its summer tour. While in town, Boczkowski heard Terné sing and accompany herself on the piano. Upon return-

ing to Warsaw he sent her a letter asking her to come to the city
and audition for Qui Pro Quo. He liked what he heard and signed
her to a contract as Ordonka's understudy.

Terné had arrived in the capital naive and frightened. She
boarded with family friends rather than take a flat. By all accounts
she was a tiny but well-proportioned blonde with a resonant voice
that belied her fragile figure.[9]

"At first, I was given songs that Ordonówna rejected," she told
me. "At that time Tuwim, Lechoń, and Hemar were writing lyrics
for Hanka and were being paid *not* to write for others. I plunged
right into Warsaw's café life. My days were quite full – morning rehearsals, a rest period, then two performances in the evening."[10]

Terné made her Qui Pro Quo debut with a sentimental song
titled "So Many Cities . . ." (*Tyle Jest Miast*) written for her by Marian Hemar. It was a tale about her home city in Lwów, and she sang
it in front of a setting reminiscent of Lwów. The song ends with
the words "Go wherever you want, do whatever you want, but if
you want to fall in love, you must fall in love in Lwów."[11] The audience loved her and brought her back onstage for an encore. "So
Many Cities" became a hit that year, and from then on Zosia Terné
was known as the "Nightingale of Warsaw."

Just before we left the dining room at the Ognisko Polskie
club, I asked her to sign my notebook. On a blank page she
scrawled, "To my beloved Ronald – your tortured Zosia."

By the end of 1927 Qui Pro Quo was getting stiff competition from
the Eye of the Sea (*Morskie Oko*). This cabaret had been around for
a number of years in various incarnations – first as the Persian Eye
(*Perskie Oko*), then as the New Persian Eye, and now with yet another name. Its first production of the season was titled *Miss
America*, directed by Jerzy Leszczyński. Ludwik Sempoliński, the
veteran actor and comic, recalled that the show was good, although

the performances were a little uneven. This was followed by a skit called *Tarzan*.

Andrzej Włast was now coming into his own as a director, having departed Qui Pro Quo. His show, *Warsaw Courier*, ran for one hundred performances in March 1928. Zula Pogorzelska, with her beautiful legs, had also defected to the Eye of the Sea and was still a star in her own right.

The club had a talented, extremely attractive chorus line, the eponymous Koszutski Girls, and the lively Halama sisters—Zizi, Loda, and Alicja. A beautiful actress and dancer, Lena Żelichowska, made her debut at the Eye of the Sea and went on to become one of Warsaw's top stars, appearing in numerous shows and films. She later lived in San Francisco.[12]

It was to counter this competition that Fryderyk Járosy turned to Madame Tatiana Wysocka's School of Theatrical Dance. Many of Warsaw's cabaret chorus girls were trained by Wysocka and were skilled in the art of dancing topless or in the flimsiest of costumes. At the school, Járosy met an attractive young dancer named Stefania Górska. Before long they were having an affair. This required some subterfuge on Járosy's part, since he and Ordonka were still living together.[13]

The Járosy-Górska affair finally came to light when Qui Pro Quo was on its summer tour. Until then Hanka had not been aware of what was going on. In Lwów she and Járosy had a confrontation, and she dismissed him from her life.

She then made her first solo tour of Europe, giving impressive performances in Paris, Vienna, and Berlin. The other Qui Pro Quo stalwarts were off doing other things. Julian Tuwim had produced another volume of poems, *Czarnola's Speech*; Mira Zimińska and Marian Hemar had formed an alliance; and the comic Adolf Dymsza had married.[14]

In 1929 Qui Pro Quo celebrated its tenth anniversary. One of the first programs of the year was titled *The Ministry of Foreign Affairs*, *or Remember Me (MSZ, Czyli Pamiętaj o Mnie)*. Zimińska did a skit titled "You Must Become a Minister," written by Marian Hemar. The story concerned a woman who wanted her reluctant husband to become a government minister. She taught her husband how to behave, whom to talk to, what presents to give to which lady in order to gain the necessary influence. Zimińska played the wife, the one who made appointments with the prime minister and so forth. In her autobiography, she noted that she was later accosted by Mrs. Józef Beck, wife of the deputy foreign minister, "whom I liked a lot and who was very nice, elegant, and a humble person. She told me, 'Mira, I know who you had in mind.'"[15]

The show's finale was the song *Remember Me (Pamiętaj Mnie)*:

Goodnight, and in your dreams
Remember me!
Know that I love you
and so much—
And if you love me
Then sigh to me.
Good night and in your dreams
Smile...

Dobranoc, a we śnie
Pamiętaj o mnie!
Wiedz, że kochałam cię
I to ogromnie,
A jeśli kochasz mnie,
To westchnij do mnie!
Dobranoc, a we śnie
Uśmiechnij się...[16]

Boy-Żeleński, in his *Morning Courier* review, called it Qui Pro Quo's best performance ever. His article had a bittersweet note to it, as if he knew that the cast had reached a peak and would soon be moving on. *Remember Me* ran for a hundred performances.[17]

This year, 1929–before the depression and forebodings of war changed Warsaw's mood–ended with one of Poland's last truly uninhibited New Year's Eve celebrations.

One woman who had celebrated many a *Sylwester*, as Polish New Year's Eve is known, was extravagant in her description of the holiday: "The New Year's Eve celebrations in Warsaw were as joyous and spontaneous as the ones anywhere. The streets of Warsaw, which we referred to at this time as 'Little Paris,' throbbed with songs and music coming from houses, hotels, and cafés. Cars crawled from Ujazdowskie Avenue through Nowy Świat and Krakowskie Przedmieście to the Old [Town] district, the center of the celebration. The most beautiful ballrooms and dance halls were located there: Europejski Hotel, the Bristol, Resury Obywatelska i Kupiecka [Citizens' and Merchants' Club], the Great Theater, with its traditional *Sylwester Reduta*, an elegant masquerade ball. It's impossible to forget the fashionably designed Adria on Sienkiewicz Street with its great Kahan and Gold's orchestra. The best Warsaw society gathered in these nightclubs.

"The costume balls in the Academy of Fine Arts were also very popular, thanks to the participation of the Gypsies. It was worth it to go to the balls just for the decorated rooms and colorful costumes."[18]

In March 1930, Qui Pro Quo celebrated with a show titled *Qui Pro Quo's Jubilee*, starring Zimińska, Ordonówna, Dymsza, Járosy, Krukowski, Konrad Tom, and Ludwik Lawiński. Ordonówna sang a new song titled "It's Difficult" (*Trudno*), about trying to hold the love of her man. You can hear it on the same scratchy disc that holds her theme song, *Love Forgives Everything*.

In the *Morning Courier,* Boy-Żeleński called it Qui Pro Quo's finest hour.[19]

A banquet to honor the cast was held at the Bristol Hotel, attended by hundreds of people in gowns, white tie and tails, and assorted military uniforms. The honored guests sat around a horseshoe-shaped table, with Ordonówna in the center, flanked by such luminaries as Julian Tuwim, the directors Jerzy Boczkowski and Seweryn Majde, Mira Zimińska, and the ever-present Colonel Wieniawa-Długoszowski. Qui Pro Quo had reached a milestone in its illustrious history.

Hanka's life took on a further luster when she met a count. In his excellent biography of her life, Tadeusz Wittlin records their first meeting. Count Michael Tyszkiewicz was a minister at the foreign office and a member of one of Poland's most socially prominent families. He also dabbled in popular music and was an amateur lyricist. He sometimes attended rehearsals at Qui Pro Quo and on one occasion brought with him the lyrics for a tune called "Streets of Barcelona" (*Uliczka w Barcelonie*). Boczkowski coaxed Ordonówna into singing it, and it turned out to be a minor success. Count Michael's thank-you note became the prelude to a long courtship that was the talk of Warsaw. He was seen frequently at the theater, and the couple dined in the city's best restaurants. This was more than the singer had bargained for when she began her career.

Like the other cabarets, Qui Pro Quo was always dodging financial bullets, but in 1931 it finally staggered to its end. A combination of factors—salaries, the effects of the depression, and an unusually high number of free passes to the shows—brought the club to its knees. Unable to secure financing to keep it going, Boczkowski closed the doors in April 1931.[20] One of the city's bright lights had gone out, and there would never again be a cabaret that rivaled Qui Pro Quo for popularity.

Insatiable

By 1930 the mood of Polish literature had changed. Czesław Miłosz notes that the writing of Słonimski and Witkacy, in particular, took on an ominous tone in the thirties. Słonimski's poetry began to include references to the worldwide depression, unemployment, and the unmistakable rise of totalitarianism. "The joy, even euphoria, that followed the recovery of independence in 1918 was faithfully noted by literature. Around 1930, the tone changed. The economic crisis, the violation of the constitution by the military junta, the emergence of fascist groupings on the right, propagating anti-Semitism and announcing 'a night of long knives' for 'Jews and intellectuals,' converged with Hitler's grab for power in neighboring Germany. . . . In intellectual circles a feeling of impotence and presentiments of an imminent European catastrophe prevailed. It is no wonder, then, that the literature of the thirties was marked by apocalyptic or humorously macabre visions."[21]

Witkacy, who by now had stopped writing plays and had turned his attention to fiction, produced his apocalyptic and darkly humorous novel, *Insatiability* (*Nienasycenie*). It takes place in a future world in which Russia has rejected communism and Poland is governed by a dictator who is also a genius. Meanwhile, Western Europe has been overwhelmed by communism and faces the threat of invasion by communist China. The latter is ruled by Murti-Bing, an ideologist who might have been the fictitious forerunner of Mao Ze-dong.

Insatiability presents a mad parody of a collapsed society desperately searching for salvation and eager to accept any scheme that might bring it. An unidentified pill is introduced to the population that induces bliss, relieves anxiety, and obliterates the will to resist. Before a crucial battle against the marauding Chinese, the Polish leader declines to fight and is beheaded with great ceremony. Afterward, the conquered people are permitted to exist as "has-beens" and are governed by a "Minister of the Mechanization of Culture."[22] This was not the first time Witkacy attacked authority in his writing, but now there was a sense of panic, of hopelessness, that had not been present before.

Not only Witkacy's subject but also his style provoked controversy. Karol Irzykowski turned his attention to Witkacy's theory of pure form. In his book *The Struggle for Contents: Studies on the Literary Theory of Cognition*, he attacked Witkacy's theory. In defense of his novels, Witkacy maintained that pure form did not enter into the experience of reading to oneself; he maintained that his novels need not adhere to any formula or literary tradition and — despite Irzykowski's challenge — went right on writing as he pleased.

The year after *Insatiability* was published, Witkacy began work on his fourth novel. Titled *The Only Way Out*, it was an effort to create "a new form of novel in which intellectual and artistic adventures would replace events and emotions as the soul of the plot." The novel has two main characters: a man who is a philosopher, dilettante, and a drug addict; and an artist who was once the lover of the philosopher's wife. Witkacy had planned a dramatic ending in which the artist cuts the philosopher's throat — the very means by which Witkacy tried to commit suicide — but the work was never completed.

Drugs and destruction — these themes recurred throughout Witkacy's work. A passage in his early novel *Farewell to Autumn* described the aftereffects of cocaine so realistically that *The Pharmaceutical News* decided to review the book. It quoted Witkacy, who had obviously sampled the drug itself, describing cocaine as "one of the most harmful narcotics, producing terrible hangovers and leading ultimately to madness and suicide."[23]

Witkacy had had a strong interest in drugs ever since his World War I wounds had been treated with morphine. He was especially interested in studying the effect of drugs on the artistic mind. Unlike the poet Stanisław Przybyszewski who was an admitted addict, Witkacy never became drug-dependent. But in his work—paintings, novels, and plays—he pushed human consciousness to new levels.

Though his behavior and some of his work reveal the influence of narcotics, Witkacy's experimentation with artificial substances was controlled. These experiments—for example, his effort to paint while under the influence of various drugs—were observed by a friend, Dr. Birula-Białynicki. This doctor-friend defended Witkacy's experiments, insisting, "Witkacy's childlike nature...led him to seek escape from reality."[24]

In 1932 Witkacy published the results of his drug experiments in a book titled *Nicotine, Alcohol, Cocaine, Peyote, Morphine, and Ether*. After this book much of Polish society concluded he was stark raving mad; at best he was seen as an intelligent drug addict. He was neither, though he was unable to surrender his affection for cigarettes and alcohol.

A personality such as Witkacy's sent shock waves through the more conservative elements of Polish society. Certain critics and writers recognized his unusual talent, but like many great artists, Witkacy was acknowledged as a genius only years after his death.

I will go sated
With life which is great, difficult, and tempestuous

Usnę, syty życia
Które jest wielkie, trudne i burzliwe

Jarosław Iwaszkiewicz
"To my wife" (*Do Żony*)
Translated by Czesław Miłosz

CHAPTER 6

Melody of Warsaw

■ 1931–1933

On the Political Front

Early in the new decade Piłsudski's health took a turn for the worse. He suffered a series of illnesses and his wife and close associates reported that he aged suddenly. A weight loss was accompanied by a loss of energy and lack of enthusiasm. The years of turmoil had begun to take their toll on him, aided and abetted by his unhealthy personal habits, in particular his heavy smoking. He suffered from both influenza and bronchitis.

Travel abroad seemed to revive Piłsudski's health somewhat, but it also gave him time to reflect on his own future. Upon returning to Warsaw he set up an office in a small apartment and seldom visited government offices. He continued to perform his duties as minister of war and inspector general but ignored domestic politics. His devoted follower Walery Sławek had resigned as prime minis-

147

ter to devote more time to the BBWR. He was succeeded by a man who held the rank of colonel, and from then on there was a steady stream of officers moving from the army into cabinet posts, not always with the best results.

Political tensions remained high, and in August, Tadeusz Hołowko, BBWR vice-president and a Sejm deputy, was assassinated by Ukrainian conspirators. The Ukrainians remained the largest minority in Poland throughout the interwar period, larger even than the Jewish minority, who received more attention. The 1931 census counted nearly five million Ukrainians living on Polish soil, compared to three million Jews.

There were movements in Poland's volatile relationships with its two immediate neighbors. The on-again, off-again contact with the Soviets improved with the signing of a nonaggression treaty in January 1931. After the hostilities of the late 1920s, the Soviet Union had had a change of heart toward Poland, influenced no doubt by the looming confrontation with the Japanese in Manchuria and, to a lesser extent, by the failure of its Five-Year Plan. Signing the nonaggression treaty had a twofold advantage for Poland: It would soothe relations with its eastern neighbor for a while, and it would keep the Germans in line.

The situation with Germany was rather tense. The dispute over control of the Baltic port of Danzig (Gdańsk) was never far from the minds of either the Poles or the Germans. But with the opening of the Gdynia seaport in 1932 Poland became less dependent upon Danzig's facilities. The loss of Polish shipping revenues and the continuing depression forced Danzig to obtain a series of loans from Germany.

When the Danzig senate requested that the League of Nations force the Poles to redirect some of their business to the port, it was met with stubborn resistance on the part of the Polish government. Danzig then withdrew its permission for Poland to use the port at all.

Piłsudski and his deputy foreign minister, Józef Beck, decided to use this opportunity to test Germany's strength. Without notifying the Danzig senate, Piłsudski ordered the Polish destroyer *Wicher* into Danzig's waters to pay a call on a fleet of visiting British ships. Piłsudski had also instructed *Wicher*'s captain to open fire on Danzig if challenged. The event went off without any confrontation, but both the Danzigers and the German government protested to the League of Nations. Nothing came of their protest, although the Allies were not particularly pleased with Piłsudski's boldness.

This was not Piłsudski's only attempt to draw out the Germans. After the *Wicher* affair he initiated secret contacts with the French government with the purpose of provoking the German military. By now news of Hitler's arms buildup had begun to leak out, and Germany's neighbors were anxious to discover just how strong Hitler really was.

Using personal contacts instead of diplomatic channels, Piłsudski sent a message to Paris in which he suggested that the two nations cooperate in a peremptory strike against Hitler. At first noncommittal, the French government eventually rejected Poland's overtures, thus assuring that Hitler could go on strengthening his forces.

Rebuffed by France, Piłsudski now knew that Poland stood alone against Germany and the Soviet Union. But instead of a policy of reconciliation he was determined to pursue a policy of toughness against the two powers.

The foreign minister Piłsudski chose in 1932, Józef Beck, reflected this tough style. As a young officer Beck had played an important role in the Polish-Russian war. Afterward he rose rapidly in Polish diplomatic ranks. He was a tall, educated man with crisp manners and a frankness that his opposite numbers took for arrogance. Piłsudski believed Beck had the makings of a great foreign minister, the kind of man the marshal hoped would maintain his foreign policy in the difficult times that lay ahead.

Decadence and Construction

Polish intellectuals were well aware of their position between Germany and the Soviet Union. Polish Communists and left-wing intellectuals, Wat, Jasieński, and others, made trips abroad to see how the revolution was faring. They were especially encouraged by what they saw in Germany. German Communists were well armed and seemed about ready to take over the collapsing society. In his book-length conversation with Czesław Miłosz, Aleksander Wat described the Berlin of 1928:

"Decadence, decadence, a Babylon of debauchery. On Friedrichstrasse, a main street, in broad daylight, in the afternoon, there'd be prostitutes walking side by side, taking up the entire sidewalk. That was very striking, impressive. But they were all very maternal, fair-haired German women proudly walking the streets. Three, four, side by side, so that sometimes the other pedestrians had to step off the sidewalk for them. In broad daylight. On Kurfurstendamm, an amazing number of faces straight out of Grosz, Otto Dix, the hideous snouts of spectators.

"Once I was taken to a side street off Kurfurstendamm, to some sort of nightclub for homosexuals. That was the first time I had ever seen that. Some of them were wearing women's clothes, their faces made up. The way they danced was monotonous; they danced like automatons. The cheap glare of the Chinese lanterns, the incredible sadness, the theatricality — above all, the sadness got to me. . . .

"Unemployment was horrible by then. Once, around eleven in the evening, an older prostitute, decently dressed, elegant, stopped me in the street. I gave her a very cold look. She said, all right, but I have a fifteen-year-old daughter; I can take you to her; the price is such and such. Selling daughters. Terrible poverty, you see. I ventured in that district — people were dying of hunger, starving to death. Side by side with all that luxury."[1]

Both Wat and the Nazis were affected by scenes such as those. Both felt this decadent milieu represented capitalist society at its worst, and both had specific, though divergent, thoughts about how the situation could be remedied. While in Berlin, Wat met with German Communists and was impressed by their organizing skills. He returned home to Warsaw full of ideas for the future.

Wat also noted that in Berlin, in 1928, "practically no one spoke to me about Hitler."

The other side of this sense of foreboding was the excitement described by novelist and screenwriter Kazimierz Brandys in his *Warsaw Diary*, speaking of his first contact with Warsaw:

"In no great capital did I ever again experience any such entrance into an image, into the living stuff of concepts, ideas, and fantasies. New York reminded me of a gigantic Łódź, a hundred bristling Łódźes with skyscrapers. Paris revealed its charms gradually, different ones with each trip. But such a breathtaking confirmation of what I had imagined and such happy amazement at my own presence at the source of those fantasies as I felt that first summer of 1932 in Warsaw—no never again, and nowhere else.

"After smoky industrial Łódź, Warsaw was synonymous with worldly glamour.

"Warsaw didn't dazzle foreigners in the twenty years between the wars. Gray, its layout chaotic, its back turned to the Vistula, it might have seemed a city of no interest. But for me, the world was interesting then."[2]

Between the wars, Brandys wrote, "the world seemed far-flung and great, but normal; it could be comprehended. . . . now I sometimes think that the world is small, stupid, and bloodstained. But less was known in those days. There can be no error cruder than to think that the more information we have about the world, the more comprehensible it becomes. On the contrary. The contemporary media only reveal the unpredictability of our planet . . . "[3]

Speaking to fellow novelist Tadeusz Konwicki, Brandys continued: "The war destroyed our way of life, and afterward, everything smelled of surrogates. I began listing restaurants and little
theaters in Warsaw between the wars, describing how racing fans
used to meet in the cafés on Marszałkowska, the ones near
Mokotowskie Field, to pick their favorites over a glass of café au
lait. I named the cafés where members of the actors' guild used to
congregate, the writers' and painters' bars, and other bars, with Chinese lanterns on their terraces, on Aleje Jerozolimskie, where
crowds of people would saunter on hot evenings until late in the
night. And I recalled the moment [at the end of World War II]
when I first became aware that all these colorful details of daily life
had been replaced by new backgrounds and props."[4]

Observers of contemporary Polish history refer to the period from
1931 to 1934 as the time of the Great Slump. The country continued to suffer the aftereffects of the worldwide depression in the
thirties, but paradoxically the early years of that decade saw continued growth and cosmetic improvement in Warsaw. The city began to expand from its small center and spread outward, especially
to the north and the south, adding a great deal of acreage to its original boundaries. There was an increase in the number of buildings
under construction, existing structures were repaired, more city
roads in Warsaw were paved, and plans were laid for new schools,
museums, and theaters.

   Jan Merkiel was born in the capital in 1918 and lives there
now, retired from his medical practice. He was on the verge of
adolesence at a time when the city seemed to be changing and growing. He remembered the transition of Marszałkowska from a street
of small shops to a boulevard replete with new stores, cafés, and restaurants announcing their presence with neon signs. "On my way
to school I used to count the number of neons, and I remember that
at one time there were about seventy of them on one side of the

street alone. On the corner of Marszałkowska and Złota a blinking neon announced Emil Wedel, *bonbonnière,* with a flashing arrow pointing out the location of the store.

"There were also many banks on Marszałkowska—the Swiss, the French, the German, as well as some small, family-owned banks, and also the Stock Exchange. On Napoleon Plaza the fourteen-story, British-owned Prudential Insurance building had recently gone up."[5] That modest skyscraper was the subject of a "Polish-American" joke that Merkiel told:

"An American of Polish origin came to visit Warsaw. He hired a horse-drawn cab for a tour of the city. The driver first took him to the Royal Castle. The visitor asked 'How long did it take to build this?' The driver replied, 'About ten years.' 'In America,' the visitor retorted, 'it would have taken only four years.' Next they visited the huge Staszic Palace. 'How long did it take to build that?' asked the American. The driver estimated four years. The American snorted and bragged that in the United States it would have taken only three months. They then went on to the Prudential building. 'What is that?' the American asked. To which the cabdriver shrugged and replied, 'I don't know. It wasn't there yesterday.' "[6]

Merkiel loved the many parks in Warsaw. It was a tradition in his family, after his twelfth birthday, for him and his father to promenade along Ujazdowskie Avenue and through Łazienki Park on Sundays after Mass. His mother and sister stayed at home to prepare the Sunday meal. On one of these occasions they came across the serene figure of President Mościcki seated on a bench, decked out in a top hat, chatting with one of his officers. The Merkiels greeted the president as one would greet a friend, and pleasantries were exchanged.

Halina Mendelsohn also witnessed President Mościcki strolling in Łazienki Park, wearing a top hat and tails and accompanied by several men who seemed to be bodyguards. Whenever she and her friends approached the great man, they would all curtsy politely. Today, it is hard to imagine the president of any country strolling through the park on a Sunday afternoon – or on any day, for that matter.

Marszałkowska and Kraków Suburb developed into the city's main shopping thoroughfares. On these boulevards the shopper could visit a tailor shop or purchase a dress at a BATA outlet, or choose from a plentiful supply of goods at the large department store, Jabłokowscy Brothers (*Bracia Jabłokowscy*). Fabrics for a new dress or drapes could be purchased at AGB or at Bierański's. For fine china one went to Łakoński on Szpitalna Street and for cutlery to Norblin's. The streets in the center of town were studded with grocery stores, meat markets, and bakeries, all dispatching their rich aromas into the downtown air.

Merkiel remembers one street with special fondness, the cross-town Holy Cross (*Świętokrzyska*) Street. There Merkiel browsed through the many antique shops and used bookstores. The Jewish proprietors of these shops were very knowledgeable about books of every sort.

"I didn't buy many books, though, because my father owned a printing house and had a large library of unusual, wonderful books, including a first-edition Mickiewicz. But everything was burned in a few hours, in September 1939."[7]

Polish architects, influenced by movements abroad and spurred by the need for municipal buildings and public housing, were enjoying full employment.

One of the capital's most pressing needs was for housing of all types. Work on the housing problem had actually begun, on a limited scale, as early as 1921. Polish architects, in cooperation with the Warsaw Housing Cooperative (*Warszawska Spółdzielnia Miesz-kanowia*, or WSM) and similar organizations led by left-leaning organizers, erected a series of estates, as they were known, which consisted of moderately priced apartments with anywhere from one to four rooms, designed for workers and middle-income families. The teachers' co-op in Żoliborz (Estate IV), designed by Barbara and Stanisław Brukalski, was one of the best known. Spearheaded by the WSM, throughout the twenties, blocks of apartment buildings sprang up away from the old city center.

Warsaw's architects seemed to prefer the Bauhaus style, so the buildings they designed were boxlike, characterized by a singular lack of ornamentation and the planes and sharp angles of Bauhaus architecture. Critics said these buildings did not take the mental or physical well-being of their inhabitants into account, but inside, they were comfortable and imaginatively designed, with decor by Polish interior designers who were making a name for themselves in this field. The simplicity of Bauhaus afforded factories the opportunity to mass-produce the components for high-rise apartment buildings and thereby accelerated the building program, which helped alleviate the shortage caused by World War I. Yet the Bauhaus style received plenty of criticism from designers and architects whose ideas were considered more avant-garde. On the other hand, the public occasionally insisted on a return to the old classic style architecture, mainly in private villas and some public buildings.

In addition to the vast apartment complexes being built, more attractive residential neighborhoods were created in Mokotów and Ochota, and across the river in the Saska Kępa district. The latter was one of the few areas relatively untouched by the Nazi occupation later.

The WSM also took the lead in city planning, although many of its schemes never got off the drawing board because of lack of financing. These plans envisioned new landscaped boulevards, overpasses, and a subway system. Some of the ideas survived the Nazi occupation and were used in reconstructing the capital after World War II.

The center of Warsaw was rebuilt at the end of the twenties.

The sixteenth- and seventeenth-century townhouses surrounding Old Town Square were rehabilitated. The square itself replaced the old Town Hall, and the houses facing it were painted bright colors.

The old airport at Mokotów, southwest of the city's center, was moved to its present location at Okęcie farther away from downtown, and the racetrack was removed to Służewiec. Later, a new racetrack was built near Mokotów.

Among the notable public buildings constructed near the end of the decade were the offices of the newspaper *Warsaw Life* (*Życie Warszawski*) on Marszałkowska, the Post Office building on Nowogródzka Street (which was to play a key role in the 1944 Uprising), the Physical Training Academy, the National Economic Bank, and the Ministry of Transport. Many of the best works of the architects who designed these structures, such as the project adjacent to Paris Commune Square, were destroyed in World War II.

Other notable buildings that went up in the early 1930s included the massive YMCA building, with its swimming pool and restaurant, the Polish Teachers' Union, the PKO Bank with its Renaissance-style facade, the Ministry of Education, and the Law Courts.

Bohdan Pniewski, one of the leading architects of this period, was responsible for the Foreign Ministry building, which was a wing of the Brühl Palace. Built in a traditional style, it featured baroque-style staircases and colonnades. The wing was destroyed by the Nazis and never rebuilt, but one of Pniewski's villas, on Rzymska Street, was rebuilt after the war. Yet another of his villas is now the Museum of the Earth on Na Skarpie Avenue, so the visitor to Warsaw may get at least some idea of his work.

With all of its building and rebuilding in the twenties and thirties Warsaw was girding itself to become a fitting capital for a reborn nation. Poles were quite aware of their historical achievement, of coming back from the dead, in a manner of speaking. Few conquered nations have ever made such a dramatic comeback. This feeling was shared by the peasants as well as the upper classes; it ran like a current through Polish society. Despite the political squabbling of the interwar years, the nation as a whole felt that it had achieved something spectacular and that it was destined to become one of Europe's great nations again.

Between the wars Poland's population and army grew, and the strength the nation felt was manifest in the muscle of its architecture. The construction that took place in the capital before 1939 reflected the power felt by its people, a power wielded with some arrogance and resulting in the construction of buildings most distinguished for their size. In fact, many of the interwar buildings can best be described as massive or huge.

Unfortunately, many of Warsaw's public structures, built in the twenties and thirties with great hopes for the future, were reduced to rubble during the war. Though a number of buildings were reconstructed using photos and drawings as blueprints, the materials used were not the same as in the original construction. Knowing that one is gazing at a replica instead of the original somehow dilutes the joy of discovery. It is impossible to measure not only the physical but also the psychological damage done to Warsaw by the Nazis.

Art and Fashion

As a complement to Warsaw's new architecture, a bustling trade in interior design sprang up. The field was dominated by ŁAD, a co-op whose members were graduates of the Academy of Fine Arts, while their competitors were graduates of Warsaw's Technical University. These interior designers were true innovators. Following their inspiration, interiors of villas, cafés, and public buildings took on a distinctive modern appearance, as up-to-date as the interiors in any western European city of the day. Young Polish designers eagerly took up the task of helping to beautify the city; they tackled such diverse projects as the interior for the popular Adria Café, the Bristol Hotel ballroom, and even the salon at the power station.[8]

Among those sharing in this rebuilding renaissance was Zofia Arciszewska. For the last half-dozen years before the war, her café Art and Fashion (*Sztuka i Moda*, or SiM) was one of the most innovative, if not important, cafés in Warsaw.

"The SiM Café was founded by me. It opened on May 18, 1932, and was located on Piłsudski Square [formerly Saxon Square] in front of the Europejski Hotel. Its abbreviated name stood for Art and Fashion and was selected in an informal competition organized among my friends. It was won by Zdzisław Kleszczyński, a famous poet, playwright, and columnist for the *Warsaw Courier* (*Kurier Warszawski*) where he wrote under the pen name Sek. He and his wife belonged to my circle of friends.

"While thinking about a name for the new café, Kleszczyński took into consideration my admiration for art and my intention to make the café a center for its support and propagation. At the same time he cleverly 'smuggled' in a compliment, referring to my way of dressing. . . .

"The entrance to the café was at 11 Królewska Street in a big garden belonging to Prince Czartoryski. An orangery used to be in the building; the presence of a large variety of exotic cactuses reminded me of its past. Because I loved cactuses I used to visit the orangery frequently. Once while I was there, the owner told me he was going to close the business because the cactuses and his other flowers weren't selling well and he was in debt.

" 'Sell it to me,' I said, 'I'll pay your debts and I'll take care of your plants. For sure, they will feel well surrounded by my art. I'll make an art display here.'

"He took me to the building's administrator and introduced me as the wife of Lieutenant Franciszek Arciszewski, who was a deputy in the Polish parliament. He added that I was also a painter.

" 'I know the lieutenant and I've heard a lot about you,' the administrator said politely. 'But somehow I can't imagine how your paintings, porcelain, and highly polished furniture will fit into this place.'

"I didn't share his doubts. I paid the deposit and started to work immediately. My husband, as usual, was surprised by my sudden decision, but he didn't even try to protest; he knew me too well. My entire staff—forty women—was from my studio on Emilia Plater Street. The elegant Janina Zabłocka was the supervisor.

"Soon the news about SiM reached the neighboring IPS Café and from there it spread around Warsaw. Painters, poets, and others began looking in the windows where I could be seen working from morning till late at night among a crowd of assistants, all girls. 'So,' they thought, 'it will be a café for ladies . . . an exhibit of paintings with soft music in the background . . .' It was difficult to imagine this at a time when jazz was triumphant. The closer we got to the opening, the more the journalists tried to learn about this strange place.

"From the outside the building looked impressive. High double columns at each entrance no longer reminded one of an orangery. Nor did its beautiful windows. The interior was divided into three rooms: a large one in the center and two smaller ones on each side. . . . There were cactuses and huge porcelain lamps painted by me with matching shades in the open spaces between the middle room and the smaller ones. Only the glassed-in ceiling covered with yellow fabric betrayed the past of the building. The paintings were displayed in the middle room and were changed every month.

"SiM seemed to be sunny even on a cloudy day, thanks to the light coming through the fabric on the ceiling. Comfortable sofas and armchairs covered with yellow, orange, or blue linen gave a different light effect in each room. The waitresses developed a reputation for good service and pleasant attitude. Their uniforms, trays, and the coffee cups matched the colors of each room.

"The specialty of the café was a variety of teas and appetizers:

pastry filled with meat, mushrooms, and cheese, served hot, and all kinds of toast and sweet cakes. There was a piano in the center of the room and there were three different pianists whose music made everyone feel at home. The regular customers of SiM never interrupted the music by being noisy."[9]

Monday evenings at Art and Fashion were taken over by the Association of Literates. At these gatherings, writers and laypeople alike would discuss the newest books. Well-known poets like Bolesław Leśmian and Adolf Nowaczyński frequented the place. Authors sometimes came to discuss their books and take part in heated exchanges with the audience.

Tuesday, Saturday, and Sunday evenings were reserved for poetry recitations, and there were regularly scheduled musical events. In the café's garden was a small cottage where American women had their club meetings and played bridge.

The women who came to Arciszewska's café came to be seen. "They knew how to show their dresses with elegance," she said, while lamenting that most of their dresses were purchased abroad. But women of all classes strove to be fashionable, improvising when they could not afford the latest Paris fashions. Maids copied the dresses of their mistresses, using hand-me-downs and cheaper materials.

Some newspapers referred to Art and Fashion as a beauty salon. Its owner did not object. "SiM hosted elegant women who were not only beautiful but also intelligent with a good sense of humor. They created in SiM an atmosphere of joy and flirtatiousness; they wanted good fun but they were also sensitive to beauty and art."[10]

Mrs. Arciszewska has preserved a complaint book she kept for her patrons. The comments recorded in it reflect the tone of the establishment: "Please change the colors of the blue-yellow ashtrays. I'm sick of seeing them at my house and at my friends' places." "Please move the phone from the hallway to another location. It's obvious that a wife doesn't call her husband from here and a husband doesn't call his wife."

But Art and Fashion was not all frivolity. As soon as the café opened, groups of poor newsboys started congregating at its doors. They soon learned the names of the café's important patrons and called them out by name, imploring them to buy their newspapers. Arciszewska herself frequently fed the boys and gave them handouts, though she was also the target of their sob stories about needing money for a sick mother or dying aunt. Once, her fox terrier disappeared, and she asked some of the boys to help her find it. Within hours ten fox terriers were reported missing in Warsaw, all of which mysteriously turned up on Arciszewska's doorstep. The police retrieved them, and her own dog was later found unharmed.

A group of her patrons, including Konrad Tom and artist Józef Czapski, got together and formed a club called the Supporters of the Newspaper Boys. In addition to helping the boys outside the café, they also sent money to other organizations in Warsaw that were helping the children of the poor. At Christmas the boys were treated to a huge supper and given gifts of warm clothing.

The QPQ Family Breaks Up

Shortly after Qui Pro Quo closed, Tuwim, Járosy, and Hemar formed a cabaret of their own called Band of Comedians (*Kabaret Komików Banda*), always referred to as Banda. They rented the Nirvana Theater on Mokotowska Street and split the duties of writing, directing, and composing lyrics, although Hemar provided most of the lyrics. Their shows included faces familiar to Warsaw audiences — Mira Zimińska, Zosia Terné, Konrad Tom, Zula Pogorzelska, Adolf Dymsza, and Ludwik Lawiński.

There was one new face, a handsome matinee-idol of the old school name Igo Sym. His name popped up in the 1992 biography of Marlene Dietrich, in which he was named as one of her many lovers but was described as a "Bavarian." The directors' decision to hire Sym reflected the uncertainties involved in starting a new cabaret. Banda certainly did not lack talent, but it needed to be assured of the box office that Sym might attract.[11]

On top of the demise of Qui Pro Quo, Julian Tuwim suffered a more personal injury when his wife left him for the dashing Colonel Wieniawa-Długoszowski. While he was undergoing the agonies of separation, Tuwim wrote a long poem for Ordonówna, titled "Melody of Warsaw" (*Melodia Warszawy*). She recited it at a Banda revue, against a musical background. It was not a paean to the city; rather, it reflected Tuwim's bitterness at being cuckolded.

Tuwim became physically ill before collapsing in a nervous breakdown. He temporarily left the city to recuperate at a spa.[12]

Hanka Ordonówna, in the meantime, had great success with a one-woman show that she produced and performed. Her success marked her gradual drift away from the old Qui Pro Quo crowd. She had literally grown up there, having been associated with it for most of the twenties. But her popularity in Poland and her success abroad gave her confidence to strike out on her own.

On March 26, 1931, Hanka married Count Michael Tyszkiewicz in a quiet ceremony at Warsaw's Holy Cross Church. The service was attended by only a few close friends. After a reception at a nearby hotel, the Tyszkiewiczes went to the family estate near Wilno. There, Hanka ran into the barriers of the Polish class system. The family had vacated the estate, leaving only the servants to greet the newlyweds. She soon realized that she was considered the black sheep of the family.

Back in Warsaw, Hanka received her first taste of negative reviews for one of her own shows. After it closed she invited one of her critics to lunch. While driving to the restaurant a tree felled by a construction crew crashed down on the car. Hanka suffered two broken arms and her companion sustained severe facial injuries. The singer withdrew from public life to recuperate.[13]

Sports Clubs and Competition

Warsaw not only supported nightclubs and cafés celebrating art and fashion but also supported athletic clubs. By the early thirties Warsaw had more than one hundred athletic clubs, some of which participated in only one sport. In the midthirties boxing, skiing, archery, and basketball emerged as popular sports.

In 1927 there were no major playing fields in Warsaw; yet by 1931 there was one stadium for soccer and two others, used for various sports, that had covered grandstands. Before the next war almost half of Warsaw's schools had their own athletic fields.

The prowess of Polish athletes was transferred to both European and international venues such as the Olympics. The Polish contingent to the Olympics in the summer of 1932 repeated its success of 1928. Stella Walsh (Stanisława Walasiewicz) won the 100-meter dash and Janusz Kuśociński triumphed in the 10,000-meter run.

In the artistic competition the sculptor Władysław Klukowski won the gold medal for his work, *Ballplayer*. He was to repeat the success in 1936 at Berlin with his sculpture, *Crowning of a Competitor*.

In 1936 the Poles also picked up two silver medals (100-meter dash and women's discus) and one bronze (women's javelin). These numbers may seem small when compared to entries from larger nations, but when one considers the disorganized state of Polish athletics after World War I, they are remarkable.

Problems in Polish athletics went back even before the war. Sport in Poland got off to a late start, with the first recorded competitions in the late nineteenth century when Warsaw was under Russian rule. Almost all early competition was on either a university or a secondary school level. Even these efforts were interrupted by the Russians, who impressed would-be athletes into civilian jobs at the outset of World War I.

When the German army arrived in Warsaw in 1915 it sometimes encouraged, sometimes ignored Polish efforts to organize sports. At this time, and indeed throughout the interwar period, sports and the military were closely interconnected.

During the war, organizations such as the Falcons (*Sokół*) Gymnastic Society encouraged young people to engage in athletic competition as a way to train military manpower for Poland's future. Sokół even opened a military academy in 1917. At the height of the war, in 1917 and 1918, sports organizations and competitions were encouraged by the Council of State. This was done through a multilayered bureaucracy with the Ministry of the Interior at the top, followed in descending order by the Department of Health Services, and the School of Hygiene.

In 1918 supervision of athletics was transferred to the Ministry of Religion and Public Education. Within the capital itself there was yet another governing body for sports. Interested nongovernmental parties formed an umbrella organization, the Union of Polish Sports Unions (*Związek Polskich Związków Sportowych*), which attempted to coordinate athletic activities until the late 1920s.

In the meantime Polish athletics suffered from a lack of funding and the absence of a governing body with real authority. The Division of Public Health was nominally in charge of overseeing athletics, though it was really rather powerless. The schools supervised their own athletic teams and budgets, but in the early years of independence it was the army and private organizations that held together Poland's sporting world.

The most prominent of these private bodies were the Army Rowing Club, Sokół, Polonia, and Korona whose funds—except for the Rowing Club—were supplied by dues and donations collected at the events or in fundraising drives.

Religious, ethnic, and special interest groups also fielded teams in a variety of sports. The Warsaw Housing Cooperative sponsored teams, as did Catholic Action, the Socialist party, and Jewish groups. The Socialists' sports club, Skra, was one of the first winning clubs. The Jewish Academy Sports Association oversaw the Jewish community's athletics. The Polish Division of Maccabee International, which also played against Catholic teams, produced some of the strongest athletic teams of the interwar years.

Finally, in 1927 the government was persuaded to play a more active role in national sports, with the argument that superbly trained athletes could quickly be integrated into the Polish armed forces. National athletic organizations were then brought together under the supervision of the State Office of Physical Education and Military Training Program (*Państowy Urząd Wychownia Fizycznego i Przysposabienia Wojskowego*, or the PUWF-PW), a government office that reinforced the connection between athletics and the military.

Poland was not the only European nation emphasizing mass physical fitness programs. European governments, especially in Nazi Germany, saw a healthy, disciplined civilian population as a second line of defense in case of war and as a breeding ground for future soldiers.

Under the PUWF-PW, which worked closely with the Ministry of Defense, sports were coordinated on national, regional, and local levels, with the government providing the budget.

Despite being the headquarters for virtually every kind of athletics, Warsaw did not entirely dominate Polish sports. In soccer, for example, the best teams were to be found in cities such as Poznań and Lwów. Where the capital did hold sway was in the more specialized sports, those that required expensive equipment, such as yachting, rowing, canoeing, equestrian events, skating, and cycling. The Warsaw Cycling Association saw to it that its teams captured most of the national championships.

Athletes from Warsaw won most of the medals awarded to Poles in interwar competition. Warsaw also had the best track and field teams, mainly because of the participation of the military. Between 1930 and 1937 Warsaw boxers captured a string of European titles, and one Varsovian, Janina Kurkowska-Spychajowa, won the world archery title five years in a row (1935–39).[14]

The YMCA, introduced into Poland by General Józef Haller, was involved in some strange controversies. Poland had received its charter from the American YMCA in 1923, and branches were erected in other Polish cities before the one in Warsaw was finally completed, in the early thirties. Once it was firmly established in the country, it involved itself in promoting athletics. In Warsaw the Y was run by Paul Super, an American, who had a staff of Americans and Poles.

Super had originally opposed membership for women but eventually gave in because "the Poles, Slav fashion, wanted the women in their buildings as coparticipants, and I had come to see that their presence contributed to the strength and influence of the work."[15]

Despite its adherence to Christian values, some older Poles were still suspicious of the Y's activities. Jan Merkiel used the swimming pool twice a week until his parents objected that it was an unhealthful pursuit. They took him to a doctor who advised him to stop using the pool because it was unhygienic. The finest American technology could not convince them otherwise.

The Jewish Population

The Jewish population in Warsaw had continued to grow over the past decade even before German Jewish emigration began. Many emigrés gravitated to the Jewish neighborhood though they were free to live anywhere in Warsaw they chose. Professor Wacław Lednicki stresses in his memoir: "One should not confuse the free settlements of the nonassimilated mass of Jews in interwar Poland in separate quarters of the towns and cities with the ghettos forcibly organized by the Germans."[16]

The centuries-old Jewish district was an irregularly shaped jumble of streets that stretched from the edge of Old Town west to include the Jewish cemetery, which is still standing. Its headstones, a combination of the simple and the very ornate, were not uprooted by the Nazis. Fortunately, for the survivors and for posterity, the Germans were able to find plenty of material elsewhere to use as paving stones and for building.

The southern border of the Jewish sector skirted the Saxon Gardens and ended several blocks below it. To the north it faded into a maze of railroad tracks and the outskirts of New Town. The Gdańsk station was there on Stawki Street. Next to it was a railroad siding, and it was from there, called the Umschlagplatz by the Germans, that in the 1940s Jews were forced onto cattle cars for the trip to their final destination.

During the twenty years of Poland's independence, the Jewish district was a bustling, noisy neighborhood, the heart of Europe's Jewish culture, a city within a city. There were theaters, libraries, cafés, musical groups, and periodicals all in Yiddish or Hebrew. Many of the Jews within the community never spoke any Polish, though they lived their entire lives in Poland.

There were, of course, synagogues and schools. The largest and most famous of the religious centers was the Great Synagogue on Tłomackie Street, said to be the largest in Poland. Its squat, powerful presence stood as a monument to Jewish culture and learning. It was across Bielańska Street from the magnificent palace of the Radziwiłłs and the Bank of Poland. The synagogue was designed by the Italian architect Leandro Marconi and built between 1872 and 1878, the more remarkable since the city was under Russian occupation at the time. Next to the synagogue stood the Judaic Library at 3/5 Tłomackie Street. It now houses the Jewish Historical Institute. The synagogue was totally destroyed by the Nazis during their occupation.

Of the Jewish houses of worship only the Nożik Synagogue on Twarda Street, where holocaust survivor Hanna Hirshaut had been married, remains. Its interior was gutted by German soldiers, but its walls were left standing. It was refurbished after the war and is now open to visitors.

Jews lived throughout Warsaw, but it was in the densely populated section later known as the Warsaw Ghetto under the Nazis that the poorer Jews lived. There they were crowded in apartment buildings, in small rooms that sometimes housed two or three families.

Hirshaut experienced living there and elsewhere in Warsaw. "The streets around the neighborhood I grew up in were lined with apartment buildings of a very unappealing architecture – rather simple, gray, four to six stories high. There were no private homes at all. . . . I, or rather my parents, lived at two places in Warsaw. First at the corner of Franciszkańska, Freta, and Zakroczymska streets. It was rather a blue-collar, gentile neighborhoood.

"My parents' bedroom windows looked out at the big Franciscan church and from the dining-room balcony one could see a patch of the river Vistula and the church of Panna Maria. . . . I remember the military parades that passed under our balcony on the way from the Citadel to Plac Zamkowy. I knew the tunes of every military march before I knew how to read. Our balcony was always decorated with white and red petunias, the colors of the flag, because this was the route of all the military parades. . . . Many dignitaries passed in the parades, . . . the king of Rumania, the prime ministers of Italy and France, and many others. . . .

"I think around 1932 we moved to Plac Muranowski, a rather nice Jewish neighborhood. My father had business relations with the Polish army. In our house there were often Polish officers of high rank. My father himself was an officer in the reserve. . . .

"On Franciszkańska there was a huge indoor market stretching for three blocks, called Bazar Yarszeskiego. There were countless stores—groceries, and of course bakeries—the best breads, rolls, pastries, and cakes in the world. . . .

"We were right across from Nalewki Street, an extremely busy section always teeming with people. This was actually the commercial center. The buildings there were like huge compounds of houses with two or three courtyards. On the ground level were countless businesses and small shops. Many wholesale representatives had their showrooms there. I remember my friend's father had the exclusive representation of BATA [a chain of women's clothing stores]. Another one had the exclusive representation for Trader Horn. There were wholesale businesses selling French perfumes and cosmetics. Contrary to [popular] opinion Nalewki Street was not some backward market place.

"Gęsia Street was mainly crowded with wholesale textile businesses, Franciszkańska Street with shops selling leather skins and goods. . . . On the Sabbath the stores were closed and there was a serene peace; people attended services. In the afternoon families would stroll toward the Saxon Gardens dressed in their best. . . . We skated in Krasiński Park and Saxon Gardens or in Dolina Szwajcarskiej during the winter months, which were bitter cold. . . ."[17]

Hirshaut, who now lives in New York, emphasized that, while there was poverty among a "significant segment of the Jewish population, there was a large middle class—businessmen, manufacturers, teachers, artisans. Some of those who were more affluent, like industrialists, professionals, people in the arts, were living in the more elegant sections of Warsaw." In spite of the hardships caused by the economic depression of the thirties and rampant anti-Semitism, Jews managed to live a decent and rich cultural life. The Jewish community of Warsaw was vibrant, creative, and deeply involved in new political ideas and cultural progress.[18]

Others saw the Jewish community in another light. Helena Wasiutyńska, a National Democrat supporter, feared walking through those crowded streets on her way to school.

"To get to our school we crossed Nowe Miasto and turned left to Freta Street. The middle section of this street was very narrow, on either side were neglected houses in which Jews lived. But only the very poor ones. They looked strange to me, especially the boys with their long black coats, yarmulkes, and side curls. There were a lot of them and they played in the narrow, foul-smelling hallways. On the doorsteps very old Jewesses wearing wigs and dark and untidy dresses sat selling broad beans. I tried not to look at them, not to look into the hallways, to pass this part of the street as quickly as possible. But never in all the years I lived in that part of the city did I ever witness any act of aggression or animosity from either side. We did not mix, we belonged to different circles, but in my home and in my school there was not a trace of anti-Semitism."[19]

Stanisław Meyer made similar observations: "the bulk of the Orthodox Jewish population kept to their traditional dress of black frock-coats reaching to their ankles and small black caps — the married women wearing wigs, and the rabbis large headdresses made of fox fur and often long frilly side-whiskers. All the men had beards. [There were some exceptions. As Isaac Bashevis Singer wrote, better a Jew without a beard than a beard without the Jew.] Much of Polish Jewry lived in extreme poverty, which accounted for the dirty and overcrowded condition of their dwellings. They were chiefly occupied with petty commerce, house industry, worked as carriers, in factories, and so on. Their black-bearded figures moving constantly to and fro in the city gave it a certain strange aspect unknown to Western Europe. A large number of prominent people sprang from this black and miserable crowd."[20]

In addition to the working-class Catholics and Jews, a number of notorious people also dwelt in the neighborhood, mainly on lower Krochmalna Street, noted for its petty thieves, prostitutes, and pimps. Singer described this aspect of the street in his stories. Janusz Korczak set up his orphanage at 92 Krochmalna, at the upper end, and rescued children from the crime and poverty of these streets.

Jewish merchants also set up shop outside the neighborhood. In his profession as an antique dealer, Meyer was quite knowledge-able about where to do business:

"One street, Holy Cross [which connected New World Ave-nue and Marszałkowska just below the Saxon Gardens], . . . was full of small antique shops. These shops, crowded with bric-a-brac, were all in the hands of Jewish dealers, nearly all related to one an-other.

"They had been in this trade for generations, and it was astonishing how much knowledge and flair they possessed. Bargain-ing was a rule, and the shopkeeper seemed to feel quite uneasy when a customer simply paid the first price named; they imagined that the price demanded was probably too small and the object of unexpect-edly great value. Most of these shops were crammed with new 'an-tiques,' things that never pretended to be really old. A shopkeeper told me once that they had to keep this stuff because this was what the public wanted; they had neither the money nor the knowledge to help buy the real things and were quite prepared to cheat them-selves; they hoped also to get the better of the dealers; the primitive instinct of searching for hidden treasures is often the motive of col-lecting. When a real collector entered one of the shops he would be invited into the back room to see some good things and asked not to look around the shop. If asked about the authenticity of a suspect object, the shopkeeper would answer, 'How can I know? I am not educated,' thus saving his conscience and exciting the buyer's curiosity. Holy Cross Street in Warsaw was bombed out of existence in September 1939, and now all the shops are gone. The dealers shared the tragic fate of the Jewish population of Warsaw."[21]

Aside from the marketplace, there seemed to be little social contact between Catholics and Jews, a situation sometimes mirrored within the Jewish community at large. I once introduced by phone two Jewish women who had grown up in Warsaw but were not acquainted. One had lived in a Jewish neighborhood; the other had lived on the boulevard Marszałkowska and seldom strayed into that area. After a brief conversation the one who had lived on Marszałkowska said, "I didn't understand a word she said." The woman who lived strictly among Jews was well educated and had used words and inflections that baffled the other. Both spoke fluent Polish and the one with the better education (from the Jewish neighborhood) announced to me that she spoke "excellent Polish." One understood Yiddish, the other did not.

What they did have in common, besides their Jewishness, was pride in being Polish. Both described themselves as being Polish in nationality and Jewish in their religious beliefs. And like other Jews who once lived in Poland, they expressed hurt, some fifty years after the fact, at being forced from what they considered their homeland.

Could it be that time is too narrow for all events?
Could it happen that all the seats within time
might have been sold? Worried, we run along the
train of events, preparing ourselves for the
journey.

Bruno Schulz
"Age of Genius" (1938)

CHAPTER 7

Sorrow and Laughter

■ 1933-1935

On the Political Front

Soon after Hitler assumed the position of Germany's chancellor, he
was again challenged by Piłsudski. Rumors had reached the Belvedere Palace that Hitler had a certain respect for Piłsudski, but the
feeling was definitely not mutual. The Polish leader tried to nip Hitler's rush for power in the bud with another provocative move,
again in the Danzig harbor.

The League of Nations had given the Poles permission to use
the promontory of Westerplatte in the harbor as an ammunition
dump and had put a strict limit on the number of Polish troops to
be stationed there. In March 1933, Piłsudski ordered the ship *Wilja*
to land more than 130 troops on Westerplatte, exceeding the limit.
It was, he said, in response to German threats against the minority
Polish population in Danzig. The German government immedi-

ately protested to the league's council. As a compromise the Harbor Police would resume responsibility for harbor traffic (its mandate had expired earlier), and the excess Polish troops would be withdrawn.

The Poles were elated that they again had embarrassed the German government, and at the same time had demonstrated their strength. Again the Allies were not so enthusiastic but the incident was quickly forgotten.

Hitler's announcement, after his inauguration, that Germany was withdrawing from the League of Nations sent shudders through the European community. Everyone now assumed that the Germans would begin rearming, with another conflict in the offing.

Through Joseph Goebbels, the German government let it be known that it would be interested in a nonaggression treaty with the Poles. The new Nazi leadership seemed to be courting Poland's goodwill. High-level meetings were conducted between the Polish ambassador in Berlin, Józef Lipski, and the Nazi leaders, including Hitler. The Germans then offered Piłsudski the draft of a treaty, and the marshal teased them by taking a holiday, during which he promised to study the proposal.

In January 1934 a nonaggression treaty was signed between Poland and Germany, to have a life of ten years. The pact alarmed both the French and the Soviets. The former accused Foreign Minister Józef Beck, who had clashed with the French as a young officer in Paris, of plotting against them. They quickly sent a minister to Warsaw with plans for a wide-ranging defense treaty that would include most of Eastern Europe and Germany. The Poles were not convinced of the treaty's effectiveness and declined to sign it. In another year's time the French and the Soviets entered into their own accord.

Goebbels became the first Nazi official to visit Warsaw, in what would be a series of reciprocal visits between the Poles and the Nazis over the next five years. While Goebbels was winding up his so-called goodwill tour of Poland, Ukrainian nationalists murdered Colonel Bronisław Pieracki, minister of the interior. After the assassin had been tried and convicted, Piłsudski established a concentration camp at Bereza-Kartuska, for political prisoners. Though it was nothing like the camps soon to be established by the Nazis, the fact that it was intended for political opponents brought forth both public and private criticism of Piłsudski.

Hermann Göring was the next Nazi to visit Poland, in January 1935. The announced intent of his trip was to go hunting in the Białowierza Forest, but the game he really sought was a German-Polish alliance against the Soviet Union. Piłsudski did not trust the Nazis any more than he did the Soviets, and he declined Göring's proposal.

Even before Göring's visit, Piłsudski's health had begun a rapid and serious decline. In March 1935 he showed all the symptoms of a serious internal problem and at times was too weak to stand. As the disease progressed the Polish public was kept in the dark; only the marshal's immediate family and close friends knew that he was seriously ill.

In the spring another proposal was made for an Eastern European defensive pact, this time by British Foreign Minister Anthony Eden. Piłsudski's meeting with him, with Beck in attendance, was to be his last of any consequence.

In late April a cancer specialist, Doctor Wenckenbach, was summoned from Vienna to examine Piłsudski. Three other doctors were also brought along, and behind closed doors they concluded that their patient had inoperable cancer of the stomach and liver. What treatment was available in those days was begun but without much hope. Madame Aleksandra Piłsudska was not told of her husband's impending death, though she must have suspected it.

Piłsudski was granted one last wish before his death: the signing of a revised constitution, something he had been hoping to achieve for years. The new document—written with Piłsudski in mind—gave the president extraordinary powers. He could select the prime minister and cabinet members; he could choose the heads of the supreme court, army, and navy; and he could appoint up to one-third of the senators. He was also given the authority to dissolve the parliament and to block proposed legislation by referring it back to both the Sejm and the Senate for reconsideration.

In early May the marshal, realizing he was dying, asked to be moved to the Belvedere Palace. A bed was set up for him in one of his favorite rooms, and Doctor Wenckenbach came again from Vienna to see him.

The Polish leader was too ill to see Pierre Laval, the French foreign minister, when he passed through Warsaw on his way to Moscow. Beck played host to Laval instead. The French minister was about to sign a defense treaty with the Soviets, and even on his deathbed Piłsudski railed against it.

On Sunday, May 12, the marshal lapsed into unconsciousness. Doctor Wenckenbach was called from Vienna, but Piłsudski was dead before he arrived. His body lay in state for two days at the Belvedere; then it was moved to St. John's Cathedral in an elaborate procession up the Royal Way, led by Cardinal Kakowski. Hundreds of thousands of weeping Poles paid their respects, and condolences were sent by leaders from around the world. The Polish press gave Piłsudski's life and death full coverage. Bruno Schulz composed a tribute for the *Morning Courier,* and Janusz Korczak prepared a special edition of his "Old Doctor" radio program. The Polish Radio directors at first refused to allow it to be aired—it was titled "A Pole Does Not Cry"—fearing it would portray the deceased leader as a weak man, for Korczak had written that there were times in Piłsudski's life when he must have wept out of frustration. In December, Madame Piłsudska insisted that the program go ahead as planned.

After a pontifical Mass Piłsudski's body was taken to

Mokotów where the military was to pay its last respects. High-ranking officers filed past the bier, and bemedaled representatives arrived from many nations, among them Laval and Marshal Pétain from France, Lord Cavan from Great Britain, and Göring from Germany. The ceremony ended with a 101-gun salute and the singing of the Polish national anthem, "Poland Has Not Yet Perished" (*Jeszcze Polska Nie Zginieła*). The weather, which had been balmy, changed suddenly, and the mourners were caught in a thunderstorm.

Piłsudski's body was borne by special train to Kraków, on a flat-bed car illuminated by spotlights. There, the marshal was laid to rest in St. Leonard's crypt of the historic cathedral of Wawel Castle, across from the tomb of another great Polish warrior, King Jan III Sobieski.[1]

Love Forgives Everything

For Julian Tuwim, 1933 was a productive year despite his recent breakdown. He was hired by the Blok-Muza film company to write two songs for an upcoming film, *The Masked Spy* (*Szpieg w Masce*).

Hanka Ordonówna was signed as the female lead in the film to play opposite two of Poland's best-known actors: Bogusław Samborski, artistic director of the Polish Theater, and Jerzy Pichelski, a handsome leading man.

One of the songs Tuwim wrote was "Love Forgives Everything" (*Miłość ci Wszystko Wybaczy*), which became Hanka's signature tune. It was a sensation the moment the film opened, and she later recorded it on one of her albums. Perhaps Tuwim was still pining for his recently departed wife when he wrote it.

Love will forgive you everything
it will change sorrow to laughter,
Love excuses so beautifully

infidelity, lies, and sins.
Even if you curse it in your despair,
that it's cruel and very bad,
Love will forgive you everything
because Love, my dear, is I.[2]

The movie opened at the Adria Theater on Theater Square, next door to the popular Oaza nightclub. It was a popular success.[3]

Ordonówna's desire to become a serious dramatic actress and the financial difficulties of the Reduta Theater intersected in the person of Juliusz Osterwa. Along with Leon Schiller, Osterwa is ranked as one of the greatest directors of the Polish stage. He had begun his career as an actor at the turn of the century, giving outstanding performances in both dramatic and comedic roles. His most memorable stage appearances were in Żeromski's *My Little Quail Has Flown Away*, Słowacki's *Fantazy*, and as Don Carlos and Alexander the Great.

During World War I Osterwa lived in Russia and came under the influence of the great Russian director Stanislavski and the Moscow Art Theater, developing a penchant for excessive text analysis and grounding himself in realism. In Warsaw he was appointed the first director of the National Theater and also assumed control of the Słowacki Theater in Kraków. Still, he wanted a venue of his own where he could put his theories into practice, and in 1919 he cofounded the experimental theater Reduta, located in the basement of the Social Insurance offices on Copernicus Square. There he dedicated himself to producing Polish plays.

From realism he moved briefly to expressionism, then very popular in Europe. Among Polish dramatists, his influences were Słowacki and Stefan Żeromski, with whom he shared the vision of "theater as a moral institution."

For most of the interwar years Osterwa shuttled between his

theaters in Warsaw and Kraków. He was a boyishly handsome man and carried his theatricality into his offstage life, where his dramatic gestures were regarded by observers as a sign of pretentiousness. In the course of his work he came into contact with the great beauties of the Polish theater, and eventually, Hanka Ordonówna.

Reduta was in the same financial straits as the rest of Warsaw's theaters. Faced with the possibility of closure, Osterwa hit upon the idea of hiring Ordonówna, sensing correctly that her name on the playbill would boost attendance. Fortunately for him she was also interested in legitimate theater and agreed to a contract. Her first appearance in Kraków was in *Night of the Three Kings* (*Wieczór Trzech Króli*), directed by Osterwa. Later she played opposite him in a comedy, *Einstein's Theory* (*Teoria Einsteina*). It was also the beginning of an affair between the actress and the director, described in detail in Tadeusz Wittlin's biography of Ordonówna.

They met one another in both Kraków and Warsaw, with Hanka's husband playing the innocent bystander. Their affair lasted for some time, and one wonders what the count was doing in the meantime. He apparently had refrained from interfering in Hanka's career. It seems that he had not insisted that she make a home for him or have children.

There is some question about whether Ordonówna and Osterwa actually consummated their love, but Benno Rand and Lola Kitajewicz, who were part of their milieu, insisted that it was a full-blown love affair, with Osterwa the pursuer.

According to Wittlin, it was Ordonka who terminated the relationship, but not before she had written Osterwa some incriminating letters. After he had been rejected, Osterwa showed the letters to Count Michael. Whatever the count's reaction was, the marriage continued.[4]

To Osterwa's dismay Hanka next accepted a role in the operetta *Arena of Stars* (*Gwiazda Areny*), a Hungarian farce with a plot that centered on a young aristocrat who leaves his family to join a circus. His stern father tries to lure the son back home but winds up joining the show himself. It was directed by Andrzej Włast and opened in March 1935.

To ensure box-office success, Włast brought together stars from Warsaw's cabaret circles as well as from opera and the film industry. Ordonówna was to play the role of a bareback rider. Others featured included Polish cabaret and comedy giant Ludwik Sempoliński; the beautiful opera star Tola Mankiewicz; and film star Igo Sym. All threw themselves into their roles with great relish. Hanka feverishly practiced with a training pony; Sym did tricks as a trapeze artist; Sempoliński was to do a trick with a pack of dogs while Mankiewicz sang to a flock of doves.

Opening night was a disaster. Sempoliński's dogs refused to cooperate and ran around the ring urinating; a dove alighted on Mankiewicz's coiffure, then flew off, leaving telltale stains on her costume; Hanka's saddle slipped, and for a few frightening moments she dangled upside down from the horse, her head only inches from the turf.

Eventually all the kinks were worked out, and the show continued to run with Hanka singing from the back of a horse and Sym serenading her from his trapeze. Despite all of the operetta's faux pas, Boy-Żeleński gave it a "nice" review in the *Morning Courier*.[5] Because of the enormous cost of mounting the production, however, *Arena of Stars* had a short life, and the performers rushed back to their own, safer venues.

Age of Genius

Bruno Schulz entered Warsaw's literary life in December 1933 with the publication of his first book of stories, *Cinnamon Stores* (known in the United Kingdom and in the United States as *Cinnamon Shops* and *Street of Crocodiles*). Aleksander Wat was one of the many writers Schulz met when he quickly established his literary credentials with this first book. One of the stories, "Birds" (*Ptaki*), had appeared earlier in the year in *The Literary News*. Critics gave *Cinnamon Shops* favorable reviews, especially in the *Morning Courier* and *The Literary News*. For Schulz, it was the culmination of almost a decade of writing and searching for a publisher.

Schulz had been born into a Jewish family in the village of Drohobycz, in the province of Galicia. Except for his excursions to Warsaw and academic study in Lwów, he remained a member of the Drohobycz community all his life. He toiled at the secondary school there as a drawing teacher, a modest, almost obsequious man, whose collected letters offer a portrait of a novice worshipful of the already established Polish writers—Tuwim, Witkacy, Gombrowicz.

Schulz at one time had studied, but never pursued a career in, architecture, contenting himself to teach in Drohobycz and executing his own odd, revealing drawings. He produced dozens of erotic pen-and-ink and wash drawings, many of them showing a man groveling before the naked or stockinged feet of a woman, or sometimes groups of women. One of his exhibitions at the Truskowiec spa was called "abominable pornography."

His works of course include many other subjects—self-portraits, sketches of friends, scenes of Jewish life in his village—all eerily childlike in their execution. Some of the figures appear to be out of proportion to their surroundings. Many of them are in the collection of the Museum of Literature in Warsaw.

Though he had been to Warsaw before as an artist, he came again in 1934, now slightly more confident as a writer, eager to meet with his publisher, Rój, and receive introductions to others in the Warsaw literary establishment. His humility did not prevent him from complaining about lack of payment from his publisher.

Among his friends was the author Zofia Nałkowska, who had already achieved a solid reputation as a writer of psychological novels. At Nałkowska's salon he met Ryszard Ordyński, the film director. Critics who have studied Schulz's life maintain that he and Nałkowska had at least a brief affair in the course of their relationship. It was she, the more experienced of the two, who was instrumental in getting his book published in the first place.

In a letter describing his visit to the capital, he said, "I had six days there. I spent them mainly with Nałkowska, my patroness, and, I can say, friend."[6] Aside from these few remarks, the self-effacing Schulz did not leave much of a record of his relationship with his benefactor, nor did Nałkowska herself leave any evidence of the amatory side of their friendship. Virtually all the correspondence to Schulz was destroyed at his death, and Nałkowska apparently also destroyed any record of her correspondence with him, even though she had promised to turn over the letters to Jerzy Ficowski, a poet, translator, and essayist who has collected much of Schulz's correspondence to others.[7]

After *Cinnamon Shops* was published, Schulz's name began to appear regularly in Warsaw periodicals. His story "Age of Genius" was published by *The Literary News* in 1934, and he later became that paper's reviewer of foreign novels. One of the authors who intrigued him most, and to whom he has been compared, was Franz Kafka.

As his next project after *Cinnamon Shops* Rój asked Schulz to do a book of illustrations, and at Piłsudski's death he wrote a commemorative essay titled "The Formation of Legends," published in *The Illustrated Weekly* (*Tygodnik Ilustrowany*).

He was ever so polite to his female correspondents, of whom there were quite a few, though Nałkowska was probably the only one with whom he was intimate. He also became engaged to a Catholic woman, a relationship that caused him much concern because of their religious differences.

Intolerance

After being released from prison, Aleksander Wat took an editorial job with the publishing firm, Gebethner and Wolff. They were among the most prestigious of a relatively small group of Polish book publishers that included Rój and M. Arct. The company had been in business for more than seventy years, and Wat was the first Jew ever to work there. He performed a variety of editorial tasks and was eventually appointed the director of the firm's wholesale division.

Jan Gebethner, the executive director of the firm, and Aleksander Wat became as good friends as employer and employee can be. This was an unusual relationship, for Gebethner was a member of parliament representing the National Democrats and a staunch Catholic. By the time he went to work for Gebethner and Wolff, Wat had achieved a certain notoriety in Warsaw, and his presence at this respected publishing house did not go unnoticed by the authorities and the clergy.

Because of his activities with *The Literary Monthly* and the Communist party, Wat had become a marked man and had enemies on all sides. As a measure of his political importance, he was sought by the Nazis when they invaded Poland, but he escaped, only to be arrested later by the Soviets.

In 1933 the Polish government sent a high-ranking official to Gebethner to urge that Wat be fired. Catholic priests threatened to boycott the company, but Jan Gebethner refused to be bullied. Wat's membership in the Communist-front League of Human and Civil Rights caused more problems. When his affiliation with the league became known, he was again arrested, though he was held for only one night. The Catholic press, led by *The Little Daily* (*Mały Dziennik*), featured the story of his arrest prominently, pointing out that he was the literary editor at Gebethner and Wolff.

Still, Jan Gebethner would not dismiss him. Hoping to ease

the pressure on him, Wat went to his employer and offered to resign. In a heated exchange, Wat, referring to what seemed an impossible situation, said sarcastically, "You can't break glass with your dick." Gebethner angrily responded with an obscenity of his own, then invited Wat to go out for a drink.[8]

■   Julian Tuwim, who published another book this year, *Gypsy Bible and Other Poems* (*Biblia Cygańska i Inne Wiersze*), came under attack again, this time by Karol Rostworowski. Rostworowski was a playwright whose best-known work is *Surprise: A True Event in Four Acts* (*Niespodzianka*) (1928). Its plot concerns a peasant woman who robs and murders a man recently returned from America, who turns out to be her son. Not surprisingly, one of Rostworowski's favorite historical characters was Judas Iscariot, about whom he wrote a play titled *Judasz*.

Criticism of Tuwim was nothing new; he had frequently been attacked by the critics for being "too Jewish" in his work. His antagonism toward the right wing was no secret, and he was often critical of contemporary Polish society. Rostworowski claimed that Tuwim's poetry was a threat to Polish culture and cited his "sensualism, his lack of feeling for nature" as examples of his Jewishness.[9]

In response, the Jewish journalist S. J. Imber wrote a spirited attack on the concept of racial purity and indirectly defended Tuwim in his book *Aces of Pure Race* (*Asy Czystej Rasy*), published in 1934. Imber demonstrated that some Polish Catholic writers had traits similar to those of Tuwim, and therefore this had nothing to do with defining Jewishness. Rostworowski remained unrepentant, blinded by his anti-Semitic stance.

■   Janusz Korczak again turned his talents to the theater and wrote a three-act children's play titled *Children from the Playground* (*Dzieci*

Ulicy). It was performed as a ballet, starring pupils from Madame Wysocka's school and premiered on March 12, 1933, at the Eye of the Sea theater. Unfortunately, no copies of the play survived the war.

Korczak's orphanage celebrated its twenty-fifth anniversary, and a number of publications were issued, some by Korczak, to commemorate the event. He put into print for the first time the rules that governed the orphanage, with the statement that both he and his staff were answerable to the children for their behavior. He wrote a separate essay called "The Jewish Child," which baldly labeled the practice of searching for differences between Jewish children and gentiles "psychosis" and called it an unscientific undertaking that only divides and sows discord.

In 1934 Korczak also began broadcasting a children's program on Polish Radio. On the show Korczak went by the name the "Old Doctor," also the show's title. While his disguise was cloaked in good humor, it was also a ploy by the station's management to conceal the fact that they were allowing a Jew to broadcast to Catholic children. Nevertheless, everyone knew that voice. Judging from the flood of mail he received from children, the show was a success.

Korczak's orphanage was not doing as well, however; it suffered from a severe lack of financing. Economic conditions in Poland had curtailed the donations that had kept it alive until now. Korczak made a widespread appeal for money and had limited success but enough to continue. In the summer he made the first of his visits to Palestine, where he met with friends, some of whom had once worked at the orphanage. He was impressed with the climate and apparent success of kibbutz life, and may have considered living there, although he returned to the harsh conditions of Warsaw and to his children.[10]

In 1935, Stanisława Przybyszewska died alone, in a squalid shack near Danzig. Her funeral was a dismal affair with only a few mourners, a stark contrast to the pomp that had attended Piłsudski's funeral three months earlier. She had written only two plays, *The Danton Case*, which survived her, and an earlier, little-known play, *Thermidor*, also dealing with the French Revolution. (Thermidor was the revolutionary name for July.) She produced a torrent of letters, however, and numbered among her correspondents Jean Cocteau and Thomas Mann. In her last letter to Mann, dated 1934, she wrote: "I've used myself up, I've misused myself. . . . I know only one thing: I can't go on."[11]

Little Paris

Wanda Stachiewicz, founder of the Polish Institute of Arts and Sciences at Canada's McGill University, returned to Warsaw in June 1935 from Częstochowa; her husband had just been appointed chief of the general staff. It was yet another move in her glamorous life as the wife of a Polish officer.

In the two decades before the war Captain Stachiewicz had been posted to Paris, Warsaw, Wilno, and Częstochowa, and now he was back to Warsaw again. Because of his position the captain and his wife were invited to many official occasions and receptions, where they mingled with the leaders of Polish society. These included "the very exclusive tea parties" given by Madame Aleksandra Piłsudska, wife of Marshal Józef Piłsudski, at the Belvedere Palace.

"The parties were usually held in the large bay-window salon overlooking the magnificent public park. It was a great honor to be invited. These parties were attended by ambassadors, other high-ranking officers, diplomats, government officials and their wives, the Papal Nuncio, and some community leaders. The atmosphere was congenial and informal. Toward the end of the party Marshal Piłsudski usually appeared. He was a man of captivating charm and informality and, in General de Gaulle's words, a man emanating a kind of magnetic force. Most of the population loved him and some idolized him for his boundless devotion to his country and his clear vision in governing it. He was the symbol of the fight for independence, and they felt secure under his protection. But of course he also had opponents, as always in politics. Yet when he died a few years later in 1935, all of Poland felt deserted and orphaned."[12]

Captain and Mrs. Stachiewicz quickly adapted to their new life in the capital. "The Staff headquarters were located in the center of the historic section of Warsaw. The entire complex was built in the seventeenth century, in the Renaissance, in early baroque style, as a palace for one of the Polish kings of the Saxon family. Two large buildings were connected by a tall colonnade under which lay the tomb of the Unknown Soldier [killed in 1918 in the defense of Lwów]. The offices faced the huge Piłsudski Square. Our apartments, located in the rear, looked out on a beautiful garden in the style of Versailles, adorned with replicas of Greek sculptures, water fountains, and a summer theater. After the end of the Polish kingdom, the garden was converted into a public park full of flowers, and to this day it is a favorite with the people.

"After ten years of life in the provinces, the move to the metropolis known as Little Paris was enjoyable and full of tempting opportunities. The best concerts, the International Chopin Competition, superb theaters, excellent lectures, and a very good university were all available. The prestigious Institute of Music invited me to teach the History and Theory of Music. As I have always liked to study I enrolled in several courses, one on the Scientific Organization of Work, the first of this kind in Warsaw, which later was very helpful in my battle for survival as an emigrant with three children.

"We were in the highest stratum, meeting important people from foreign countries. One's behavior was observed, criticized, and commented upon, and one ceased to be a private person. Since my husband was extremely busy he reduced his participation in social life to a minimum. He attended only a few receptions for very important foreign visitors who came to Warsaw for political and military talks. I had to accept many invitations and participate, for both of us, in all sorts of entertainments, usually escorted by his aide-de-camp. I attended innumerable cocktail parties, dinners, sports events, festivals, and benefit affairs, and often showed our historic landmarks to the wives of visiting dignitaries. I just do not know how I managed to fit it all in, since I also spent much time with my children.

"I considered these engagements to be part of my duties as the wife of the chief of the general staff, but I must admit that some were quite stimulating, particularly when I met important world politicians, such as the foreign ministers of France or Italy, with their wives. The Italian foreign minister Galazzo Chiano and his wife, Edda, Mussolini's daughter, were a particularly interesting couple. I also met the stern German Foreign Minister von Ribbentrop, jovial Hermann Göring, head of the German air force, and the heads of state: Emperor Haile Selassie, the autocratic ruler of Ethiopia since 1930 [exiled to England in 1935 by the Italian occupation and reinstated in 1941]; Miklos Horthy, regent of Hungary from 1929 to 1944; and King Charles [Carol] of Rumania, who was accompanied by his minister of foreign affairs, Gafencu.

"I was considered to be the first lady of the military staff, because the wife of the commander-in-chief of the army never participated in social life [because of poor] health, so at formal receptions I usually found myself seated next to one of the top visitors. I took advantage of these situations to find out what they really thought about our nation and to learn about their country, its customs, way of life, and so on.

"When we entertained, I did my best to perform my duties as hostess satisfactorily. At small parties I tried to make people feel at home by avoiding formalities. When we had large receptions for the military attachés, or the diplomatic corps, I would also invite people from the artistic, literary, and musical world, who would give a special accent to the party. I remember an actor, Juliusz Osterwa [actually more noted for his directing], who possessed a magic charm and was a great attraction. Another, a young pianist named Witold Małcużyński, winner of the International Chopin Competition, played Chopin at one of our dinner parties for the diplomatic corps. I introduced him to the ambassadors, hoping that he would receive an invitation to perform abroad. I succeeded, as the Swedish and French ambassadors invited him to come to their respective countries. Malcuzyński went to America after the war and became a well-known concert pianist.

"All these parties and receptions required many pretty dresses. However, I could not spend too much money on haute couture.

"It may seem strange to an American that my husband, holding such a high position, did not command a very high salary. One of the reasons was that our country was rising literally from the dust and ashes after a hundred and fifty years of brutal occupation. Rebuilding the nation required enormous funds, and lack of foreign loans made the situation very difficult.

"In 1936 we went to Paris again, this time on a very important mission. My husband accompanied the Polish commander-in-chief for final negotiations and signing of the Franco-Polish military and economic agreement at Bouillet. It guaranteed French assistance to Poland and strengthened the alliance between the two countries.

"It was on this occasion, when my husband was a member of the Polish delegation, that we were invited by the president of the French Republic, Lebrun, to the Palais l'Élysée. The reception was set in great splendor, and I remember that I wore a very pretty sequined formal dress that looked like a shining 'waterfall of little stars,' according to a description that later appeared in the newspapers.

"On the way back to Poland my husband decided to travel by car through Germany and to get some firsthand impressions of Germany under Hitler. I went to Berlin by train and stayed there for several days with the family of the Polish military attaché, waiting

for my husband. I was invited . . . to many parties and official receptions and had a chance to meet some of the most high-ranking
officials of the Nazi party, including Hitler. The most memorable
event of my stay in Berlin was a really big rally during which Adolf
Hitler made one of his famous speeches. Watching him, one had
the impression of seeing a fanatic who exerted an almost hypnotic
effect on the crowd. Thousands of people excited to the point of
mass hysteria were raising their arms and rhythmically shouting
'Sieg Heil.' It was obvious that this man was blindly accepted as
leader and that he had aroused the dormant impulses of the German
soul. Staring at this performance, I had a feeling of intense fear and
foreboding. . . ."[13]

Take each other's hand and sing:
pax, pax, pax —
To signify the brotherhood of Man.

Jarosław Iwaszkiewicz
The Brotherhood of Man
Translated by Adam Gillon
and Ludwik Krzyżanowski

CHAPTER 8

Progress and Other Problems

■ 1935–1936

On the Political Front

Piłsudski's death left an enormous void in Polish political life. There was no one in the country who commanded such admiration and nonpartisan respect. His passing also opened the floodgates for the anti-Semites.

The maneuvering to succeed the marshal was played out over the summer and in the end the man Piłsudski hoped would succeed him, Walery Sławek, did not. The ever-loyal Sławek was a modest man of dignity but not very aggressive. To everyone's surprise but his own, President Mościcki, now in his late sixties and nearing the end of his first term, decided to stand for another term.

There was a third entry in the competition for leadership, in the person of General Edward Śmigły-Rydz. His name reflects his status as war hero and legionnaire: Śmigły — Polish for the flight of an eagle—was the code name Rydz used in that part of Poland still under Austrian domination. He was known to eschew politics, but his wife was more of an opportunist and at her urging he began to fancy himself a leader in the Piłsudski mold.

Both Mościcki and Śmigły-Rydz had coteries of followers large enough to cause trouble should one or the other become Poland's new leader. Mościcki proved to be the more nimble. He approached the general with a plan that would allow him to retain the presidency and at the same time would grant Śmigły-Rydz more power and prestige. He would become commander-in-chief of all the armed forces, and the government would begin a campaign to promote him as Piłsudski's successor.

In the meantime, Sławek became a victim of his own political manipulations. He had been instrumental in drafting a new election law that would reduce the number of seats in both houses and give the government control over the electoral process. Outraged by the BBWR's control over the selection of candidates, much of the opposition boycotted the 1936 elections. Mościcki remained as president, now with more power, thanks to the 1935 constitution. He acted immediately to force Sławek out of his premiership and appointed a man more to his liking.

In a fit of pique, Sławek then announced that the BBWR was to be disbanded. Even though he did not have the power to make such a decision, the party's members, thoroughly used to his leadership, dispersed, leaving the government without any party backing. Most of the electorate then chose to support either Mościcki or Śmigły-Rydz. Mościcki remained true to his promise to cede more power to the general, and he next elevated him to the rank of marshal, a promotion that offended many Poles because in their eyes there was only one marshal, and that was Piłsudski. Mościcki went even further to protect his own position by replacing his prime minister with one more amenable to Śmigły-Rydz, General Sławoj-Składkowski, a man of little ambition who was to remain prime minister until September 1939, thus making him the longest-serving premier of the interwar period.

With Hitler consolidating power in Germany and becoming more vituperative, the new marshal played upon people's fears of another war, assuring them that he was the man to save Poland in time of crisis.

Yet another military officer, Adam Koc, was appointed in 1936 to form an all-government party to replace the recently departed BBWR. Like Sławek, Koc hoped to attract a wide following to this new creation, known by its Polish acronym OZON (*Obóz Zjednoczenia Narodowego*), or the Camp of National Unity. Unlike its predecessor, OZON set more restrictive conditions for membership. For example, one was expected to be a Polish national. This would ensure that no members of the ethnic minorities would become OZON members. The policy did not take into account, however, the thousands of Jews who had assimilated into Polish society. As an afterthought, Koc announced that OZON members were expected to be Christians, preferably of the Catholic variety.

The sudden rise to power of OZON alarmed a number of people, including Ignacy Jan Paderewski, then living in Morges, Switzerland. At a meeting at his home the Morges Front was formed with Paderewski, General Sikorski, former Prime Minister Witos, and General Józef Haller. They hoped to lead the center-right opposition to the government but were never able to arouse widespread support in Poland.

After Piłsudski's death, attacks on Jews became more prominent, and the Mościcki government did little except to denounce physical violence. Even the archbishop of Poland, Cardinal Hlond, publicly denounced the Jews. Some typical Polish complaints during the interwar period were that fifty percent or more of Poland's doctors and lawyers were Jews, that enrollments in universities favored Jewish students, and that banks, other financial institutions, department stores, and some small businesses were dominated by Jews.

Still, non-Jews dominated the military, the government, civil service, heavy industry, and agriculture. Few Jews owned farms. In a typical Polish village, there were, as Ludwik Łubieński pointed out, two familiar institutions – a church and a wine bar. After Mass on Sundays the villagers, Catholics and Jews alike, would gather in the Jewish-owned bar.

Łubieński expressed the ambivalence felt by many Poles toward Jews when we met at his office at the Sikorski Institute in London. He reiterated the arguments about the Jewish domination of the medical and legal professions and others, and how this engendered resentment from Polish Catholics. Yet he described Jewish tradesmen he had known politely and without any apparent trace of resentment of his own. He believed, as did others I spoke to, that Poland was not an anti-Semitic nation and pointed out that his institute cooperated with Jewish organizations around the world, including a library in Tel Aviv with whom the Sikorski Institute exchanged books, sometimes supplying works that were unavailable in Israel. "In Tel Aviv," he said, "Polish was the second language."[1]

No one has satisfactorily explained the disproportionate number of Jews in certain professions in Poland. The fact is that by the time the nation regained its independence in 1918, a terrific amount of resentment against Jewish success had built up within a significant portion of the Catholic population.

Whatever the reasons for Polish antipathy toward Jews, the government after Piłsudski's death made it clear that it wanted the Jews out of Poland. It supported the Zionist-led movement for emigration to Palestine, even contributing money toward the effort, which failed because the British had put severe limits on the number of Jews they would permit to enter Palestine.

At the universities, too, particularly the University of Warsaw, OZON found surprising support. Groups of faculty and students, angry at the large Jewish enrollment in areas such as law and medicine, instituted bench ghettos, a vicious form of discrimination that forced Jewish students to stand either beside their desks or in the rear of the classroom. While the government did not encourage such behavior, it did little to discourage it. Attempts to boycott Jewish businesses petered out because the Jews formed the underpinning of much of Poland's commercial life.

This surge in anti-Semitism also opened the door for the formation of small fascist groups, such as Falanga, whose prescription for treatment of Jewish citizens was almost as irrational and hideous as that of the Nazis.

Large numbers of Poles openly expressed anger and embarrassment at such a climate of hate. OZON lost many members but other parties were too weak and divided to overcome its influence.

Novelist Kazimierz Brandys observed the bench ghettos firsthand while a student at the University of Warsaw and took the lead in writing letters of protest to the government. Some Poles who were students then denied seeing any such activities.

One of the Jewish students at the university's law faculty was Menachem Begin, later prime minister of Israel. Begin did not take a degree, however; he left his studies to become more actively involved with the Polish Zionists.

Another of anti-Semitism's victims was Korczak's "Old Doctor" radio program. When his contract expired in 1936, Korczak was simply not offered a new one. The unspoken reason for his dismissal was right-wing pressure on the radio's directors to prevent Catholic children from being exposed to stories told by a Jew. No one asked the children how they felt about it.

In the summer of 1935 Germany and Poland signed a trade agreement, formally bringing to a close the tariff wars begun ten years earlier. Hitler now believed he was safe from any Polish aggression. In 1936, freed from the constraints of the Treaty of Versailles, he moved an army into the neutral Rhineland. The French watched with trepidation but did not resist, even though Polish Foreign Minister Józef Beck offered military aid.

The following year Hermann Göring made another trip to Warsaw, again with the express purpose of involving the Polish government in an anti-Comintern pact. Beck, who had retained his own portfolio and had even greater authority after the Mościcki – Śmigły-Rydz power struggle, refused Göring's request. This did nothing to allay the suspicions of the Russians, who still suspected Beck of plotting against them.

Later in the year the Poles and the Germans signed another agreement, this one guaranteeing the rights of each other's minorities living on opposite sides of the border. And Hitler again assured Ambassador Lipski that he had no designs on Danzig.

The Barber of Warsaw

The satirical magazine *The Barber of Warsaw* (*Cyrulik Warszawski*) also got into the act, so to speak, by putting on evening readings of its own satires in 1934. The magazine's editor, Jerzy Paczkowski, is credited with this brainstorm, which had the support of Julian Tuwim. The writing and the acting were performed by the magazine's staff. Posters were supplied by the staff artist, Feliks Topolski. Paczkowski asked each of the participants to write a biographical note for the program, describing themselves as "carefree pranksters."[2]

In 1935 the Warsaw Opera produced several highly praised operettas. The "first success" of that year, according to Ludwik Sempoliński, was Franz Lehar's *The Happy Land* (*Kraina Uśmiechu*). It opened in March and ran through April. That was followed in May by Lehar's *The Princess of Luxemburg* (*Hrabina Luxemburg*) and in August by Rudolph Friml's *Rose Marie.* A number of the Qui Pro Quo veterans moved over to the Barber of Warsaw cabaret, where in 1936 Járosy mounted the comedy *The Barber's Shampoo* (or *Head Wash*) (*Mycie Głowy*) starring Mira Zimińska. In March the troupe presented the revue *Garden of Delight* (*Ogród Rozkoszy*) with Lena Żelichowska and Stefania Górska heading the cast. Járosy had a busy year producing and directing shows, including one starring his former lover, Hanka Ordonówna, in the revue *A Smiling Face* (*Frontem do Radości*). The cast also included Igo Sym, Kazimierz Krukowski, and Ludwik Lawiński.

Not all the cabaret shows were simple comedies or musical numbers. In August Tuwim wrote a political satire, *The Career of Alpha Omega* (*Kariera Alfa Omegi,*) a send-up of the popular and talented opera star Jan Kiepura. It may have been just coincidental that Kiepura was also a favorite in Berlin.[3]

There was now a rash of new spaces available to cabaret-style shows, including the Summer Theater (*Teatr Letni*), the Café Club, and even the Ziemiańska café, heretofore known for the quality of the intelligentsia who congregated there. The Café Club, at the intersection of New World and Jerusalem avenues, headlined Zimińska in November, in a show titled *Mira and Satire* (*Mira i Satyra*).[4] Zimińska also starred in one of her best-known roles, *Soldier of the Queen of Madagascar* (*Żołnierz Królowej Madagaskaru*), a musical comedy. It was the result of a collaboration between Tuwim and Tadeusz Sygietyński, who later became Zimińska's husband and cofounder of the Mazowsze Dance Troupe.

On New Year's Eve 1935, Ordonka did a production of her own called *Spectacle No. 1* (*Widowiska Nr 1*). The program included her recital of Mickiewicz's "Ode to Youth" (*Oda do Młodości*) and a host of patriotic songs. The show's odd patriotic overtones were an unusual theme in an Ordonówna performance. It did not go down well with the critics.

Nevertheless, Ordonówna continued to be a hit on the cabaret circuit and occasionally staged one-woman shows in which she would sing, dance, and recite poetry. She also toured the continent again and was well received in Paris and in several German cities, despite the growing anti-Polish sentiment there.

Other Qui Pro Quo alumni also continued to star. In May 1935 Járosy produced a revue titled *The Gypsies* (*Cyganeria*). He leased the Hollywood cinema on Jasnej Street and brought in a cast that included Zosia Terné, Zula Pogorzelska, Lena Żelichowska, Igo Sym, Zizi Halama, his lover Stefania Górska, Adolf Dymsza, and an American named Gloria Grand. Sadly, this was to be Pogorzelska's last performance.

For the past several months she had been complaining about back pains. After seeing a doctor she had been taken to a hospital in Wilno by Konrad Tom.

Zula's best friend among the cabaret people was Mira Zimińska. "I always liked Zulka. She was a good friend, a good buddy. She had great taste, damn it! I used to take advantage of it. We were exactly the same size. I'd say to her, 'Zula, I have a rehearsal to go to. Please go and try on my dress.' On returning from the tailor she'd say, 'Mira, the fabric you've chosen is the wrong color,' or this or that has to be changed, and I'd say, 'Zula, you can go ahead and change what has to be changed.' And she always did. I could go to a gala opening night in a dress chosen by Zula. Such was life with my competition.

"At some point Zula moved to another theater. She called me one night and said, 'Mira, there's a premiere soon and I don't have even one good song! It's going to be a disaster.' Neither Tuwim nor Hemar could help her because they had exclusive contracts with Qui Pro Quo. What did I do? I gave Zula a very good song of mine, under the table. It was illegal, but I knew that even though she was my rival I couldn't leave her without a good program. After all, she was my friend. We remained good friends for the rest of her life.

"She liked cards. It used to be fashionable among the performers to play. [Zula and Konrad] took me a couple of times to their clubs. I was lucky maybe once, but it wasn't my cup of tea at all. There was also a lot of cigarette smoke in those places and I didn't smoke.

"All of a sudden Zula fell ill. I was very concerned and called Doctor Rose in Wilno, a brain, back, and nerves specialist. He came to Warsaw, examined Zula, and said, 'I'm taking her to my hospital.' But he said to me: 'Mira, it's hopeless—spinal cancer. She'll suffer for a while, she might even be able to walk for some time.'

"She performed for a short time, limping slightly. But she struggled. One day she took something hot into her hands and burned her skin; she was able to smell it but felt nothing. She said to me, 'Mira, I'm really sick.'

"She stayed in a hospital in Warsaw. I came in a luxurious limousine, all perfumed and dressed up. I told Zulka about the ball, how wonderful it was.... 'Imagine, so-and-so was there'... and I noticed that Zulka had become very sad. 'Oh, you idiot,' I said to myself, 'what a way to talk to your sick friend.' I curbed my oh's and ah's and told her about my headache and how miserable I felt.

"The following day I went to see her without my usual makeup on. From then on I'd say, 'You know, I feel awful today,' and she'd answer: 'You know, me too.'

" 'I had such a headache last night I couldn't sleep at all.'

" 'Yes, neither could I.'

"I was telling her about *my* problems and she tried to comfort me.

"Zulka went to see Doctor Rose again. He called me late one night and said, 'Zulka is dead.'

"Konrad Tom intended to erect a big marble monument on her grave, with angels carrying flowers and holding hands. It was

supposed to be the most beautiful tombstone at the Powązki cemetery, but it never was done. The one there is from me. The city gave
me a beautiful piece of red granite from an old Russian church that
had been torn down. I loved Zulka very much. She was a great
friend."[5]

Pogorzelska died in February 1936 at the age of forty.

Tadeusz Wittlin has also written movingly of Zula's funeral,
telling how Konrad Tom met the train carrying her coffin into Warsaw, and describing the scene at Powązki cemetery, with her elderly
mother and her friends from Qui Pro Quo standing around her
grave in the rain, some of them weeping uncontrollably.

■   By the midthirties Ordonówna had become Poland's equivalent of
a superstar. Her performances always played to a full house. Her
records were selling well, especially her recording of "Love Forgives
Everything," from the movie *The Masked Spy*. Other performers
tried to emulate her. Some did impersonations of her singing, others
tried to bribe music publishers to sell them her copyrighted material. Artists caricatured her, comics parodied her, and she did not
mind in the least. She had not succeeded in becoming a great
Shakespearean actress but there were other compensations. And of
course, there was her marriage to Count Michael Tyszkiewicz, who
gave her the emotional support she needed.

The Catastrophists

As the political situation began to turn ugly, Warsaw's poets reacted
strongly. Julian Tuwim, an opponent of the Endecja as well as a
mocker of bourgeois society, composed a controversial poem so
blasphemous that it was not published until after the war. It was
titled "Ball at the Opera" (*Bal w Operze*), and it painted a scathingly
dark scenario in which "diplomats, generals, bankers, whores," and

other recognizable Warsaw types converge at a ball given by a fictitious dictator of Poland. In a scene rivaled only by those of Fellini,
the party moves from the ball to the city's outskirts where there is
a very symbolic and obvious encounter between trucks carrying
waste matter to a disposal site and farmers and peasants streaming
into the city with their fresh produce.[6]

Tuwim's sometime friend, Gałczyński, offered his view of
contemporary society in his poem "Ball at Solomon's" (*Bal u Salo-
mona*). While not as acid as Tuwim's poem, it still drew a depressing
portrait of events and people, obviously meant to symbolize Poland.

■ Bruno Schulz introduced Franz Kafka to Poland in 1936 with his
translation of *The Trial*. In 1937 Schulz's second, and final, work
of fiction appeared. It bore the unwieldy title *Sanatorium under the
Sign of the Hourglass* (*Sanatorium pod Klepsydrą*), but it was well
received by the critics. Schulz was then awarded a golden laurel and
highly praised by the Polish Academy of Literature.

Later that year Antoni Słonimski produced his satirical novel
Two Ends of the World (*Dwa Końce Świata*) in which Warsaw is destroyed in an air raid directed by a madman named Retlich. Only
two men survive, one a Jewish book salesman and the other a Catholic laborer, but they are unable to communicate because they have
no common language. The city is then overrun by Lapps, and the
two men wind up in a camp.

Even the ebullient Wierzyński had taken to writing darkly
apocryphal poems, including the 1936 volume *Tragic Freedom*
(*Wólność Tragiczna*).

■ One future Nobel laureate, Isaac Bashevis Singer, moved to
America in 1935 but was replaced by another, Czesław Miłosz,

who arrived in Warsaw in 1937. Miłosz took a job at the state-run radio and did not become a part of the capital's literary milieu until the war years.[7] The young poet came from Wilno, where he had already published several volumes of poetry, including his first, *A Poem on Time Frozen* (*Poemat o Czasie Zastygłym*). Another of his books, *Three Winters* (*Trzy Zimy*) was nominated for the best book award for 1937 by *The Literary News*. A panel of authors selected the best books annually, and its members included such well-known writers as Maria Dąbrowska, Jarosław Iwaszkiewicz, Tuwim, and Józef Wittlin.

Miłosz was categorized by at least one critic as a "catastrophist," a school of poetry that enjoyed a brief vogue in Polish letters during the interwar period. According to the Polish critic Kazimierz Wyka, "catastrophism" was "an intellectual-artistic phenomenon in Polish poetry of the second decade between the two wars, which consisted of a symbolist-classicist elaboration (sometimes with a surrealist or expressionist tinge) of themes suggesting and announcing the approach of an inevitable historical and moral catastrophe."[8]

■ Catastrophe waited on all sides of Poland: The Marxist poet Bruno Jasieński's career was interrupted by his arrest in the Soviet Union. He subsequently died in a Soviet concentration camp. He was one of the first caught in the net of Stalin's paranoia, which was eventually to destroy the Polish Communist party as well as the lives of millions of Soviets he suspected of being involved in plots.

Health and Hygiene

The gloom of Poland's poets was pierced, if only temporarily, by the country's continued success in Olympic competition. In the famous games held in Berlin in the summer of 1936, in which Hitler stalked out rather than shake hands with the great American Olympian Jesse Owens, the Polish contingent picked up two silver medals—in the 100-meter dash and the women's discus—and one bronze, in the women's javelin throw.

The Poles also scored in the arts competition. Władysław Klukowski again won a medal for sculpture, this time for his work titled *Crowning of a Competitor*. Novelist Jan Parandowski won a bronze medal for his book *The Olympic Discus*.

■ Warsaw had a new mayor, Stefan Starzyński, whose energy revitalized Warsaw, both its arts and its amenities. Starzyński was a great lover of opera, and even though the Warsaw Opera received government subsidies, it never seemed to have enough money. At the mayor's urging, the Committee of the Friends of the Opera was formed to raise additional financing for the opera.

With Warsaw's new city planners plus Starzyński's leadership and the innovations promoted by Stanisław Różański and others, Warsaw continued to offer its citizens an improved standard of living. In 1935, in an effort to urge the city's leaders to adopt his suggestions, Różański, an engineer and city planner, mounted a public exhibit titled *Warsaw of the Future*. Starzyński viewed the display of models, plans, and maps, was very impressed, and the following year created the Bureau of Urban Planning with Różański as its head.

Różański deserves much of the credit for Warsaw's surge toward modernization. He envisioned a city with wide boulevards, districts segregated according to function—residential, commercial, industrial—separated by large patches of green. Visitors to today's Warsaw are impressed with the many parks, the squares, and the boulevards that allow the free flow of traffic.

For years the capital had been heated and lit by gas and coal. One of the mayor's first moves was to bring all the private sources of electric production under municipal ownership and offer cheaper power to consumers. Within a few short years consumption of gas decreased as more and more public buildings and private homes were hooked into the city's electric power supply.

The building of housing units continued apace, and the banality of high-rise apartment buildings was occasionally relieved by the construction of homes in the style of old manor houses.

The transportation system too was greatly improved, as long-distance rail lines were added, and transportation within the city — by bus and electric tram — and to the suburbs was enhanced by the purchase of more rolling stock and continued expansion of the highway network.

To cope with the ever-increasing traffic — there were more cars on the city's streets by 1936 — barriers were erected at major intersections to act as deterrents to jaywalking, and to protect pedestrians from out-of-control vehicles.

Tram stops were modernized, and in 1938 the first automated traffic signals were installed in downtown Warsaw. Safety lighting on the streets had been introduced around 1929, but it took a major leap forward by 1939 when more than two-thirds of the city's growing number of streets had safety lighting.

Starzyński's efforts also extended to Warsaw's suburbs, whose population saw a rise in standard of living. In the last half of the 1930s Warsaw added significantly to its acreage by incorporating many outlying areas.

The number of telephones in use in Warsaw was still quite small at this time, but besides the basic service the telephone company offered, for an additional fee, such luxuries as wake-up calls; a service that would answer incoming calls and provide a message to the caller; a system whereby one could order local or long-distance calls for a specific time; and a paging service that would send a taxi to one's home or office. The Astronomical Observatory would also give the caller the correct time. These additions were lumped together under the rubric of the Request Office.[9]

By the time the war began there were almost a hundred thousand listings in the Warsaw phone directory, a small percentage of the overall population but a decided improvement for the capital. (Because of years of neglect under the Communists there is currently no comprehensive phone directory for central Warsaw, and the phone system is woefully inadequate, though steps are being taken to correct this.)

■   Despite improvements in health care, interwar Poland was unable to contain the spread of tuberculosis, particularly among the poor and working classes. Other serious diseases, such as typhoid fever and smallpox, were brought under control, but there were still high rates of alcoholism and venereal disease.

This last-named scourge was the result of a combination of readily available prostitutes and disregard for personal hygiene. Because of Warsaw's importance as a center for commerce, government, and tourism, large numbers of visitors from abroad were attracted to the city, and prostitution became a thriving business, one that the government was reluctant to curtail. There were, no doubt, women who turned to prostitution as a means of support in an economy that was never completely stable.

The Catholic church was unable to use its influence to stem the flow of alcohol and proliferation of prostitutes; leaders of other denominations were equally powerless in the face of the demand for these vices, as a visit to Krochmalna Street would attest.

Gradually health clinics were established throughout the city. These offered such services as prenatal care, testing and treatment for venereal disease, and outpatient care. Warsaw had its version of Alcoholics Anonymous, but the appeal and availability of vodka were undiminished.[10]

Nimbly we dance in the wind; through abysses of
space we go sweeping...

Kazimierz Tetmajer
"Song of the Night Mist"
Translated by Watson Kirkconnell

CHAPTER 9

The Last Dance

■ 1937-1938

On the Political Front

By early January 1938 Hitler had already decided to grab Austria,
but he had to be sure that Poland would not intervene. Polish Foreign Minister Józef Beck and German Foreign Minister Joachim
von Ribbentrop had a series of meetings in Berlin and Warsaw,
primarily to ascertain the Polish response to the German move.
Beck assured his opposite number that his country had no interest
in Austria; in fact, Beck had other matters on his mind, namely relations with Lithuania and Czechoslovakia.

Since the coup in Lithuania in 1920, there had been no relations of any kind between it and Poland, and their borders remained
sealed at Lithuania's insistence. Lithuania had no desire to become
part of the Polish empire again. A border incident, however, com-
promised this tough stance. During a clash between Lithuanian

agents and a Polish border guard, a Polish soldier was killed. The Polish government quickly mobilized its troops and sent them to the Lithuanian border. After some days of tension and a conference with the French government, Lithuania agreed to reopen its borders and to exchange ambassadors with Poland.

Hermann Göring visited Warsaw again in February, to monitor the Polish position on Austria, and found it unchanged. While in the capital he took time out to relax. Professor Wacław Lednicki, a noted Slavicist and former minister in the foreign office, commented in his memoirs on the German air marshal's visit: "When, in connection with its political game, the government invited Germans and Mussolini's ministers to Poland for hunting parties and brilliant social receptions, some circles of Polish society participated in these activities, and they accepted invitations from Göring and others to similar hunting parties and receptions in Germany...."

These "circles" constituted only a small and elite part of Polish society. The majority of the population, especially those in the political center and on the left, remained suspicious and indeed antagonistic toward Germany.

With Austria under his control, Hitler focused his attention on Czechoslovakia. In the spring of 1938 he announced to his military staff his intention to invade and seize it. In order to prevent any intervention on the part of the Allies, he would claim it in parcels. First, he demanded the coupling of the Sudetenland with "mother" Germany, since this region held a huge German population that was supposedly being mistreated by the Czechs.

Negotiations between the Czechs, the Germans, and the British took place during the late spring and summer, with the immediate result that the Sudetenland was ceded to Germany. Before Hitler could take the rest of the country, Poland made its own demands on Czechoslovakia. The Poles had always claimed that

Teschen (*Cieszyn*) was properly their territory and pointed to the large Polish population living in the region. Beck demanded that if the Sudeten Germans were to be given special consideration, then the Poles in Teschen were to be accorded similar rights. His demands were backed up by an implied military threat.

The Czech government, anxious to avoid any armed conflict, gave in to Beck's demand, and Polish troops moved into Teschen. This move found widespread support in Poland, but it alienated important segments of the American and Allied governments. The foreign press began to question openly whether Beck was in league with the Germans. Even within his own country there was dismay over his bullying tactics. Professor Lednicki wrote: "Everyone remembers the painful impression of Poland's participation in [Czechoslovakia's] dismemberment. This soiled Poland's international reputation for a long time." But Lednicki asserted, "It is true that the lands of the Cieszyn region that Poland annexed were ethnographically Polish—her action was a correction of the St. Germain Treaty—and that when Poland was fighting desperately against Soviet Russia in 1920, the behavior of the Czechs was not at all edifying."

Still Lednicki was embarrassed by the hyperpatriotism that seized some of the populace, especially the young men volunteering to be part of the special force to be stationed in the Teschen province. "I don't think," he continued, "that the majority of the Polish population was at all enthusiastic about Beck's policy. And the fall of Czechoslovakia frightened many of us."[1]

Ambassador Józef Lipski was the next guest at Berchtesgaden, Hitler's headquarters in the Bavarian Alps, where the deposed leaders of Austria and Czechoslovakia had been bullied into surrendering their nations. In late October Lipski met there with von Ribbentrop, who suggested that Germany be allowed to build a highway and rail lines across the Polish Corridor. The German foreign minister also said it might be time to reconsider the Danzig question. Lipski was now quite alarmed and related his fears to Beck, who utterly rejected the German "suggestions." Furthermore, Beck warned von Ribbentrop that any move on Danzig would lead to open conflict.

Beck had adopted a frank stance of defiance against Poland's neighbors. When the Soviets expressed their concerns for Czechoslovakia, he told them bluntly to mind their own business, and they did. He rendered useless a Czech-Soviet defensive treaty by refusing to permit the Red Army to cross Polish territory, thus making it easier for Hitler to seize Czechoslovakia.

Surprisingly, von Ribbentrop reacted to Beck's response without rancor. He even suggested that the Polish minister visit with him and Hitler in January 1939, upon his return from a holiday in Italy.

The government by the "colonels," and its right-wing supporters, cemented its control over Polish politics in the elections of November 1938. The opposition's leader in parliament, Stanisław Car, had died and the Piłsudski-ites replaced him with Walery Sławek. President Mościcki saw this as a challenge to his authority, and so, using his presidential powers, he dissolved parliament in September.

In the campaign before the November elections the government stressed the themes of a militarily strong Poland and an improving economy. Even though unemployment was quite high, particularly among the Jews, industrial output was at its highest in Polish history, and the average Pole was not doing that badly. The finance minister, Eugeniusz Kwiatkowski, who had built the port at Gdynia, had pumped money into heavy industry and the manufacture of arms and other military needs.

The opposition, particularly the old Piłsudski supporters, boycotted the election, hoping that the mass of Polish voters would be fed up with authoritarian government. Unfortunately, fear of war ranked higher in the voters' minds. The OZON group won 161 out of 208 seats in the Sejm and had an even larger majority in the Senate. Sławek lost his seat and several months later committed suicide, shooting himself at precisely the same day and hour when Piłsudski had died four years earlier.

President Mościcki and Marshal Śmigły-Rydz were now in firm control and would lead the nation in the coming war.

Merrily We Roll Along

The imminence of war did not dampen spirits in Warsaw, outside of politics. There were now sixty-eight cinemas in the city and a revitalized theater scene thanks to municipal and government subsidies, which assured that at least a dozen professional theaters could continue operations. Qui Pro Quo had been closed for more than half a dozen years, but other cabarets were providing light entertainment as well as operettas. The opera, symphony, and smaller companies offering classical music continued to have full schedules.

Film-going easily became the most popular form of entertainment, for it was cheap and available to everyone. Poland was well on its way to developing its own film industry, but in terms of quality it still had a long way to go. As a young man Leopold Łabędz, later the editor of the political journal *Survey,* sampled a little bit of it all. "The literary life was very lively," he said, "as was the theater — theater was first-class, comparable to that of the French and the British [but] films were lousy...."[2]

A host of American films were playing in town, among them *The Prince and the Pauper* (*Książe i Żebrak*), starring Errol Flynn, at the Atlantic cinema; *Grand Illusion* (*Towarzysze Broni*) at the Baltic; *Double Wedding* (*Dwa Wesela*) with William Powell and Myrna Loy at the Palladium; and *The Scarlet Empress* (*Hrabina Władinów*), starring Marlene Dietrich and Jacques Feyder, which thrilled audiences at the Style (*Stylowy*).

As befitted its role as the hub of the nation's cultural life, Warsaw was also the focus of the film industry, for two reasons: It had the money, and it boasted a large pool of talent. Budding actors, directors, and technicians gravitated to the place that offered the greatest number of possibilities, and that was the capital city. The Polish film industry produced documentaries and newsreels as well as commercial films.

The earliest major studio, Sphinx, was owned by Aleksander Hertz, whose production of the soap-opera-ish *Trędowata* was so roundly criticized by Słonimski. One of his brightest actresses was Pola Negri, but he could not hold onto her once she had achieved some success.

It has been estimated that by 1937 Warsaw studios alone were producing twenty-seven major films annually.[3] Though the number of films produced in Poland increased dramatically between the wars, the number of major studios could be counted on one hand. Hertz's most serious rival was the inappropriately named Falanga, founded in 1923, which had produced Ordonówna's successful film, *The Masked Spy.*

The studios made the switch from silent to sound films without any problem. The early talkies tended to be either comedies or musical programs featuring entertainers currently popular on the cabaret circuit. Celebrities such as Mira Zimińska, the comedians Adolf Dymsza, Kazimierz Krukowski, and Romuald Gierasiński all appeared in numerous films. Konrad Tom made the transition from cabaret to film enthusiastically and became a director and writer of screenplays. Historical films almost always concentrated on Poland's struggles against Russian domination. Comedies tended to predominate.

Toward the end of the 1930s the studios were turning out more films adapted from popular Polish literature. Stories dealing with major social problems were quite common. One such movie was *The Girls from Nowolipki Street.* The story followed the lives of five girls brought up in the Jewish section of Warsaw, their loves, careers, successes, and failures. (Boycotts of Jewish businesses and exclusion of Jews from political parties were not carried into cultural and entertainment ventures. Anti-Semitism in Poland tended to be uneven and selective.) *The Girls from Nowolipki Street* was revived with some critical approval at the San Francisco International Women's Film Festival in 1985.

One of the all-time favorites of the Yiddish cinema, *The Dybbuk*, directed by Michael Waszynsky and starring Lili Liliana and Leon Liebgold, opened in Warsaw in 1938. There was a very noticeable Jewish presence in Poland's film industry, in all sectors — studio owners, producers, directors, actors. It is no coincidence that many of the Hollywood pioneers came from Poland and Eastern Europe.

To add to the attractions available in the capital, the glamorous Clara Seglovitch opened the Young People's Theater, with productions mainly for children but with some evening programs for adults. The first show was *Kolduny*, by the well-known Yiddish playwright Goldfaydn.

Segalovitch's company moved into the Nowości Theater, replacing the group led by the legendary Ida Kamińska. One of the most memorable shows of the Young People's Theater was a production of Shakespeare's *Tempest*, directed by Leon Schiller.

Varsovians continued to enjoy a wide variety of theatrical performances. In January they had the opportunity to see two imports, George Bernard Shaw's three-act comedy, *Candida*, at the Malicka Theater and at the Atheneum a production of the Moss Hart — George S. Kaufman musical, *Merrily We Roll Along* (*Cieszmy Się Życiem*).

The Atheneum was loosely designated the "workers' theater." It was housed in the Railroad Trade Union Building in a working-class district of the city. As a rule its programs appealed to the progressives and, more specifically, to the intelligentsia, although attempts were made to draw in workers. But the economic exigencies of operating a theater forced certain compromises. Musicals like *Merrily We Roll Along* were often scheduled to attract a larger box office.

The stage of the Atheneum was less deep than those of the other major theaters, hence the set designers had to be more creative in their stagings. Sets were often satirical, even grotesque, and at times they resembled the artwork seen in advertisements.

The personalities most frequently associated with the Atheneum in its interwar years were the great Polish actor and director Stefan Jaracz and his associate Stanisława Perzanowska. Like Schiller, Jaracz had a streak of rebelliousness, and this was evident from the shows he mounted at the Atheneum.

Perzanowska was one of several highly successful female directors who were active at this time, including Stanisława Wysocka, who combined the careers of acting and directing. In this respect Poland was way ahead of the West, including the United States, where female directors are still rare. Perzanowska was known for her interpretations of Molière, Beaumarchais, and the great Polish playwright Aleksander Fredro, whose work was frequently ignored by other Polish directors of this period.

Other Polish classics continued to be popular. Juliusz Osterwa directed Słowacki's *Balladyna* at the National Theater in February; in April Wyśpianski's *November Night* (*Noc Listopadowa*) played at the Polish Theater, directed by Aleksander Węgier. An adaptation of Charles Dickens's *Little Dorrit* (*Mała Dorrit*) opened at the Polish Theater in February 1938. The French were represented by several productions: Molière's *Tartuffe: The Impostor* (*Świętoszek*), directed by Perzanowska in October, using Boy-Żeleński's translation; and *The Brothers Thierry* (*Rodzeństwo Thierry*) by Roger Martin du Gard.

Polish cabaret shows were overshadowed in May, when Josephine Baker appeared in Warsaw with her Paris revue. Her show, which played for three evenings, was a tremendous success. Baker used a hand-held microphone, an innovation previously unknown to the Warsaw stage. For the finale she performed the Charleston, nude except for her trademark string of bananas around her hips. Sempoliński thought her singing was much better than her dancing.

Apocalypse Now

Witold Gombrowicz's novel *Ferdydurke* was the big success of the publishing business in 1937. Until then the author had been known mainly for his eccentric short stories and essays and his long exchange with Bruno Schulz in *The Literary News*.

Gombrowicz was one of a number of European writers of the interwar period whose work reflected the uncertainty of the times and the coming breakdown of accepted social structures across Europe. Fortunately, *Ferdydurke* is one of the works of Polish interwar literature available in English. It offers the reader an excellent example of the frenetic confusion that prevailed before World War II. At this point in history it seemed that an apocalypse of historic proportions was required for Europe to shake off the last vestiges of imperialism, of class-dominated cultures, and to settle the conflict among the predominant ideologies – a flawed democracy with fascism, communism, and socialism to the right and left of it.

The novel's hero, or antihero, Ferdydurke, is something of a buffoon, a character who cares little for society's straitjacketing mores. He was in that sense a reflection of Gombrowicz's own thought, for he was in rebellion against tradition, against the rules of polite society, which he considered to be outright hypocrisy. Gombrowicz also wanted to stretch the limits of familiar literary forms, and he certainly achieved this in *Ferdydurke*. In this section from the first chapter, Dr. Philifor, described as "the greatest synthesist of all times," confronts his opposite from Columbia University, an analyst known as Anti-Philifor:

The doctor and master of analysis said:
"Gnocchi!"
"Gnocchi," the synthetisiologist retorted.
"Gnocchi, gnocchi, or a mixture of eggs, flour, and water," said Anti-Philifor, and Philifor capped this with:
"Gnocchi means the higher essence, the supreme spirit of gnocchi, the thing-in-itself."
His eyes flashed fire, he wagged his beard, it was obvious that he had won. The professor of higher analysis recoiled a few paces, seized with impotent rage, but a dreadful idea suddenly flashed into his mind. A sickly and puny man in comparison to Philifor, he decided to attack Mrs. Philifor, who was the apple of her worthy professor-husband's eye.[4]

Later in the year Gombrowicz's play *Yvonne, Princess of Burgundy* (*Iwona, Księżniczka Burgunda*) also appeared for the first time. It is perhaps the clearest, least complex statement of his defiant attitude toward the accepted rules of society. The protagonist of the drama is a young prince whose family expects him to marry a beautiful, socially acceptable mate. Instead, while walking in a park he encounters an unattractive, mute girl and selects her to become his wife, much to the disgust of his family. All the members of his family insult and mistreat the girl, and they finally murder her by serving up a plate of unboned fish on which she chokes.

Few other novels of note were published in Poland that year. The versatile Jarosław Iwaszkiewicz, whose talent encompassed all literary forms, published a play titled *Masquerade* (*Maskarad*), dealing with the last year in the life of Pushkin. At least among the intelligentsia, Pushkin was one of the most popular Russian authors. The

Polish embrace of romantic, tragic figures must have played some part in Pushkin's popularity in a nation where the Russians were otherwise hated, especially the vehemently anti-Polish Dostoyevski.

Adam Ważyk, known today for his poetry and his translations of Guillaume Apollinaire more than for his fiction, wrote a novel titled *Family Myths* (*Mity Rodzine*). Of the three most popular female novelists, only Maria Kuncewicz wrote anything of importance after 1935. Her novel *The Everyday Life of Mr. and Mrs. Jones* (*Dni Powszednie Państwa Kowalskich*) was the first to be serialized on Polish radio. Zofia Nałkowska had not written any novels since *Boundary Line* (*Granica*) in 1935. She did resume her career after the war. Maria Dąbrowska was perhaps the most active of the three in the years just before the war. She published a collection of stories, *The Signs of Life*, in 1936 and a study of peasant life, *The Crossroads* (*Rozdroże*), in 1937.

Among the poets, the idealist and supporter of the Russian Revolution Władysław Broniewski wrote *The Last Cry* (*Krzyk Ostateczny*). Jan Lechoń, whom Polish critics believe to be the interwar poet with the most potential for greatness, withdrew from writing, blocked by a combination of emotional problems and despondency over the coming war. In the late 1930s he joined the Polish diplomatic corps and was posted to Paris, where he was stationed when the German invasion finally came.

The Literary News became a forum for those speaking out against anti-Semitism. A spate of articles, such as *The Tragedy of the Jews* by Józef Labodowski, and *Antysemityzm* by the respected essayist Alek Świętochowski, demonstrated that there was a significant opposition to this destructive prejudice.

In January 1938, the *News* devoted most of a ten-page issue to the life and work of composer Karol Szymanowski, who had died the year before. There were articles and tributes by his librettist, Jarosław Iwaszkiewicz, his sister Stanisława, the director Ryszard Ordyński, Leon Schiller, and Zofia Nałkowska. Szymanowski's death left a gaping hole in the country's musical life. Paderewski and Rubinstein lived and performed almost exclusively outside of Poland. Future stars—Witold Lutosławski, Stanisław Skrowaczewski, and Krzysztof Penderecki—were still young men about to embark on their careers.

The café IPS (Institute for Artistic Propaganda), which was a gathering place for right-wing intellectuals, according to Zofia Chądzyńska, opened a series of art exhibits. One outstanding show featured the paintings of Henryk Gottlieb and Xawery Dunikowski along with the sculptures of Karol Hiller. Another memorable exhibit featured the work of Józef Czapski, arguably Poland's most talented artist of the interwar period (still living in Paris at the time of this writing).

In June 1938, Janusz Korczak's "Old Doctor" radio program was reinstated, thanks to the intervention of friends such as Jan Piotrowski, a writer and illustrator of children's books. The program was broadcast two afternoons a week. It was later canceled for a second time, and Piotrowski was even forbidden to write about the "Old Doctor" in the radio magazine *Antenna*.

A Last Fling

While Josephine Baker was entertaining Warsaw, Hanka Ordonówna accepted an invitation to tour the United States. She traveled in great style aboard the ship *Batory*. During the trip, according to Tadeusz Wittlin, she struck up a relationship with a handsome first officer that continued after the ship had docked in New York.

Ordonka's month-long tour included shows in New York as well as in American cities with large Polish populations.[5]

While Ordonówna was in America, a lovely actress-singer with great potential made her debut at the Barber of Warsaw cabaret. Her name was Lola Kitajewicz, and, unlike many of the top performers, she had studied at the University of Warsaw. Her first club appearance in June was in the comedy *Romance with the Tax Officer* (*Romans z Urzędem Skarbowym*).

Lola's interwar career was brief, but she managed to squeeze some memorable performances into the time remaining before this cabaret world disappeared. In November she performed in *Warsaw for Sale* (*Sprzedajmy Warszawe*) with Fryderyk Járosy, and in December she had a part in the last show ever performed at the Barber. It ran until March 1939. The Barber had a relatively short life — about three-and-a-half years — and like many clubs of this era simply did not have the financing to continue.

Lola and her husband, Benno, were a young couple with high aspirations. He was the son of a carpet manufacturer, a man-about-town with a splendid office on Senatorska Street, not far from the old Qui Pro Quo, and a roadster with white sidewalls and semiautomatic gearshift. His office was the envy of his friends because it had a bar and refrigerator built into the wall.

He recalled Warsaw with great joy, without a trace of sadness, at their comfortable home in North London. To him it was a city "of very lively people with a colossal sense of humor. Life was so exciting, so rich, beautiful women, elegant restaurants. It was a time when it was simply out of the question for men to go out on the town without a dinner jacket."[6]

The couple's favorite club was the Adria, whose manager, Franciszek Moszkowicz, carried two pairs of glasses: One he wore to greet his wealthy customers, the other to announce to the poorer ones that there were no tables available. Another of his idiosyncracies was a daily inspection of the waiters. While they stood at attention he would carefully look over their uniforms and mark a red "x" across the chest of anyone wearing a dirty shirt.

During his courting days Benno had been acquainted with the young Marian Hemar, a writer so nimble of mind that for a few pennies he would create poetry on demand for young men to include with the bouquets they were sending to their dates. This custom now seems hopelessly outmoded, but in the 1930s a young woman expected no less. Benno hired Hemar to write a love poem for him to present to Lola, but when the magic moment arrived he discovered that her date the previous week had given her the same verse.[7]

A premier stage and cabaret actor for thirty years was Ludwik Sempoliński, a man well remembered for his many comic roles but who in fact performed admirably in dramas as well (and who, one Polish gentleman reminded me, owned the first Fiat in Warsaw). In his memoirs Sempoliński wrote that by 1938 there were only two outstanding cabarets remaining in Warsaw, the Barber and a new club known as Little Qui Pro Quo.

Sempoliński starred in the last show at the Barber, one that featured a crowd of faces also familiar to audiences—there were Zosia Terné, Fryderyk Járosy, and Ludwik Lawiński. Choreography was by Madame Tatiana Wysocka.

With the closing of the Barber, Little Qui Pro Quo—so-called because many of its cast had performed at the old Qui Pro Quo—remained the most popular on the circuit. The club produced a number of shows in late 1938 featuring Adolf Dymsza. As the year drew to a close another popular night spot, Café Club, staged several cabaret-style revues, including one titled *Political Monkey Business* (*Szopka Politycznej*). The club hosted a gala party on December 31, with a program recalling the good times. Sempoliński sang a song from his early career. The well-dressed crowd was determined to have a good time, and the celebration was reminiscent of the days of Carnival in another, more pleasant era.[8]

"I don't remember a New Year's Eve as marvelous, pompous,

and as joyous as the one of 1938," wrote Zofia Arciszewska. "It was
a tradition in Warsaw to celebrate New Year's Eve in several nightclubs, which were usually located in the same neighborhood. After
supper in our own restaurant, Under the Golden Duck, I went with
my husband and our guests to the Raspberry Room in the Bristol
Hotel. We were accompanied by the graphic artist Tadeusz Gro-
nowski and his wife, as well as by my husband's brother, Lieutenant
Stanisław Rola-Arciszewski. We enjoyed ourselves as never before,
as if we knew for some of us it would be the last New Year's Eve
party."[9]

There is no country whence I shall not yearn
In grieving anguish for the old, gray streets.

Julian Tuwim
"There Is No Country"
Translated by Watson Kirkconnell

CHAPTER 10

The Curtain Falls

■ 1939

On the Political Front

The last round of talks between Poland and Germany began in January 1939. Returning from an Italian holiday, Józef Beck stopped over in Berlin where he met separately with Hitler and von Ribbentrop. The führer was reassuring on the question of Danzig, though he hinted the situation would have to be resolved eventually. Von Ribbentrop was more formal. He again asked for highway and rail lines to be built across the Polish Corridor and also raised the issue of Danzig. Beck made no commitments, but he sensed that things were coming to a head. He conveyed his impressions to President Mościcki and Marshal Śmigły-Rydz as soon as he returned to Warsaw.

In late January 1939 von Ribbentrop made a reciprocal visit to Warsaw. He brought with him demands for the transit rights and

221

again urged the Poles to join an anti-Comintern pact. This time Beck told the Germans in no uncertain terms that there would be no highway or rail lines across the corridor, and that Poland would not join any pact against the Soviets.

In March the Germans seized the balance of Czechoslovakia, giving the territory of Ruthenia with its population of Hungarians and Ruthenians to Hungary.

Ambassador József Lipski was summoned to von Ribbentrop's office in Berlin where it was made clear to him that the German government was very unhappy with what they saw as Poland's lack of cooperation. Before the meeting ended Lipski inquired about rumors of Germany's impending seizure of the Lithuanian port of Memel, with its sizable German population. Von Ribbentrop stated that Hitler had no plans to invade, but shortly afterward the Lithuanians were presented with an ultimatum that German troops must be stationed in Memel to protect their minority. The Lithuanians offered no resistance, but Polish troops were mobilized – by mail, so as not to alert German espionage agents. German troops were now stationed on three sides of Poland.

Count Edward Raczyński, now the ambassador to Britain, approached Lord Halifax for assistance, and without hesitation the prime minister, Neville Chamberlain, assured the count that both Britain and France were ready to assist Poland should it come under attack from Hitler. In April British officials suggested to Minister Beck a coalition of several nations, including the Soviet Union. Beck resolutely refused, fearing that it would open the door for Red Army troops to enter Polish territory.

Later that month Hitler delivered one of his patented, hysterical speeches, denouncing all the Allies including the Americans, and abrogating the Polish-German treaty of nonaggression signed in 1934.

The Italians, who remained on friendly terms with Poland, sent Count Ciano, Mussolini's son-in-law, to Warsaw to hear

Beck's plea that his country dissociate itself from Hitler. The Ruma-
nians also sent an emissary, to sign a treaty of mutual assistance, in
the event that either they or the Poles were attacked by the Soviet
Union.

   With the situation beginning to look more desperate, the Polish government sent its minister of war to Paris to present a plan
that called for the French to respond to a German attack on Poland
with an air assault followed by a land invasion of Germany. British
General Ironside visited Poland in July and confirmed his country's
offer of assistance.

   The Soviet Union was also getting anxious about events in the
West and sent its foreign minister, Maxim Litvinov, to London
with a proposal for a defensive pact to include Great Britain,
France, the Soviet Union, Poland, and perhaps other European nations. The British asked for time to consider the proposition (during
which time Litvinov was removed from office),[1] knowing full well
that the Poles would not agree to any alliance with the Soviets.

   In July representatives from Britain and France traveled to
Moscow for further discussions. The Soviet government insisted
that the Baltic states and Poland must be a part of any defensive
treaty. Still at loggerheads the Allied delegation left the Soviet capital without any agreement.

   In late August, with the political situation at a stalemate,
rumors suddenly surfaced that the Nazis and the Soviets were about
to sign a nonaggression pact themselves. The news stunned political
leaders and observers all over the Western world, astonished that
the fascists and the communists would enter into *any* agreement.
The rumor was confirmed on August 22 when von Ribbentrop
departed for Moscow.

   In the last week of freedom, in August, there was a final flurry
of activity between Great Britain and Germany and between Poland and Germany. Prime Minister Chamberlain sent a note to Hitler declaring his country's willingness to come to Poland's aid.

Hitler was furious and postponed the original invasion date of August 25. At the same time Mussolini notified the führer that Italy was not prepared to go to war.

The Mościcki government made desperate efforts to bring other countries into the negotiations. The Swedes proposed to mediate a meeting between Poland and Germany, but Hitler insisted on a face-to-face meeting with a Polish representative empowered to make on-the-spot decisions. Ambassador Lipski was still in Berlin but Beck refused to give him such authority. The Polish army had now been mobilized.

The British ambassador to Germany, Joseph Henderson, met with von Ribbentrop, who claimed to have a list of sixteen conditions the Poles had to meet in order to stave off war. But the German minister refused to give Henderson a copy of the list and instead read off the items so fast that Henderson could barely note them.

Messages flowed in from abroad, urging the Poles to give in. Appeals came from Pope Pius XII, the king of Belgium, the queen of Holland — all pleading with the government to give in to the German demands (whatever they were), to give away Danzig. British and French diplomats begged Beck to call off his troops. He refused, and the delegation then went to Marshal Śmigły-Rydz who first agreed but then changed his mind and reinstated the mobilization order on August 28. By then the Poles had lost two precious days of preparation.

Ludwik Łubieński, who had become Beck's private secretary, stayed up all night to man the telephone, after the minister had retired around one A.M., exhausted. Łubieński reported: "In the morning around four o'clock on the first of September, the first phone call came, the Germans had moved in, and one hour afterward the first alarm . . . and German planes came to bomb Warsaw."[2]

Pessimism and Bravado

Warsaw's social life in 1939 seemed little affected by the impending crisis. Although war seemed inevitable, in Poland there was a mixture of pessimism and bravado. Attendance at the splendid balls did not decrease noticeably. The usual round of parties continued. Ludwik Łubieński, a former Fiat executive now in the foreign service, recalled having cocktails after work, followed by a black-tie dinner that lasted until dawn. He would then go directly to his office in his evening clothes, not having had time to change.

Stanisław Meyer continued his work in classical music circles, undeterred by the frantic intergovernment negotiations taking place.

"In the spring of 1939 the International Society of Contemporary Music held its annual meeting in Warsaw; to break the monotony of official receptions for the members of the congress we invited them to our house. The guests represented many different countries and as I knew only a few personally I had to ask every new arrival whether he spoke French or German. According to my list, among the few missing guests was a Bulgarian. Rather late in the evening a large man with a prominent dark beard appeared. 'This is my Bulgarian,' I decided. After the formal greeting I discovered that he preferred to speak German. 'I am sorry I do not speak Bulgarian though I understand quite a little,' I said in the course of our conversation. The bearded musician looked at me somewhat suspiciously, but noticing that I was quite sober answered: 'Is it so important to speak Bulgarian? I on my part do not know a word of it.' 'But then, who are you, Sir?' was my astonished exclamation. 'Don't you know? Allan Busch, one of the British delegates!' "[3]

Professor Wacław Lednicki, returning to Kraków from a lecture engagement in Brussels, stopped over in Warsaw to see friends, some of whom held high government positions.

"When I arrived in Warsaw, where I spent two days, I learned in the Foreign Office that my intimate friend, W. Grzybowski, our ambassador to Moscow, was in Warsaw. . . . . I was happy to hear of his return, but also astonished, for at that very time France and Britain were attempting to come to some understanding with Stalin, and the French and British delegations were then in Moscow. It was difficult for me to understand how a Polish ambassador in Moscow could have left his post under these circumstances. But . . . this apparent unconcern of the Polish ambassador was, in a way, typical. Diplomats and statesmen often at the time of grave circumstances take such attitudes of detachment. . . .

"As soon as I heard about Grzybowski's presence in Warsaw, I called him, and he immediately invited me out for a luncheon at a small but famous Warsaw restaurant, Krzemiński, which, unfortunately, does not exist any longer. It was ruined in the last war with the rest of Warsaw. This restaurant had only a couple of small rooms around a liquor and wine shop; the furniture was that of an ordinary bar, with plain chairs and marble-topped tables on which waiters would simply put a piece of paper under the plates. But the food, the cellar, the Polish *wódka-starka* [old Polish hard liquor] were all excellent — also very expensive. The restaurant was a tradition.

"As soon as I arrived in the restaurant, I was told by the manager that the ambassador was already there in a separate room. I entered and was struck by the table laden with the finest appetizers and with a bottle, the shape, dust, and mold of which eloquently confirmed my great expectations. Polish ambassadors were well paid, and they became easily accustomed to the luxuries granted by the diplomatic service abroad. . . .

"My friend Grzybowski knew how to entertain, not only in embassies and legations but in restaurants in Warsaw or in any European capital; I know this because I have often enjoyed his hospitality myself. When I appeared in the door, he stopped me and said,

'Before you take a seat, please answer a question. Will there be a war or not?'

" 'I have a very slight hope that perhaps it may be avoided.'

" 'Well, unfortunately you are right; the war probably will not occur *yet*.' "[4]

Professor Lednicki did not trust either the Germans or the Russians, but Ambassador Grzybowski was quite confident that Poland could withstand an assault, at least until the Allies arrived. He then announced he was about to go to the Adriatic for his annual holidays.

As Lednicki walked about Warsaw, he felt an air of optimism, buoyed by the sight of men in uniform on the streets, in the restaurants, and in the theaters. Others were not so hopeful and had begun either moving to the countryside after storing their valuables, or leaving Poland altogether.

Actually, no one really knew where safety lay. Lednicki's friend, the Princess Casimir Lubomirska, told him, "The war is coming. Poznania [Poznań] will be invaded by the Germans, so I have left my estate and am on my way to Kraków where one may be safer."[5]

In late August, Professor Lednicki was on his way home after a brief holiday in Paris. A Polish diplomat had asked him to deliver an attaché case to the Foreign Office in Warsaw. En route, he passed through Germany.

"In the morning the train stopped for a while in Berlin at Schesischer Bahnof. I was shaving in the bathroom close to my compartment, and from time to time I had to get some things that were on my bed. As the curtains of the window in my compartment were up, I suddenly saw on the platform Ryszard Ordyński, a Polish stage manager and movie man whom I knew well. I opened the window and greeted him.

" 'Do you know what has happened?' he asked me.

"I said, 'What?'

" 'A pact!'

" 'With Hungary?' I asked, as this was expected.

" 'No—with Russia!'

" 'Then it is war. Where are you on the train? Will you take your breakfast in the dining car so we may talk? . . .' "[6]

As soon as he arrived in Warsaw, Lednicki went straight to the Foreign Office housed in Count Raczyński's former home, the Brühl Palace. Inside there was pandemonium, with clerks, ministers, and journalists crowded in the corridors seeking information. Some of them had heard about the pact on the radio and had rushed home from their holiday retreats.

There were still a few officials who believed that there would be no war, but they were now in a rapidly dwindling minority. There was also a tangible change in the air, as Lednicki noted: "The atmosphere of Warsaw, as I circulated on the streets, had been obviously apprehensive. One sensed in the crowds, and even in the traffic, something of the kind of thing one sees in nature when a big storm is approaching. I felt the same in Kraków the next day. . . . "[7]

"It was a wonderful, hot, dry summer in Poland before the war in 1939," wrote Wanda Stachiewicz. "The sun poured down its brilliance, to make one forget the menacing threat of Germany. Warsaw . . . with nearly two million inhabitants, an attractive modern city full of gaiety and wit, was now completely changed. War was in the air. Every week increased the tension . . . "[8]

Stachiewicz continued, "Throughout the year, we were preparing ourselves for war. The Women's Auxiliary Service . . . doubled its work, organizing courses. We received antigas as well as rifle training and various kinds of instruction. Before the outbreak of the war women were told to prepare their husband's or their son's knapsacks in case they should be unexpectedly called up; to prepare their own and their children's things so as to be ready to leave abruptly in case of bombing.

"Each family had to have provisions for one month. Each child had to have a label with his name and address stitched on his clothes — in case he was lost. I remember how depressing it was, when we sat in silence and sewed on those labels. Everybody offered one day of work to dig shelters in the parks. Each woman and girl, trained in antigas defense, had ten blocks to look after in case of bombing.

"I had completed a Liaison Service course and in July I started work at General Headquarters, happy to be useful and near my husband. I had sent my little daughter . . . to a small cottage just outside Warsaw so that he could see her sometimes. The cottage, hidden in the forest, seemed to be very safe in case of war, because I did not realize then what war would be like. . . ."[9]

Years later Kazimierz Brandys recalled making preparations for war: "We were called upon to dig antitank and antiaircraft ditches. I reported with two colleagues from the university to the assigned point, a long courtyard, on the even-numbered side of Nowy Świat, where, as I recall, there used to be a skating rink in the winter. Everyone got a shovel; we dug along strings stretched out as markers. It was a warm day. A woman in a dressing gown and high-heeled slippers was working beside me. She was having a hard time of it — I, jamming my shovel into the ground, could see her out of the corner of my eye, her slender white feet sinking into the clayey earth. A woman who looked like a maid was digging alongside her. 'You should rest, ma'am,' [the maid] advised her when the sun grew stronger. The woman in the dressing gown took out a pack of cigarettes but didn't have a light. She bent toward me when I brought a lit match over to her cigarette and I could see two black trickles of sweat running alongside her nose. It was then that I recognized her. A year and a half before I graduated from the Gymnasium she had solicited me as I was walking down Nowy Świat, somewhere between Warecka and Chmielna streets. I had heard about her before: My classmates Andrzej Rudnicki and Jurek

Lichtenstein knew her. Her name was Zosia Bergy. Her real name was Gadomska or Gostyńska; her father was a respectable doctor. She solicited me in a passageway, whispering a few words in French."[10]

His eyes opened, Brandys continued to work alongside her in the streets of Warsaw.

Count Władysław Zamoyski spoke with British General Ironside on his visit to Warsaw right before the war, and the general expressed his pessimism over Poland's military preparations. It so happened that the count and Professor Lednicki shared a compartment on the train from Warsaw to Kraków where Zamoyski mentioned this to the professor, almost in passing. As Lednicki related it, their trip began in high spirits:

"On the platform of the station I met Count W. Zamoyski, a still marvelously handsome man in his sixties, a member of a distinguished Polish aristocratic family. . . .

"He greeted me with his usual charming friendliness and said, 'Are you going to Kraków? Then we shall have dinner together. I brought from Wilno some *sieławki* [a renowned Lithuanian freshwater fish]. They will broil them for us in the dining car.' I of course eagerly accepted his invitation and told him that I would reciprocate because I had a bottle of Armagnac that I had brought from Brussels. . . . The sun had already begun to set, but it was still possible to see the countryside, and Zamoyski showed me the new racetrack of which he was extremely proud, having played an important part in its establishment as a member of the racing board in Warsaw. 'Do you know that General Ironside, who just visited Poland, marveled when he saw our track and said that it was certainly one of the best in Europe, but he was much less enthusiastic as far as our military preparations were concerned.' . . . We spent the rest of the evening in rather depressed conversation."[11]

Even with the threat of disaster heavily in the air, many Varsovians continued their annual custom of spending the summer, or part of it, in the countryside. Some were still at their favorite retreat when the war began; others, sensing danger, hurried back to the city earlier.

Leopold Łabędz had been a student in Paris for the past two years but in mid-August, certain that there would be a war, he returned to Warsaw to join the army. Before settling down to soldiering, he and a friend went on holiday to Duszniki, a popular spa near Wilno. He was there when the Hitler-Stalin pact was signed and said it came as no surprise to him. Then he headed back to Warsaw.

"There was a panic because everyone who wanted to get back couldn't get a ticket on the train, so we went by taxi all through Poland. I reached Warsaw on August 27. . . .

"On August 31 I was rushing back and forth between Powązki and a shop on Nowy Świat, a good shoemaker, Poznański, who made officers' boots. My father was already mobilized . . . and had ordered the boots and they were not ready and he was in the barracks at Powązki. They were going to leave at any moment for an unknown destination and the boots were not ready. I went back and forth by taxi and finally got the boots one hour before they left. . . ."[12]

Stefania Kossowska had left the university a year earlier and married the artist Adam Kossowski. Their combined families took their usual vacation in August. "My parents had a country house near Poznań and we spent our last summer holiday there—my husband, cousins—a big family affair. The atmosphere was extremely uneasy. There were many Germans living in this part of Poland. Many had lived there before the war. They were considered to be Poles, but when the war came nearer they suddenly discovered they were Germans, and they started to parade in these Hitler Jungen uniforms, and so on.

"We usually stayed until the beginning of September, but this last year we left at the end of August because we realized something was coming to an end. We went to Warsaw at once, just time enough for my husband to arrange for his family to come to Warsaw because no one knew what was going to happen."[13]

Casimir Sabbat, a future president of the government-in-exile, was taking part in a scout camp on the Baltic Sea. "On August 26 the mobilization was announced but then halted at the request of Great Britain. On my way home I passed through Gdańsk which was still a free city. From the train I saw the city covered with Hitlerite flags."[14]

While the international cable lines were overheating with exchanges of last-minute proposals, the Polish army was put on alert at the beginning of the week, told to stand down, then put on alert again at the end of the week.

These contradictory orders left large numbers of Polish reserves in a state of confusion and resulted in the last-minute spectacle of men rushing about the country trying to find their units. Many of them never reached their destinations in time.

Optimists Rising

In early 1939, according to Tadeusz Wittlin, Poland's optimists seemed to be in ascendance. By that time the radio airwaves were humming with martial music. There was an air of anticipation and, depending on whom one spoke to, a variety of opinions not so much about whether there would be a war but about who the victor would be. Around the city posters and graffiti defiantly urged "Together – Powerful – Ready!" (*Zwarci – Silni – Gotowi*).

Rumors about Germany swept through the capital: German factories were suffering widespread shortages, German tanks were decoys made from papier-mâché or plywood, German people were starving.

At the newly opened Little Qui Pro Quo (*Mały Qui Pro Quo*), the revues mocked Hitler, and the songs rang with an air of defiance. In one tune the refrain was "In less than a month we'll be drinking in Berlin."

A reincarnation of Qui Pro Quo, this club had its stage upstairs above the Café Ziemiańska and employed some of the old hands— Boczkowski and Majde as directors, Dymsza, Górska, and Zimińska in the cast—supported by the Dana Chorus.

The early 1939 theater season opened with a performance at the Cricot Theater of the comedy *Husband and Wife* (*Mąż i Żona*), by Aleksander Fredro, a perennial favorite of theater audiences. There was more lighthearted fare to follow, including a Cyprian Kamil Norwid one-act comedy at the New Theater, *Pure Love in a Spa by the Sea* (*Miłość Czysta u Kapieli Morskich*). In March Leon Schiller mounted a production of Thornton Wilder's *Our Town* (*Nasze Miasto*) at the National. The perennial Shaw contribution did not appear until the summer. It was a production of the political fantasy *Geneva* at the Polish Theater.

Perhaps the best-remembered show took place at the Scala Theater where the Yiddish players produced a comedy revue titled *The Crazy World*. It was written by Dzigan and Shumakher, a popular pair of satirists whose shows were always sold out. Among the scenes in the revue was one titled "The Last Jew in Poland." The revue itself made only oblique references to the present political situation; otherwise it would never have passed the board of censors.

"The Last Jew in Poland" was a devastating satire of the Jewish condition in Poland. It portrayed a nation in which all Jews but one have been eliminated. The nation is so bereft of entertainment, cultural events, and commercial progress that the government pleads with the remaining Jew not to leave Poland. A student group organizes a banquet for him at which Yiddish songs are sung. As a condition for remaining in the country the Jew demands some kosher food, such as gefilte fish, only there is no one left who knows how to cook it.

In desperation the government awards the Jew its highest honors, which he defiantly pins to the tails of his coat. The skit ends with the singing of an old Polish favorite – sung to honor someone on a birthday or for an accomplishment – "May You Live a Hundred Years" (*Sto Lat*).

Its sarcasm did not escape the ears of the authorities. The two authors were hauled before the police commission the day after the opening and given a sharp reprimand.[15]

Despite the recent closing of the Barber, cabaret performers and directors found other locations for their performances. The Café Club greeted the new year with a series of revues that continued into March.

In April Tuwim, Hemar, and Włast wrote a political satire aimed at the agreements signed between Poland and Germany in the last several years, agreements that now seemed to have been fraudulent from the very beginning. Their show was titled *Facts and Pacts (Fakty i Pakty)*.

In May the revue *Eagle or Reich (Orzet czy Rzeszka)* opened, throwing down the challenge, Poland or Germany? The response of course was a defiant choice of the Polish Eagle. Parodies of Hitler were now more frequent in cabaret sketches, along with the odd send-up of Mussolini. Other well-known political figures such as Józef Beck and Britain's Neville Chamberlain were also lampooned. The cabaret revues of these last days before the German invasion were full of bravado in the face of the Nazi threat. While some of their fellow citizens were beginning to panic, the club performers were determined to stand their ground.

In July the *Warsaw Courier (Kurier Warszawski)* announced the opening of two revues. *You Beloved Old Dog House (Wesoła Buda)*, the affectionate name that had been given to Qui Pro Quo by its members, opened at the Buffo Theater. The other revue opened at the Tip-Top on the boulevard Marszałkowska, a cabaret created by Fritz Járosy. On August 12 he premiered a show titled *Who Whom? (Kto Kogo?)*. Antoni Słonimski was one of several contributors to the script. In the cast were Hanka Ordonówna, Eugene Bodo, Alicja Halama, and the Dana Chorus, among others. Járosy was planning to open another revue at the Figaro Theater on September 3; it was never produced.[16]

Tadeusz Wittlin's novel *Achilles' Heel* was published in the spring, and he celebrated with his friends by giving a floating party that began at the Adria Café, moved on to the bar of the Europejski Hotel, and finished up at the Café Club. Wittlin was getting paid well, and there was more money to come: an advance from the START group to write an adaptation of the comedy *Soldier of the Queen of Madagascar (Żołnierz Królowej Madagaskaru)* with Mira Zimińska, and an offer from the Leo Film studio to do another screenplay, to be titled *Mad Jane (Szalona Janka)*, starring the sultry Jadwiga Smosarska. Wittlin needed a quiet place to do all this work, so he retreated to the mountain resort of Zakopane.[17]

Janusz Korczak was also away from Warsaw, on a working holiday at a spa, where he was putting the finishing touches on his new book, *The Religion of the Child*. His biographer noted that from his lodgings Korczak could watch soldiers being trained for duty on the German-Polish border.

At his camp for children on the outskirts of Warsaw the season usually ended with an athletic competition, a sort of miniature Olympic Games. But in the summer of 1939 the children wanted to play war games – Poles versus Germans. Korczak described how "a large sandy area was prepared for the battlefield, fortifications built, bunkers dug. Shotguns were carved out of wood and chestnuts became bullets. Any boy hit by a chestnut fell down, played dead, and was out of the game. The girls, acting as nurses, helped the wounded from the field."[18]

Korczak had made up his mind by then to visit Palestine and Jerusalem in October. He never had the opportunity.

Warsaw's writers had slowed their output by this time, perhaps because of the political uncertainty, or perhaps as part of the natural rhythm of creativity. In an atmosphere rife with war fever, Jerzy Andrzejewski, a Catholic writer, won the literary prize offered by the Polish Academy of Literature. He later wrote the well-known *Ashes and Diamonds* (*Popiół i Diament*).

Perhaps the most significant poem of the year was Władysław Broniewski's call to arms, "Fixed Bayonets" (*Bagnet na Broń*), also known as "Bayonets Ready." It ends with the rousing stanza:

> *Bayonets ready!*
> *Bayonets ready!*
> *And should we die with our swords,*
> *We shall recall what Cambronne said.*
> *And on the Vistula repeat his words.*[19]
> Translated by Adam Gillon
> and Ludwik Krzyżanowski

Witold Gombrowicz enjoyed a certain stature now as a man of letters and as something of a celebrity. In June the management of the Polish steamship line invited him to be its guest on the maiden voyage to Argentina of the *Chrobry*. He accepted, little knowing that he would never see Warsaw again. His colleague Bruno Schulz was in his village of Drohobycz working on another book, *Messiah*.

In August Tadeusz Wittlin met with Hanka Ordonówna, who wanted his help in preparing a program of songs that she could take to the front lines where she planned to entertain troops. Wittlin recalled that the usually optimistic Hanka was apprehensive about going but nevertheless felt that she had to do something to assist in the war effort. When she asked the writer for a title for her revue, he suggested *A Pile of Laughs* (*Kupa Śmiechu*).

The program never progressed beyond the planning stage.

The next time Wittlin saw Ordonówna she was singing to wounded soldiers at the train station.[20]

It is almost as if the clock stopped on September 1, 1939. Many times when I think about my life and about my age I feel that I was robbed of my youth, of my dreams, of how different my life would have been.

Hanna Hirshaut
Letter to the author

Epilogue

For a time there was some question as to whether or not Warsaw would be defended or declared an open city. There was fighting around the city as enemy troops approached, and the capital was subjected to artillery fire and air raids. People were continually leaving the city, while villagers whose homes had been destroyed moved in. Mayor Starzyński, who distinguished himself in the uprising, called for all able-bodied men to join in the fight against the German invaders.

At the height of the bombing Stanisław Meyer sent his two sons to safety. "We gave them our car, a new Buick partly made in Poland, and under cover of the darkest night I remember, they rolled off into the blacked-out streets towards the crowded bridges, and then beyond the river towards the Russian frontier, or to the

South to Lwów. . . . For my wife and myself it was the hardest moment of our lives. I shall never forget the warm September night,
the pitch-dark streets and the last hurried embraces in the blue dim
light of torches, a parting, perhaps forever, with all that was best
and dearest to us."[1]

Neighbors whose homes had been blasted moved in with each
other, and what food was available was shared. Gradually, essential
services were cut. Meyer, who had become the de facto warden of
his street, remembers that "on Saturday the twenty-third – I am
quite certain it was a Saturday – the electricity stopped working and
with it the telephone network. . . . " The gas had already been cut
off, and the water was shut off soon afterward.

The government simply fell apart, and the city was abandoned, as ministers packed their files and fled in convoy toward the
Rumanian border. By the end of September German troops were
in Warsaw, and within a week or so they became the new occu-
piers. The utilities were switched on, more food was made available, although there was rationing, some banks were permitted to
open, and a few cabs appeared on the streets.

Then the terror began. Certain groups had been singled out
for arrest and possible extermination even before the invasion – the
clergy, the intelligentsia, university professors and teachers, civic
and political leaders, some entertainers, and, as always, the Jews.

In 1940 the Jews were walled up in the ghetto. Yellow arm-
bands became a familiar sight, as the Jews made occasional forays
outside the ghetto walls to do whatever business they could and to
purchase food.

Slowly but surely their numbers were reduced, either by death
or by relocation to concentration camps, which was simply another
form of death. Janusz Korczak had to find a space within the overcrowded ghetto for his orphanage. In 1942, disregarding offers of
safe haven, he led a column of his children and staff to the rail yards

at the northern tip of the ghetto, the Umschlagplatz, where they were loaded onto freight cars and sent to Treblinka.

In 1943, faced with extinction, the Jews of Warsaw's ghetto rose up against the Germans. From mid-April until May vicious fighting went on between Jews and Germans. The latter took surprisingly heavy losses and had to resort to heavy artillery to squelch the rebellion. In the course of the battle the ghetto was burned and torn apart. The Tłomackie Street synagogue was destroyed and has never been rebuilt. Only the Nozik synagogue, or rather its shell, survived, although it suffered extensive damage. After the last Jewish holdouts surrendered, they were carted off to the camps, and the ghetto was razed.

One year later, on August 1, the Polish Underground unleashed its own uprising, on orders from its exiled government in London. The struggle went on for sixty days as the outmanned Poles contested every street, every block, even every building. The Royal Castle, most of the palaces, the Bristol Hotel, the Ziemiańska café, the manor houses, the workers' tenements, the churches, including St. John's Cathedral, the opera house—all were heavily, and in many cases terminally, damaged.

This uprising too was doomed to failure, and, heroic though it was, in retrospect it was obviously ill-timed. No city until Hiroshima suffered the wanton destruction visited upon Warsaw by the furious Germans. Approximately 85 percent of the city's structures were badly damaged or totally destroyed.[2] All the bridges across the Vistula were brought down, the major thoroughfares made impassable and unrecognizable by tons of rubble—broken statues, splintered furniture, shards of glass, dead horses, overturned cars and trams, corpses filled the streets.

The Krasiński Library, the National Library, the Arsenal, and other private collections were burned. Some four hundred streets and plazas were either destroyed or disappeared from postwar maps. New World Avenue was bombed out of existence. (Later it was rebuilt.)

The death toll soared into the tens of thousands, including civilians and military personnel. General Bór-Komorowski finally surrendered his beleaguered forces on October 2. Every person who could walk or be carried was then forced out of the city.

Once Warsaw had been cleared of Poles, and the Germans could no longer withstand the shelling by the advancing Red Army, they retreated, and the sappers began their work. Buildings still standing were dynamited and/or burned in a frenzy of destruction. When it was all over, Warsaw was a ghost town. The Red Army and General Berling's First Polish Army entered the devastated city on January 17, 1945. It was, as one observer described it, a moonscape.

As for its inhabitants—the personalities who had once made Warsaw the Paris of Eastern Europe—they were either dead or scattered to the four winds. The lifeblood of the capital—rich and poor, Catholics, Jews, and nonbelievers, poets, writers, and architects, porters who once fought one another for jobs, bankers and beggars, nuns and prostitutes, wise guys who had hung around Qui Pro Quo and the Persian Eye—all gone, vanished as if they had never existed.

Writers Karol Irzykowski, Juliusz Kaden-Bandrowski, and Kamil Krzysztof Baczyński were all killed in the fighting. Fritz Járosy and Konstanty Ildefons Gałczyński joined the Underground. Both survived the uprising and were sent to the camps. When Járosy emerged he immediately resumed his career; in an emaciated condition he entertained the prisoners in a German displaced persons camp. He eventually emigrated to London and continued his career. In the early 1950s he visited Los Angeles as part of a touring group of entertainers.

Maria Modzelewska and Marian Hemar headed for the safety of the Rumanian border along with thousands of other Poles.

Benno Rand recalled seeing a depressed Hemar there. Maria had abandoned him and gone off with an army officer. Hemar, endlessly chain-smoking, considered suicide but somehow pulled himself together. He too went to London, where he had a successful career within the Polish community.

Mira Zimińska remained in Poland, married Tadeusz Sygietyński, and founded the enormously successful Mazowsze Dance Troupe.

Witold Gombrowicz stayed in Argentina, living in poverty and writing his diaries and novels. In the 1950s his books began to appear in the West, and in 1967 he won the Prix Formentor for his novel *Cosmos.* He never returned to Poland; the closest he came was Switzerland where he died in 1969.

Stanisław Ignacy Witkiewicz (Witkacy) headed east when the Germans invaded. When the news arrived that the Soviets had invaded too, he sat down beneath a tree and killed himself by swallowing drugs and cutting his throat.

Bruno Schulz was confined to the ghetto in his village of Drohobycz, where he continued to write and draw. One day while on an errand he was shot and killed by a Gestapo officer.

Jan Lechoń remained in the Polish diplomatic corps for a time. He and Julian Tuwim visited Gombrowicz in Argentina, then moved on to New York. But Lechoń's long-lasting despondency followed him there, too, and in 1956 he killed himself by leaping from a window at the Henry Hudson Hotel.

Tuwim escaped through Rumania, went to Argentina and Brazil, then to New York, and wound up in London, which served as a haven for fleeing Poles. After the Communists had a firm grip on Poland, he returned home, believing that Stalinism was the wave of the future. He and Marian Hemar had a bitter row over this and never spoke to one another again. Tuwim was sadly disappointed and had lost all his illusions by the time of his death in Warsaw in 1953.

Tadeusz Boy-Żeleński was caught by the Nazis in Lwów. He was working on a translation of Proust's *À la Recherche du Temps Perdu*. He was murdered by the Nazis, but there is some mystery surrounding the exact circumstances of his death.

Antoni Słonimski made it safely to London and continued writing his columns. He too eventually returned to Warsaw, more out of patriotism than a belief in communism. He managed to publish in Warsaw without much hindrance from the authorities. In 1976, he was struck and killed by a car while crossing the street.

Kazimierz Wierzyński escaped through France, traveled in South America, and then went to New York, where his *Life and Death of Chopin* was a best-seller in 1949.

Some writers remained in Warsaw. Jarosław Iwaszkiewicz, too old to be conscripted, maintained a salon of sorts just outside the city. He lived to the ripe old age of eighty-six. The young Czesław Miłosz also joined the Underground, where he wrote patriotic poems for the clandestine press. After the war the government sent him to France as a cultural attaché. In Paris, he had a change of heart, defected, and came to the United States, later settling in Berkeley. There, his career prospered, capped by the Nobel Prize for Literature in 1981.

Two of Poland's outstanding female writers, Maria Dąbrowska and Zofia Nałkowska, remained in Poland. Dąbrowska continued writing fiction and distanced herself from any political involvement. Nałkowska, like Tuwim, saw hope for the future in social realism. She resumed writing but also became more active politically, was elected to the Polish parliament, and served on the International Committee for the Investigation of Nazi Crimes.

Maria Kuncewicz left the country when the war broke out, lived briefly in Europe, and then moved to the United States in the 1950s. She continued writing there and lived to be almost one hundred years old.

Feliks Topolski left Warsaw for London in 1935 to paint

scenes of the Jubilee of King George V and never returned. He was attached to the Polish and British Defense Ministries during the war and afterward had an extraordinary career in London. His work is on display at his old studio beneath the Hungerford Bridge.

Stanisław Meyer and his wife established another salon in London, and Meyer continued his pursuit of antiques. They were reunited with their two sons, who also settled in London. Mrs. Meyer, who was a gifted pianist but did not play professionally, lived to be 101 years old.

Poland's top trio of directors—Leon Schiller, Stefan Jaracz, and Juliusz Osterwa—were all sent to Auschwitz. Jaracz and Osterwa died soon after being released, as a result of the suffering they had endured. Schiller was able to resume his career, pursuing his interest in social realism on stage. He also directed opera productions.

For some years after the war Lena Żelichowska and her artist husband Stefan Norblin lived in the Middle East, where his career flourished. They emigrated to the United States, settling in San Francisco, where his art was not as well received. Norblin subsequently took his own life. Żelichowska worked in a hairdressing salon and raised their son. She also died in San Francisco.

Zosia Terné, Hanka's one-time understudy, who also had an affair with Járosy, continued to perform in London into her seventies and died there peacefully. Lola Kitajewicz still lives in London and gives an occasional singing performance for small groups.

The actress Clara Segalovitch fell victim to the Nazi's cruel hoax on the Jews at the Hotel Polski (see note 11 to chapter 1). She and her husband were taken to Auschwitz, where they both died.

The political leaders and officers whom Piłsudski left behind were powerless against the Nazis. Top officials abandoned the capital early in September and went south, then crossed over into Rumania. They were reluctantly interned by the Rumanian government, anxious to placate Hitler. Józef Beck never left Rumania. He became ill and died there, at the relatively young age of fifty. President Mościcki was also interned but managed to make preparations for the continuity of the government. He sent word to Paris that General Wieniawa-Długoszowski should succeed him. But Wieniawa's reputation as a heavy drinker and womanizer preceded him. Both the French government and General Sikorski opposed the appointment. Sikorski was then asked to head the government-in-exile and held the twin posts of commander-in-chief and president. He died in 1943, in a mysterious plane crash off the coast of Gibraltar.

Ignacy Paderewski was in anguish over Poland's fate and did what he could to rally the West to Poland's side. But by the time of the Nazi invasion he was ill and infirm. He died in the United States in 1941 and was buried in Arlington National Cemetery. In 1992 his remains were reinterred in Warsaw.

To everyone's surprise, Marshal Śmigły-Rydz also showed up in Rumania. He left the country before its formal surrender, abandoning an army and a general staff in total disarray. He later sneaked back to occupied Poland in mufti, hoping to contact the Underground, but was unsuccessful.

And what of Hanka Ordonówna? She and some other entertainers were arrested by the Gestapo, allegedly on a tip from the director Tymoteusz Ortym. After her release, she was seen in the bar of the Europejski Hotel looking frightened and disheveled.

As things became more difficult in Warsaw Hanka and her husband left for the Tyszkiewicz estate outside Wilno, which had not yet been occupied. Other members of Warsaw's artistic community also went to Wilno, and before long they organized their own cabarets. Count Michael was soon arrested by the NKVD (later, the KGB) and taken to Moscow. After Lithuania fell to the Red Army, Hanka accepted an invitation to perform in Moscow, hoping to make contact with her husband. This proved extremely difficult. One writer who knew her described her friendships with Russian officers in Moscow as "scandalous." She did give several performances in the Soviet capital before she was also arrested and sent to a labor camp in Uzbekistan.

In the camp she fell ill with tuberculosis. However, she regained enough strength so that, when Stalin permitted the formation of a Polish army under General Władysław Anders, Ordonówna was part of the huge exodus of Polish civilians and soldiers who made the trek across the Soviet Union and into the Middle East. She was eventually reunited with Count Michael, who had been released from a Soviet prison and had also made his way to the Middle East.

Hanka never fully recovered her health and was hospitalized in several sanatoriums, including one in Jerusalem. There is a story, confirmed by several sources, that a certain Jewish doctor, identified only as Doctor B., fell in love with the singer. The feeling was not mutual, and one night, while Hanka was away from her apartment, Doctor B. went in and hanged himself.

After the war, Hanka and Count Michael settled in Beirut, which had not yet become the killing ground of the 1980s. In 1950, Hanka Ordonówna contracted typhus. She died in September, at the age of forty-eight, and was buried in Beirut.[3]

In 1989, after the Communist government had fallen, her remains were transferred to Warsaw's Powązki cemetery.

Notes

Notes to Introduction

1. Marek Żuławski, *In the Shadow of the Mechanized Apocalypse: Impressions of Warsaw and Life in Poland* (Warsaw: Czytelnik, 1980).
2. Czesław Miłosz, *The History of Polish Literature*, 2d ed. (Berkeley: University of California Press, 1983).
3. Both the British and the Soviet governments were opposed to the creation of a Polish state. Lloyd George said that Poland had won its freedom "not by her own exertions but by the blood of others." Economist John Maynard Keynes noted that the restoration of Poland "was an economic impossibility [for a nation] whose only industry is Jew-baiting." V. M. Molotov referred to Poland as "the monstrous bastard of the Peace of Versailles." As quoted in Norman Davies, *God's Playground: A History of Poland*, vol. 2 (London: Oxford University Press, 1981).
4. Interview conducted by the author. London, November 1986.
5. Ibid.
6. Stanisław Meyer, *My City: Reminiscences* (Newtown, England: Montgomeryshire Printing Co., 1947). One of Meyer's contemporaries defined the class division even more narrowly: "first there were those who belonged to the titled aristocracy; then the members of the Hunters' Club in Warsaw [the most exclusive club]; then diplomats; if one were not a diplomat, then at least one should speak English; . . . anything else was of secondary value. . . ." Wacław Led-

nicki, *Reminiscences: The Adventures of a Modern Gil Blas during the Last War* (The Hague: Mouton and Co. N.V. Publishers, 1971).
7. Interview conducted by Maika Kwiecińska-Decker. Warsaw, 1986.
8. Ibid.
9. For a detailed description of Warsaw's night life in the first days of independence see Tadeusz Wittlin, *Pieśnarka Warszawy: Hanka Ordonówna i Jej Świat* (Warsaw Songstress: Hanka Ordonówna and Her Times) (London: Polska Fundacja Kulturalna, 1985).

Notes to Chapter 1

1. Interview conducted by Maika Kwiecińska-Decker. Warsaw, 1986.
2. Ibid.
3. Stanisław Meyer, *My City: Reminiscences* (Newtown, England: Montgomeryshire Printing Co., 1947).
4. Interview conducted by the author. London, November 1986.
5. Viscount D'Abernon, *The Eighteenth Decisive Battle of the World: Warsaw 1920* (London: Hodder and Staughton, 1931).
6. W. Baranowski, *Rozmowy z Piłsudskim: 1916–1931* (Warsaw, 1938).
7. Adam Zamoyski, *Paderewski* (London: Collins, 1982).
8. Meyer, op. cit.
9. Ibid.
10. Abraham Shulman, *The Case of Hotel Polski* (New York: Schocken Books, 1982).
11. The Gestapo put out a rumor that any Jew who wanted a visa to leave Poland should come to the Hotel Polski on Długa Street, with money or jewelry. At the hotel the Jews were arrested and taken to Pawiak prison. From there most of them were sent to concentration camps where they died.
12. Meyer, op. cit.
13. Letter to the author, November 1989.
14. Ibid.
15. Interview conducted by Maika Kwiecińska-Decker. Warsaw, 1986.

Notes to Chapter 2

1. Hugh Gibson, the American minister to Warsaw at the time, wrote in his memoirs that he "confiscated" Paderewski's first resignation letter. He told the maestro that such a move would cause the United States to lose "confidence" in Poland. See Adam Zamoyski, *Paderewski* (London: Collins, 1982).

2. "White Poland" was a derogatory term implying that Poland was a fascist state.

3. Norman Davies, *White Eagle, Red Star* (London: Orbis Books, 1983).

4. Ibid.

5. Czesław Miłosz, *The History of Polish Literature* (Berkeley: University of California Press, 1983).

6. Ibid.

7. Ibid.

8. Ibid.

9. These were Polish poets, roughly of the 1920s decade, after which they were succeeded by the so-called Second Vanguard.

10. For a thorough account of Qui Pro Quo's opening, see Tadeusz Wittlin, *Pieśnarka Warszawy: Hanka Ordonówna i Jej Świat* (London: Polska Fundacja Kulturalna, 1985).

11. Interview conducted by Maika Kwiecińska-Decker. Warsaw, 1986.

12. Wittlin, op. cit.

13. For a more complete treatment of Polish film, see Edward Wynot, Jr., *Warsaw between the World Wars: Profile of the Capital City in a Developing Land, 1918–1939* (Boulder, Colo.: East European Monographs; dist. by Columbia University Press, 1983), and Stanisław Janicki, *W Starym Polskim Kinie* (Warsaw: Krajowa Agencja Wydawnicza, 1985).

14. Wynot, op. cit.

15. Jadwiga Kosicka and Daniel Gerould, *A Life of Solitude: Stanisława Przybyszewska: A Biographical Study with Selected Letters* (Evanston, Ill.: Northwestern University Press, 1989).

16. Edward Csato, *The Polish Theater* (Warsaw: Polonia Publishing House, 1963).

17. Ibid.

18. Daniel Gerould, *Witkacy: Stanisław Ignacy Witkiewicz as an Imaginative Writer* (Seattle: University of Washington Press, 1981).

19. Ibid.

20. Ibid.

21. Interview conducted by the author. London, November 1986.

22. Paul Kresh, *The Magician of 86th Street: A Biography* (New York: Dial Press, 1979).

23. As quoted in Norman Davies, *God's Playground*, vol. 2 (London: Oxford Press, 1981).

Notes to Chapter 3

1. The Inner War Council was the operational arm of the army's command system. It consisted of the corps commanders, the chief-of-staff, and the council head, who in this case was Piłsudski. Together with the larger Full War Council, which was the administrative division of the military, it was responsible for planning and carrying out Poland's military operations in peacetime as well as in war.

2. Tadeusz Wittlin, *Pieśnarka Warszawy: Hanka Orodnówna i Jej Świat* (London: Polska Fundacja Kulturalna, 1985). Trans. provided by Richard Rehl.

3. Ibid.

4. As told to the author by Tadeusz Wittlin.

5. Wittlin, op. cit.

6. Ibid.

7. Mira Zimińska-Sygietyńska, *Nie Żyłam Samotnie* (I Didn't Live Alone) (Warszawa: Wydawnictwo Artystyczne i Filmowe, 1985). Trans. provided by Zosia Osiacka.

8. Ibid.

9. Wittlin, op. cit.

10. Zimińska-Sygietyńska, op. cit.

11. Ryszard Marek Groński, *Jak w Przedwojennym Kabarecie* (Warsaw:

Wydawnictwo Artystyczne i Filmowe, 1987). Trans. provided by Irena Narell.

12. Interview conducted by the author. London, December 1986.
13. Stanisław Meyer, *My City: Reminiscences* (Newtown, England: Montgomeryshire Printing Co., 1947).
14. Interview conducted by Maika Kwiecińska-Decker. Warsaw, 1986.
15. Letter to the author, November 1986.
16. *The Literary News* was published during the war in London under the title *News (Wiadomości)*. Its editorials were decidedly anti-Soviet, much to the anger and chagrin of the British government, which was trying to convince Stalin to open a second front against the Germans. When the paper's publishing schedule was disrupted, the editors accused the government of withholding newsprint. Others maintain that the disruption was coincidental and that the British government rationed newsprint for all periodicals.
17. Interview conducted by the author. London, December 1986.
18. Meyer, op. cit.
19. Ibid.
20. Ibid.
21. Ibid.
22. For a more detailed discussion of Poland's art movements, see Andrzej K. Olszewski, *An Outline History of Polish Art and Architecture, 1890–1980*, trans. Stanisław Tarnowski (Warsaw: Interpress Publishers, 1989).
23. Edward Wynot, Jr., *Warsaw between the Wars: Profile of the Capital City in a Developing Land, 1918–1939* (Boulder, Colo.: East European Monographs; dist. by Columbia University Press, 1983).
24. Betty Jean Lifton, *The King of Children: A Biography of Janusz Korczak* (London: Chatto and Windus, 1988).

Notes to Chapter 4

1. Neal Ascheron, *The Observer*, 1989. Raczyński was knighted by Queen Elizabeth II in 1991 on the occasion of his one hundredth birthday.

2. Count Raczyński's palace was located at the intersection of Wierzbowa and Fredry streets, adjacent to the Saxon Palace. Today's Raczyński Palace is located on Krakowskie Przedmieście and is the Academy of Fine Arts. There was also once a Raczyński library in the Krasiński Palace. It is now part of the National Library.

3. Interview conducted by the author. London, November 1986.

4. Ibid.

5. Stanisław Meyer, *My City: Reminiscences* (Newtown, England: Montgomeryshire Printing Co., 1947).

6. Teresa Chylińska, *Szymanowski*, trans. A. T. Jordan (Kraków: Polski Wydawnictwo Muzyczne, 1981).

7. Ibid.

8. Ibid.

9. Ibid.

10. Peter Kurth, *American Cassandra* (Boston: Little, Brown, 1990).

11. Interview conducted by the author. London, December 1986.

12. Ibid.

13. Ibid.

14. Ibid.

15. Ibid.

16. Interview conducted by Maika Kwiecińska-Decker. Warsaw, June 1986.

17. G. K. Chesterson, *Autobiography*, edited and with an introduction by Richard Ingrams (London: Hamish Hamilton, 1986).

18. Meyer, op. cit.

19. Chesterson, op. cit.

20. As quoted in ibid.

21. Ibid.

22. Ibid.

23. Ibid.

24. Aleksander Wat, *My Century: The Odyssey of a Polish Intellectual*, edited and translated by Richard Lourie, foreword by Czesław Miłosz (Berkeley: University of California Press, 1988).

25. Interview conducted by Maika Kwiecińska-Decker. Warsaw, June 1986.

26. See Daniel Gerould, *Witkacy: Stanisław Ignacy Witkiewicz as an Imaginative Writer* (Seattle: University of Washington Press, 1981) and his preface to the collection, *The Madman and the Nun, and Other Plays*, translated and edited by Daniel C. Gerould and C. S. Durer (Seattle: University of Washington Press, 1968).

27. Jerzy Ficowski, ed., *Letters and Drawings of Bruno Schulz* (Evanston, Ill.: Northwestern University Press, 1988).

28. Betty Jean Lifton, *The King of Children: A Biography of Janusz Korczak* (London: Chatto and Windus, 1988).

29. Wat, op. cit.

30. Ibid.

31. For a full description of Korczak's life and works, see Lifton, op. cit.

32. *Kinie* (Warsaw: Krajowa Agencja Wydawnicza, 1985), a collection of articles from the Polish-language magazine of the same name published before the war. This quote was translated by Richard Rehl.

33. For a more detailed description of events surrounding this film see Tadeusz Wittlin, *Pieśnarka Warszawy: Hanka Ordonówna i Jej Świat* (London: Polska Fundacja Kulturalna, 1985).

Notes to Chapter 5

1. Wacław, Lednicki, *Reminiscences: The Adventures of a Modern Gil Blas during the Last War* (The Hague: Mouton and Co. N.V. Publishers, 1971).

2. Tadeusz Wittlin, *Ostatnia Cyganeria (The Last Gypsies)* (Warsaw: Czytelnik, 1989). Trans. provided by Richard Rehl.

3. The poem was published in the magazine *Quadriga (Kwadriga)* (1926–31). This translation appeared in *Five Centuries of Polish Poetry*, ed. and trans. Jerzy Peterkiewicz (London: Secker and Warburg, 1960).

4. Aleksander Wat, *My Century: The Odyssey of a Polish Intellectual*, ed. and trans. Richard Lourie, foreword by Czesław Miłosz (Berkeley: University of California Press, 1988).

5. Ibid.

6. Ibid.

7. Ibid.

8. Paul Super, *My Twenty Years with the Poles*. N.p.: Paul Super Memorial Fund, 1947.

9. Interview conducted by the author. London, December, 1986.

10. Ibid.

11. Ibid.

12. Ludwik Sempoliński, *Wielcy Artyści Małych Scen* (Warsaw: Czytelnik, 1977). Trans. by the author. See this title for more details on *Morskie Oko*.

13. Tadeusz Wittlin, *Pieśnarka Warszawy: Hanka Ordonówna i Jej Świat* (London: Polska Fundacja Kulturalna, 1985).

14. Ibid.

15. Mira Zimińska-Sygietyńska, *Nie Żyłam Samotnie* (I Didn't Live Alone) (Warsaw: Wydawnictwo Artystyczne i Filmowe, 1985). Trans. provided by Zosia Osiacka.

16. Translation by Richard Rehl from lyrics as they appear in Wittlin, *Pieśnarka Warszawy*.

17. Wittlin, *Pieśnarka Warszawy*.

18. Zofia Arciszewska, *Po Obu Strona Oceanu* (Sussex: Polska Fundacja Kulturalna, 1976).

19. Wittlin, *Pieśnarka Warszawy*.

20. Ibid.

21. Czesław Miłosz, *The History of Polish Literature* (Berkeley: University of California Press, 1983.)

22. Daniel Gerould, ed., *Twentieth Century Polish Avant-Garde Drama: Plays, Scenarios, Critical Documents* (Ithaca, N.Y.: Cornell University Press, 1977).

23. Ibid.

24. Ibid.

Notes to Chapter 6

1. Aleksander Wat, *My Century: The Odyssey of a Polish Intellectual*, ed. and trans. Richard Lourie, foreword by Czesław Miłosz (Berkeley: University of California Press, 1988).

2. Kazimierz Brandys, *A Warsaw Diary: 1978–1981*, trans. Richard Lourie (New York: Random House, 1983).

3. Ibid.

4. Ibid.

5. Interview conducted by Maika Kwiecińska-Decker. Warsaw, 1986.

6. Ibid.

7. Ibid.

8. For a detailed discussion of the role architects played in the modernization of Warsaw, see Andrzej K. Olszewski, *An Outline History of Polish Art and Architecture 1890–1980*, trans. Stanisław Tarnowski (Warsaw: Interpress Publishers, 1989).

9. Zofia Arciszewska, *Po Obu Stronach Oceanu* (Sussex: Polska Fundacja Kulturalna, 1976). Trans. provided by Maria Serenc.

10. Ibid.

11. Ludwik Sempoliński, *Wielcy Artyści Małych Scen* (Warsaw: Czytelnik, 1977).

12. For details of Tuwim's collapse and Ordonówna's recitation of his poem, see Tadeusz Wittlin, *Pieśniarka Warszawy: Hanka Ordonówna i Jej Świat* (London: Polska Fundacja Kulturalna, 1985).

13. Ibid.

14. For a detailed treatment of athletics in Poland, see Edward Wynot, Jr., *Warsaw between the Wars: Profile of the Capital City in a Developing Land, 1918–1939* (Boulder, Colo.: East European Monographs; dist. by Columbia University Press, 1983), and Stefan Sieniarski, *Sport in Poland* (Warsaw: Interpress Publishers, 1976).

15. Paul Super, *My Twenty Years with the Poles*. N.p.: Paul Super Memorial Fund, 1947.

16. Wacław Lednicki, *Reminiscences: The Adventures of a Modern Gil Blas during the Last War* (The Hague: Mouton and Co. N.V. Publishers, 1971).

17. Letters to the author, July 1990 and May 1992.

18. Ibid.

19. Letter to the author, November 1989.

20. Stanisław Meyer, *My City: Reminiscences* (Newtown, England: Montgomeryshire Printing Co., 1947).
21. Ibid.

Notes to Chapter 7

1. For a detailed description of Piłsudski's funeral, see Wacław Jędrzejewicz, *Piłsudski: A Life for Poland*, introduction by Zbigniew Brzeziński (New York: Hippocrene Books, 1982).
2. Translation provided by Wanda Tomczykowska.
3. Tadeusz Wittlin, *Pieśnarka Warszawy: Hanka Ordonówna i Jej Świat* (London: Polska Fundacja Kulturalna, 1985).
4. For a detailed treatment of the Osterwa-Ordonówna affair, see ibid.
5. For more on the show and Boy-Żeleński's review, see Ludwik Sempoliński, *Wielcy Artyści Małych Scen* (Warsaw: Czytelnik, 1977), and Wittlin, op. cit.
6. Jerzy Ficowski, ed., *Letters and Drawings of Bruno Schulz* (Evanston, Ill.: Northwestern University Press, 1989).
7. Ibid.
8. Aleksander Wat, *My Century: The Odyssey of a Polish Intellectual*, ed. and trans. Richard Lourie, foreword by Czesław Miłosz (Berkeley: University of California Press, 1988).
9. Czesław Miłosz, *The History of Polish Literature* (Berkeley: University of California Press, 1983).
10. Betty Jean Lifton, *The King of Children: A Biography of Janusz Korczak* (London: Chatto and Windus, 1988).
11. For details of her death and her collected letters, see Jadwiga Kosicka and Daniel Gerould, *A Life of Solitude: Stanisława Przybyszewska: A Biographical Study with Selected Letters* (Evanston, Ill.: Northwestern University Press, 1989).
12. Wanda Stachiewicz, *Journey through History: Memoirs* (Toronto: Canadian Polish Research Institute, 1989).
13. Ibid.

Notes to Chapter 8

1. Interview conducted by the author. London, December 1986.
2. For the story of this magazine and its contributors, see Tadeusz Wittlin, *Ostatnia Cyganeria* (The Last Gypsies) (Warsaw: Czytelnik, 1989). Not available in English.
3. Kiepura was admired in Berlin as the star of *Tonfilm*. Bella Fromm overheard this remark at a party: "They are very fond of him . . . perhaps because he fills their cashboxes, singing for the *Winterhilfe*. They do not tell him that the money is used for rearmament." Bella Fromm, *Blood and Banquets: A Berlin Social Diary* (New York: Carol Publishing Group, 1990).
4. For an exhaustive list of cabaret performances in interwar Warsaw, see Ludwik Sempoliński, *Wielcy Artyści Małych Scen* (Warsaw: Czytelnik, 1977).
5. Mira Zimińska-Sygietyńska, *Nie Żyłam Samotnie* (I Didn't Live Alone) (Warsaw: Wydanictwa Artystyczne in Filmowe, 1985). Trans. provided by Zosia Osiacka.
6. Czesław Miłosz, *The History of Polish Literature* (Berkeley: University of California Press, 1983).
7. For more about Miłosz's prewar activities in Warsaw, see Ewa Czarnecka and Aleksander Fiut, *Conversations with Czesław Miłosz* (San Diego: Harcourt Brace Jovanovich, 1987).
8. Miłosz, op. cit.
9. Edward Wynot, Jr., *Warsaw between the World Wars: Profile of the Capital City in a Developing Land, 1918–1939* (Boulder, Colo.: East European Monographs; dist. by Columbia University Press, 1983).
10. The material on Warsaw's modernization is summarized from Wynot's excellent study, ibid.

Notes to Chapter 9

1. Wacław Lednicki, *Reminiscences: The Adventures of a Modern Gil Blas during the Last War* (The Hague: Mouton and Co. N. V. Publishers, 1971).

2. Interview conducted by the author. London, November 1986.

3. For a detailed treatment of the business side of the film industry from 1918 to 1939, see Edward Wynot, Jr., *Warsaw between the Wars: Profile of the Capital City in a Developing Land 1918–1939* (Boulder, Colo.: East European Monographs; dist. by Columbia University Press, 1983).

4. Witold Gombrowicz, *Ferdydurke*, trans. Eric Mosbacher (New York: Harcourt, Brace & World, 1961), chap. 5.

5. See Tadeusz Wittlin, *Pieśnarka Warszawy: Hanka Ordonówna i Jej Świat* (London: Polska Fundacja Kulturalna, 1985), for an account of Ordonówna's trip and her affair with First Officer Jan Strzembos.

6. Interview conducted by the author. London, February 1992.

7. Ibid.

8. Ludwik Sempoliński, *Wielcy Artyści Małych Scen* (Warsaw: Czytelnik, 1977).

9. Zofia Arciszewska, *Po Obu Stronach Oceanu* (On Both Sides of the Ocean) (Sussex: Polska Fundacja Kulturalna, 1976). Trans. provided by Maria Serenc.

Notes to Chapter 10

1. Litvinov's dismissal by Stalin was caused by two factors: He was Jewish and he held progressive attitudes. He was replaced by V. M. Molotov.

2. Interview conducted by author. London, December 1986.

3. Stanisław Meyer, *My City: Reminiscences* (Newtown, England: Montgomeryshire Printing Co., 1947).

4. Wacław Lednicki, *Reminiscences: The Adventures of a Modern Gil Blas during the Last War* (The Hague: Mouton and Co. N. V. Publishers, 1971).

5. Ibid.

6. Ibid.

7. Ibid.

8. Wanda Stachiewicz, *Journey through History: Memoirs* (Toronto: Canadian Polish Research Institute and the author, n.d.).

9. Ibid.

10. Kazimierz Brandys, *A Warsaw Diary: 1978–1981*, trans. Richard Lourie (New York: Random House, 1983).

11. Lednicki, op. cit.

12. Interview conducted by the author. London, November 1986.

13. Interview conducted by the author. London, October 1986.

14. Interview conducted by the author. London, October 1986.

15. Condensed from material in Nahma Sandrow, *Vagabond Stars: A World History of Yiddish Theatre* (New York: Limelight Editions, 1986).

16. For a more exhaustive account of revues playing in Warsaw in the summer of 1939, see Ludwik Sempoliński, *Wielcy Artyści Małych Scen* (Warsaw: Czytelnik, 1977).

17. An account of Wittlin's activities in the final days before the war is given in his book *Pieśnarka Warszawy: Hanka Ordonówna i Jej Świat* (London: Polska Fundacja Kulturalna, 1985).

18. Betty Jean Lifton, *The King of Children: A Biography of Janusz Korczak* (London: Chatto and Windus, 1988).

19. Cambronne was the French general under Napoleon who, when confronted with a surrender demand from the Duke of Wellington, replied *"Merde!"* Some say that in French his reply could be interpreted to mean more than it usually does. For the complete poem in English, see Adam Gillon and Ludwik Krzyżanowski, eds., *Introduction to Modern Polish Literature* (New York: Hippocrene Books, 1979).

20. See Wittlin, op. cit.

Notes to Epilogue

1. Stanisław Meyer, *My City: Reminiscences.* (Newtown, England: Montgomeryshire Printing Co., 1947).

2. Estimates of the extent of the damage run from 80 to 94 percent of all structures in the city limits.

3. For details of Hanka's fate and the days in Warsaw prior to Nazi occupation, see Tadeusz Wittlin, *Pieśnarka Warszawy: Hanka Ordonówna i Jej Świat* (London: Polska Fundacja Kulturalna, 1985).

Glossary of Terms and Abbreviations

BBWR: Nonpolitical Party Bloc for Cooperation with the Government (*Bezpartyjny Blok Współpracy z Rządem*).

Belvedere Palace: official residence of the president of Poland, near Łazienki Park.

Centrolew: a coalition of left and center parties created to oppose the Piłsudski-dominated government in the late 1920s.

IPS: Institute for Artistic Propaganda (*Instytut Propagandy Sztuki*), a café frequented mainly by right-wing intellectuals that also held art exhibits and cabaret performances.

LAD: a cooperative group of interior designers whose members were graduates of the Academy of Fine Arts.

LM: *The Literary Monthly;* the Communists' literary and political magazine, 1929–32.

ND: National Democrats; the major right-wing party of the interwar years; also known as *Endecja* or *Endeks*.

OZON: Camp of National Unity (*Obóz Zjednoczenia Narodowego*), an all-government party formed in 1937, with anti-Semitic tendencies.

PCP: Polish Communist Party (*Komunistyczna Partia Polski*).

PPS: Polish Socialist Party (*Polska Partia Sociallistyczna*).

QPQ: Qui Pro Quo, probably the best known of Warsaw's cabarets during the interwar years 1919–29.

Royal Way: a route consisting of three contiguous avenues, Krakowskie Przedmieście, Nowy Świat, and Aleje Ujazdowskie, running north to south, beginning near the Royal Castle and continuing to Belvedere Palace. Today it is considered to terminate at Wilanów, at the palace of King Jan III Sobieski.

Sejm: usually refers to the chief legislative body, which is the lower house of parliament, called the Chamber of Deputies.

SiM: Art and Fashion (*Sztuka i Moda*), a popular café founded in 1932 by Zofia Arciszewska. It is no longer in existence.

Skamander: a school of poets, loosely organized in 1919. Their magazine, also called *Skamander*, was founded in 1920 and ceased publication before World War II.

START: Association of Devotees of Artistic Films (*Stowarzyszenie Miłośników Filmu Artystycznego*), a group of directors, actors, writers, and producers organized to provide more opportunities for filmmakers and to promote experimental films.

TKKT: Association for the Promulgation of Theatrical Culture (*Towarzystwo Krzewienia Kultury Teatralnej*), a government-sponsored organization, founded in 1933, whose principal function was to provide subsidies for Warsaw theaters.

WL: *The Literary News* (*Wiadomości Literackie*), a progressive weekly tabloid of reviews, essays, prose, and poetry, founded in 1924 by Mieczysław Grydzewski. It survived in various forms until 1981.

WSM: the Warsaw Housing Cooperative (*Warszawska Spółdzielnia Mieszkanowia*), founded in 1921 by a coalition of leftist parties to build cheap housing for workers and the intelligentsia.

Zamek: the Polish name for the Royal Castle.

Bibliography

Books

Abramsky, C., Jachimczyk, M., and Polonsky, A. *The Jews in Poland.* Oxford: Basil Blackwell, 1986, 1988.

Brandys, Kazimierz. *A Warsaw Diary: 1978–1981.* Translated from the Polish by Richard Lourie. New York: Random House, 1983.

Carpenter, Bogdana. *The Poetic Avant-Garde in Poland.* Seattle: University of Washington Press, 1983.

Chesterton, G. K. *Autobiography.* Edited and introduced by Richard Ingrams. London: Hamish Hamilton, 1986.

Chylińska, Teresa. *Szymanowski.* Translated from the Polish by A. T. Jordan. Kraków: Polska Wydawnictwo Muzyczne, 1981.

Csato, Edward. *The Polish Theatre.* Translated by Christina Cenkalska. Warsaw: Polonia Publishing House, 1963.

D'Abernon, Viscount. *The Eighteenth Decisive Battle of the World: Warsaw 1920.* London: Hodder and Stoughton, 1931.

Davies, Norman. *God's Playground: A History of Poland,* volume 2. London: Oxford University Press, 1984.

Davies, Norman. *White Eagle, Red Star.* London: Orbis, 1983; first published in 1972 in Great Britain by Macdonald and Co.

263

Dobroszycki, Lucjan, and Kirshenblatt-Gimblett, Barbara, *Image before My Eyes: A Photographic History of Jewish Life in Poland, 1864–1939.* New York: Schocken Books, 1977.

Ficowski, Jerzy, ed. *Letters and Drawings of Bruno Schulz.* Evanston, Ill.: Northwestern University Press, 1988.

Fromm, Bella. *Blood and Banquets: A Berlin Social Diary.* New York: Carol Publishing Group, 1990.

Gerould, Daniel. *Witkacy: Stanisław Ignacy Witkiewicz as an Imaginative Writer.* Seattle: University of Washington Press, 1981.

Gerould, Daniel, ed. *Twentieth-Century Polish Avant-Garde Drama: Plays, Scenarios, Critical Documents.* Translated by Daniel and Eleanor Gerould; introduction by Daniel Gerould. Ithaca, N.Y.: Cornell University Press, 1977.

Gerould, Daniel, and Durer, C. S., trans. and eds. *The Madman and the Nun and Other Plays by Stanisław Ignacy Witkiewicz.* Seattle: University of Washington Press, 1968.

Gillon, Adam, and Krzyżanowski, Ludwik, eds. *Introduction to Modern Polish Literature.* New York: Hippocrene Books, 1982.

Halecki, Oskar. *A History of Poland.* Chicago: Regnery Logos, 1966.

Heine, Marc. *Poland.* New York: Hippocrene Books, 1979.

Humphrey, Grace. *Come with Me through Warsaw.* Warsaw: M. Arct Publishing Co., 1934.

Hundert, G. D., and Bacon, G. C. *The Jews in Poland and Russia.* Bloomington: Indiana University Press, 1984.

Jankowski, Stanisław, and Ciborowski, Adolf. *Warsaw: 1945, Today, and Tomorrow.* Warsaw: Interpress Publishers, 1978.

Jędrzejewicz, Wacław. *Piłsudski: A Life for Poland.* Introduction by Zbigniew Brzeziński. New York: Hippocrene Books, 1982.

Klimaszewski, Bolesław. *An Outline History of Polish Culture.* Translated by Krystyna Mroczelc. Warsaw: Interpress Publishers, 1983.

Knox, Brian. *The Architecture of Poland.* London: Barrie and Jenkins, 1971.

Kościuszko Foundation. *A Chronology of the Life, Activities, and Works of Janusz Korczak.* Text by Maria Falkowska, translated by E. Kulawiec. Warsaw: Wydawnictwa Szokolne i Pedagogiczne, 1978.

Kosicka, Jadwiga, and Gerould, Daniel. *A Life of Solitude: Stanisława Przybyszewska: A Biographical Study with Selected Letters.* Evanston, Ill.: Northwestern University Press, 1989.

Kresh, Paul. *I. B. Singer: The Magician of 86th Street, A Biography.* New York: Dial Press, 1979.

Krzyżanowski, Julian. *A History of Polish Literature.* Translated by Doris Rondewicz. Warsaw: PWN – Polish Scientific Publishers, 1978.

Lednicki, Wacław. *Reminiscences: The Adventures of a Modern Gil Blas during the Last War.* The Hague: Mouton and Co. N. V. Publishers, 1971.

Lifton, Betty Jean. *The King of Children: A Biography of Janusz Korczak.* London: Chatto and Windus, 1988.

Meyer, Stanisław. *My City: Reminiscences.* Illustrated by Marek Żuławski. Newtown, England: Montgomeryshire Printing Co., 1947.

Miłosz, Czesław. *The History of Polish Literature.* Berkeley: University of California Press, 1983.

Olszewski, Andrzej K. *An Outline of Polish Art and Architecture 1890–1980.* Translated by Stanisław Tarnowski. Warsaw: Interpress Publishers, 1989.

Paderewski, Ignacy Jan, and Lawton, Mary. *The Paderewski Memoirs.* London: Collins, 1939.

Piłsudski, Józef. *Memoirs of a Polish Revolutionary and Soldier.* Translated and edited by D. R. Gillie. London: Faber and Faber, 1931.

Polonsky, Antony. *Politics in Independent Poland: Crisis of Constitutional Government, 1921–1939.* London: Oxford University Press, 1972.

Sandrow, Nahma. *Vagabond Stars: A World History of Yiddish Theater.* New York: Limelight Editions, 1986.

Shulman, Abraham. *The Case of Hotel Polski.* New York: Holocaust Publications, Schocken Books, 1982.

Sieniarski, Stefan. *Sport in Poland.* Warsaw: Interpress Publishers, 1976.

Singer, Isaac Bashevis. *Love and Exile: The Early Years, a Memoir.* London: Jonathan Cape, 1985; Penguin Books, 1986.

Stachiewicz, Wanda. *Journey through History: Memoirs.* Toronto: Canadian Polish Research Institute and the author, n.d.

Super, Paul. *My Twenty Years with the Poles.* N.p.: Paul Super Memorial Fund, 1947.

Vishniac, Roman. *A Vanished World.* New York: Farrar, Straus, and Giroux, 1983.

Wat, Aleksander. *My Century: Odyssey of a Polish Intellectual.* Edited and translated by Richard Lourie, foreword by Czesław Miłosz. Berkeley: University of California Press, 1988.

Watt, Richard. *Bitter Glory: Poland and Its Fate, 1918–1939.* New York: Simon and Schuster, 1982.

Wisłocka, Izabella. *Avant-Garde Polish Architecture, 1918–1939.* Warsaw: Arkady, 1968.

Wynot, Edward, Jr. *Warsaw between the Wars: Profile of the Capital City in a Developing Land, 1918–1939.* Boulder, Colo.: East European Monographs, Columbia University Press, 1983.

Zamoyski, Adam. *Paderewski.* London: Collins, 1982.

Periodicals

The Polish Review 37(4) (1987). New York: The Polish Institute of Arts and Sciences.

Books in Polish

Arciszewska, Zofia. *Po Obu Stronach Oceanu* (On Both Sides of the Ocean). Sussex: Polska Fundacja Kulturalna, 1976.

Baranowski, Wacław. *Rozmowy z Piłsudskim 1916–31*. Warsaw: Wydawnictwa "Zebra," 1938, 1990.

Drozdowski, Marian Marek. *Stefan Starzyński, Prezydent Warszawy*. Warsaw: Państowy Instytut Wydawniczy, 1980.

Groński, Ryszard Marek. *Jak w Przedwojennym Kabarecie*. Warsaw: Wydawnictwa Artystyczne i Filmowe, 1978.

Groński, Ryszard Marek. *Kabaret Hemara*. Warsaw: Wydawnictwo Towarzystwa Wydawców Książek, 1989.

Janicki, Stanisław. *W Starym Polskim Kinie*. Warsaw: Krajowa Agencja Wydawnicza, 1985.

Krasiński, Edward. *Warszawskie Sceny 1918–1939*. Warsaw: Państwowy Instytut Wydawniczy, 1976.

Krukowski, Kazimierz. *Mała Antologia Kabaretu*. Warsaw: Wydawnictwa Artystyczne i Filmowe, 1988.

Sempoliński, Ludwik. *Wielcy Artyści Małych Scen*. Warsaw: Czytelnik, 1977.

Słonimski, Antoni. *Gwałt na Melpomenie*. Warsaw: Wydawnictwa Artystyczne i Filmowe, 1982.

Wapiński, Roman. *Roman Dmowski*. Monograph. Warsaw: Iskry, 1979.

Wittlin, Tadeusz. *Pieśnarka Warszawy: Hanka Ordonówna i Jej Świat.* London: Polska Fundacja Kulturalna, 1985.

Wittlin, Tadeusz. *Ostatnia Cyganeria.* Warsaw: Czytelnik, 1989.

Zimińska-Sygietyńska, Mira. *Nie Żyłam Samotnie.* Warsaw: Wydawnictwa Artystyczne i Filmowe, 1985.

Periodicals in Polish

Wiadomości Literackie, various issues, 1924–39.

Kurier Poranny, various issues, 1924–39.

Permissions

For permission to quote I am indebted to: the late Stefania Meyer, for material from *My City: Reminiscences* by Stanisław Meyer; Holocaust Publications, for material from *The Case of Hotel Polski* by Abraham Shulman; Ryszard Marek Groński, for material from his books *Jak w Przedwojennym Kabarecie* and *Kabaret Hemara*; Wanda Stachiewicz and the Canadian Polish Research Institute, Toronto, for material from her book *Journey through History: Memoirs*; Polska Fundacja Kulturalna, for material from *Po Obu Stronach Oceanu* by Zofia Arciszewska; Hippocrene Books, for material from *Piłsudski: A Life for Poland* by Wacław Jedzęjewicz; the University of California Press, for material from *My Century* by Aleksander Wat; Tadeusz Wittlin, for material from *Pieśnarka Warszawy: Hanka Ordonówna i Jej Świat* and from *Ostatnia Cyganeria*; Random House, for material from *Warsaw Diary: 1978–1981* by Kazimierz Brandys; Hanna Hirshaut, for material from her letters.

Excerpts from Polish poems translated by Adam Gillon and Watson Kirkconnell are from *Introduction to Modern Polish Literature*, edited by Adam Gillon and Ludwik Krzyżanowski (New York: Hippocrene Books, 1982).

The excerpt on page 215 from *Ferdydurke* by Witold Gombrowicz is from the edition translated by Eric Mosbacher and published by Harcourt Brace & World, 1961.

For permission to use photographs of Warsaw and its personalities, I am grateful to: Zdzisław Jagodziński at the Polish Library in London; Wlada Majeska for the photo of Marian Hemar; the publishing firm

Książka i Wiedza in Warsaw and Helena Klimek; Archiwum Dokumentacji Mechanicznej in Warsaw. Acknowledgment is also made to the Historical Museum of Warsaw.

My thanks to Oxford University Press for permission to reprint the map on page 41, which originally appeared in Norman Davies, *God's Playground: A History of Poland*, volume 2 (London, 1984).

The street map of Warsaw is based on a map produced by Wydawnictwa ALFA, Warsaw, 1985.

Index

About the Author

Ron Nowicki has long been involved with the Polish communities in San Francisco and London. He was a trustee of the Polish Arts and Culture Foundation in San Francisco for a number of years and remains a member.

Nowicki was the founder and for many years the publisher and editor of the *San Francisco Review of Books,* and he has written articles for *Newsweek, Publishers Weekly, North American Review,* the *London Literary Review,* the *New York Times* Travel Section, and the *San Francisco Bay Guardian.* He currently lives in London with his wife, Diana Liu. This is his first book.

The text of this book was designed by Zipporah Collins, using Janson type with a Polish character set and Serif Gothic display. Typesetting was done by Stanton Publication Services. Editing was directed by Thomas Christensen and David Peattie; Carol Christensen was the editor. Production was coordinated by Zipporah Collins. The word processors were Kirsten Janene-Nelson and Sarah Malarkey. David Sweet and Mu'frida Bell did the proofreading. The book was printed on Glatfelter B-16 paper by Data Reproductions Corporation. The cover is Multicolor Antique Cayenne with Joanna Kennett Black cloth for the spine. The jacket was designed by Madeleine Budnick under the art direction of Sharon Smith; it is printed on Multicolor Antique Thistle.